AF411954

Televising History

Televising History

Mediating the Past in Postwar Europe

Edited by

Erin Bell

and

Ann Gray

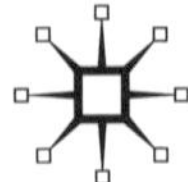

First published 2010 by
PALGRAVE MACMILLAN

Palgrave Macmillan in the UK is an imprint of Macmillan Publishers Limited, registered in England, company number 785998, of Houndmills, Basingstoke, Hampshire RG21 6XS.

Palgrave Macmillan in the US is a division of St Martin's Press LLC, 175 Fifth Avenue, New York, NY 10010.

Palgrave Macmillan is the global academic imprint of the above companies and has companies and representatives throughout the world.

Palgrave® and Macmillan® are registered trademarks in the United States, the United Kingdom, Europe and other countries.

ISBN-13: 978–0–230–22208–3 hardback

This book is printed on paper suitable for recycling and made from fully managed and sustained forest sources. Logging, pulping and manufacturing processes are expected to conform to the environmental regulations of the country of origin.

A catalogue record for this book is available from the British Library.

Library of Congress Cataloging-in-Publication Data
Televising history : mediating the past in post-war Europe / edited by
   Erin Bell, Ann Gray.
      p.   cm.
   Summary: "This fascinating essay collection examines the representation of history on television in Europe from a transnational and interdisciplinary perspective, including case studies from Britain, France, Spain, Italy, Germany, Belgium, the Netherlands, Denmark and Yugoslavia"— Provided by publisher.
   Includes bibliographical references and index.
   ISBN 978–0–230–22208–3 (hardback)
   1. Historical television programs—Europe—History and criticism.
   2. Documentary television programs—Europe—History and criticism.
   3. Documentary-style television programs—Europe.   4. Television and history—Europe.   5. History on television.   I. Bell, Erin, 1975–
   II. Gray, Ann, 1946–
   PN1992.8.H56T45 2010
   791.45′658—dc22   2010002677

10   9   8   7   6   5   4   3   2   1
19   18   17   16   15   14   13   12   11   10

Printed and bound in Great Britain by
CPI Antony Rowe, Chippenham and Eastbourne

Contents

List of Figures

Acknowledgements

We are grateful to our contributors for their patience and for providing such an interesting mix of scholarly research on this topic. The seeds for this collection were sown at the symposium 'Televising History: The Past(s) on the Small Screen' held at the University of Lincoln in 2005, which was attended by, amongst others, Tobias Ebbrecht, Emma Hanna and Jerome de Groot, who shared our enthusiasm for the topic and who have become good friends. John Corner, Brian Winston and Sylvia Harvey provided wise words of encouragement at the right moments. We thank our fellow members of the AHRC 'Televising History: 1995–2010' project team, Sarah Moody, Barbara Sadler and especially Carolyn Williams, the project administrator, for her charm and grace under pressure. Members of the project's Advisory Board have been tremendously supportive and we thank them for their guidance and valuable contributions to the direction of our work. We are grateful to the University of Lincoln for providing initial funding for the project and our colleagues in the Faculty of Media, Humanities & Technology, in particular Krista Cowman, Kate Hill, Nigel Morris, Tom Nicholls, John Simons and David Sleight, for smoothing our way. Christabel Scaife at Palgrave has been an excellent editor. Finally, our thanks to Florian Gleisner and Nick Gray for feigning interest in our project, putting up with our absences, and for their good-humoured tolerance of our distractions.

Erin Bell
Ann Gray

Note on the Cover: The façade of the Thomas-Weissbecker-Haus, Berlin Kreuzberg, which was created by those living in the house in the era and is one of few extant traces of West Berlin's liberal subculture of the 1970s and 1980s. We thank Tobias Ebbrecht who captured the image which the editors came across when lost in Berlin.

Notes on Contributors

Editors

Ann Gray is Professor of Cultural Studies at the University of Lincoln and Director of the AHRC-funded 'Televising History 1995–2010' project. She works in the fields of gender and technology, audience research and research methods.

Erin Bell was research fellow on the AHRC-funded 'Televising History 1995–2010' project and is currently a lecturer in History at the Lincoln School of Humanities and Performing Arts. She continues to work in the fields of gender and testimony and to publish on early modern history. A co-authored (with Ann Gray) book, *History on Television*, based on the 'Televising History' project research is forthcoming.

Contributors

Aileen Blaney is currently a post-doctoral scholar in the Graduate Department of Film Studies at Chung-Ang University in Seoul, where she is researching contemporary Korean cinema. Her primary research interests focus on the docudrama as an ethical mode of cultural representation and dynamic social practice. Her publications explore how post-conflict representations of historical suffering in UK/Irish film and television memorialize the past and circulate as public history artefacts.

Luisa Cigognetti has published numerous essays on film and history, and with Lorenza Servetti she has co-authored *Migranti in celluloide: Storici, cinema ed emigazione* (2003), and with Pierre Sorlin and Lorenza Servetti *La storia in televisione: Storici e registi a confronto* (2001). She has also co-edited, with Lorenza Servetti, historical films about the Italian Risorgimento and images of resistance in Europe during the Second World War.

John Corner is Visiting Professor in Communication Studies at the University of Leeds and an emeritus professor of the University of Liverpool. Recent work includes the edited collection with Dick Pels, *Media and the Restyling of Politics* (2003), and the authored volume with Peter Goddard and Kay Richardson, *Public Issue Television* (2007) together with a number of articles and book chapters, some still forthcoming, on aspects of mediated political culture, documentary form and critical aesthetics.

Jerome de Groot teaches in English and American Studies at the University of Manchester. His book on contemporary popular history, *Consuming*

History, which considers the ways in which contemporary popular culture engages with history, was published in 2008, and his *The Historical Novel* was published in 2009.

Sonja de Leeuw is Professor at the Department of Media and Culture Studies at Utrecht University. Her research and teaching interests are Dutch television culture in an international context (both history and theory) and media and cultural diversity (diasporic media, representation of ethnicity). She also co-ordinates a European research project on European television heritage, discussing issues such as creating access, contextualizing archival material, and memory and identity. Recent publications include *De man achter het scherm: De televisie van Erik de Vries* (2008) and 'TV nations or global medium? European television between national institution and window on the world', in Jonathan Bignell and Andreas Fickers (eds), *A European Television History* (2008).

Alexander Dhoest is a lecturer in media studies at the University of Antwerp and member of the Media, Policy and Culture research group. His doctoral research dealt with the construction of national identity in Flemish television drama. In his current research, he further investigates the historical and contemporary reception of domestic TV drama. He has published widely on these issues in journals and books such as *De verbeelde gemeenschap: 50 jaar Vlaamse tv-fictie en de constructie van een nationale identiteit* (2004) and co-edited with Enric Castelló and Hugh O'Donnell, *The Nation on Screen: Discourses of the National on Global Television* (2009).

Tobias Ebbrecht teaches media history at the Film and Television Academy (HFF) 'Konrad Wolf' at Potsdam-Babelsberg. His PhD research considered the representation of the Holocaust and Nazism in film and television. He has published articles on related topics including 'History, public memory and media event: Codes and conventions of historical event-television in Germany', in S. Nicholas, T.O'Malley and K. Williams (eds) *Reconstructing the Past: History in the Mass Media, 1890–2005* (2008) and, with Thomas Schick, he edited *Emotion – Empathie – Figur: Spielformen der Filmwahrnehmung* (2008).

Emma Hanna completed her PhD in history, 'The Great War on the Small Screen: British Television Documentaries about the First World War, 1964–2003' at the University of Kent in 2005, and works as a senior lecturer in History at the University of Greenwich. Her future research plans include breaking down the history versus cultural studies barrier with more inter-disciplinary work on the representation and consumption of historical imagery in British popular culture. Her first book, *The Great War on the Small Screen: Representing the First World War in Contemporary Britain*, was published in 2009.

Sira Hernández Corchete, PhD in Public Communication, is Assistant Lecturer in the School of Communication at the University of Navarra (Spain). She is author of *La historia contada en television: El documental televisivo de divulgación histórica en España* (2008) and of several articles dealing with the history of Spanish historical television documentary and the narrative and rhetorical ways that define the account of the past in images.

Amy Holdsworth is Lecturer in the Department of Theatre, Film and Television at the University of Glasgow. She has a PhD from the department of Film and Television Studies of the University of Warwick on British Television, Memory and Nostalgia. Her research interests primarily lie in the field of television theory, history and aesthetics. She is particularly interested in questions of form and genre, television history and memory, and memory and history on television. She has published in several journals including the *Journal of British Film and Television*.

Iris Kleinecke-Bates is Lecturer in Film Studies at the University of Hull. Her PhD research considered the representation of the nineteenth century on 1990s British television, and her research interests include television (in particular, British television), national cinemas (in particular, British and German cinema), costume drama, adaptation, representations of the past, memory and nostalgia. She has published in a number of journals, and her article on *The Forsyte Saga* was published in *Screen* 47.2 (2006).

Margit Rohringer is a lecturer at the University of Vienna and was formerly Research Associate in Film Studies at the University of Leicester and at the University of St. Andrews (UK) where she worked on the AHRB-funded project 'Balkan Cinema: Film and History'. She studied sociology and communication at the University of Vienna and wrote a thesis on Yugoslav cinema. Her monograph *Der jugoslawische Film nach Tito: Konstruktionen kollektiver Identitäten* was published by LIT-Verlag (2008). She has written various articles, reviews and essays related to Balkan cinema and culture and has curated film programmes featuring the cinema of the region. Her current work is on the representations of historical truths, memory and identity in Balkan documentary filmmaking. Her book *Documents on the Balkans: History, Memory, Identity: Representations of Historical Discourses in the Balkan Documentary Film* was published in 2009.

Pierre Sorlin is Emeritus Professor of Sociology in Audiovisual Media, University of Paris III, and he works at the Audiovisual Department at the Istituto Parri, Bologna. He is the author of (amongst other works) *European Cinemas, European Societies* (1991), *Mass Media* (1994), *Italian National Cinema* (1996) and *Dreamtelling* (2003).

Isabelle Veyrat-Masson is DR2 at the Centre National de la Recherche Scientifique, Paris; Director of the Centre Communication et Politique (LCP).

Her works include *Quand la television explore le temps* (Paris: Fayard, 2000). She has published, in the French language, books, articles and chapters dealing with history and French télévision. Recently she has published *Télévision et Histoire: le mélange des genres: Docudramas, docufictions et fictions du réel*; with Pascal Blanchard, *Les guerres de mémoires: La France et son histoire* (2008), and with Pascal Blanchard and Marc Ferro 'Les guerres de mémoires dans le monde', *Hermès*, 52 (2008).

Brian Winston is the first Lincoln Chair of Communication at the University of Lincoln and was formerly Pro-Vice Chancellor at the university. He won an Emmy for his script for the WNET series *Heritage: Civilization and the Jews* and has published widely on documentary film, most recently *Claiming the Real II: Documentary: Grierson and Beyond* (2008). His script for a feature documentary on Robert Flaherty, *A Boatload of Wild Irishmen*, is completing production, and he is editing the *BFI Companion to Documentary* for publication in 2010.

Introduction

History on Television in Europe: The Past Two Decades

Ann Gray and Erin Bell

Analysis of the representation of the past on screen is a rapidly developing field. In the 1990s, history programming made for TV increased exponentially in Europe, as well as the US, and a proliferation of different platforms – digital, satellite, Internet – and genres accompanied them, many of which are considered in this collection. These developments led to revived scholarly interest in the UK and continued interest in Western Europe (see, e.g., Feil, 1974; Knopp and Quandt, 1988; Kuehl, 1976; McArthur, 1978; Reimers and Friedrich, 1982; Watt, 1976) although until recently much debate has continued to focus upon the medium's inability to do 'proper' history. In 2005, at the outset of our AHRC-funded interdisciplinary 'Televising History 1995–2010' research project, there were still relatively few scholars working in this area.

Focussing on 'nonfiction' programming, the 4-year 'Televising History' project examined the different genres employed by producers during the 'boom' period, and tracked their commissioning, production, marketing and distribution histories. Through a number of case studies, including interviews with academic and media professionals involved in history programming, Ann Gray, the project's director, and Erin Bell, the research fellow, analysed the role of the 'professional' historian and producer/directors as mediators and interpreters of historical material. The project's two doctoral students, Barbara Sadler and Sarah Moody, considered regional history programming in the UK, and the use of broadcast material in the secondary school classroom and museums, respectively. The project aimed, from the outset, to ask how we get the kinds of television histories we do, and why. Starting with the relationship between the academy and media professionals, through commissioning and programme making, the project explored the often-competing professional discourses about how to 'do' history. Based on this research, key sub-genres have been identified, with analysis of how historical meanings are achieved, and these will be discussed further in forthcoming publications.

Other scholars working in the field include Graham Roberts and Philip M. Taylor, who in 2001 published their collection *The Historian, Television and Television History* with the aim of legitimizing the academic historical study of television. But arguably it was David Cannadine's edited collection *History and the Media*, published in 2004, with contributions from those involved in the industry as historians or media producers, which began to raise questions about how and in what ways history was represented on television. However, only a tiny proportion of the contributions came from scholars representing other disciplines, in particular those from media, television and cultural studies. Perhaps intended as a parallel volume in the related field of archaeology, and published only a few years later, Timothy Clack and Marcus Brittain's 2007 *Archaeology and the Media* drew together the insights of archaeologists and in some senses sought to be a guide, allowing the reader to explore the effects of media exposure – through television, but also cinema, radio and the press – on the discipline, and to reflect upon the possible implications especially for those working closely with the public. In common with the Cannadine collection, though, scholars from outside the field were largely absent.

However, unlike either of the two previously discussed volumes, Gary Edgerton and Peter Rollins' *Television Histories* (2001) successfully brought together the work of scholars from history, film, communication and television studies, as well as media practitioners, and its focus upon the US makes it an informative parallel collection to this volume, which seeks to consider European programming and identities. Indeed, several of the present volume's contributors have found it extremely useful. More recently, Enric Castelló, Alexander Dhoest and Hugh O'Donnell's *The Nation on Screen* (2009) has also sought to consider the ways in which the nation is depicted on television from a range of disciplinary perspectives, some of which consider history programming and offer insights into the different ways in which television reinforces national, and other, identities. From a specifically German perspective, Barbara Korte and Sylvia Paletschek's *History Goes Pop* (2009) similarly brings together scholars from different disciplines on the representation of the past in popular media and genres.

In the early days of our research we began to identify scholars from a range of disciplines working on this topic, and our first symposium 'Televising History: The Past(s) on the Small Screen' held at the University of Lincoln in July 2005 brought together several early career scholars together with more senior scholars, demonstrating the nascent nature of much of the field and the promise our interdisciplinary approach offered for the future.[1] Indeed, many of the key themes that emerged at that symposium are also apparent in this, extended, collection. We will now turn to important aspects of the apposite contexts of this collection identified as change and uncertainty in Europe, especially post-1990, and the consequent challenges to the television industry.

Change and uncertainty: Europe post-1990

Since the 1990s, with the fall of the Berlin Wall and the demise of Communist regimes in the centre and east of the continent, there has been renewed interest in the relationship between history, memory and identity in Europe. Myria Georgiou notes the increased mobility of people and ideas, 'both physical and mediated', in the continent. As she asserts:

> European cultural landscapes relate more to [Arjun] Appadurai's scapes... than to a stable political and bounded geographical zone... 'people, machinery, money, images and ideas now follow increasingly nonisomorphic paths'.
>
> (Georgiou, 2008, pp. 241–2)

In an example of this, the Dutch historian and journalist Geert Mak spent 1999 travelling across the continent, culminating in *In Europe*, a historical account of European memory and identity that became a bestseller in Europe and, in part, sought to determine if it is possible to pierce the 'shell of distance and alienation [which] had developed between Eastern and Western Europeans' (Mak, 2007, p. xiii). Although necessarily related to the massive political changes in former Communist states, journalists and scholars' interest has also been influenced by the development of policies – political and cultural, if the two can be separated – by the European Union, which sought to define the key areas of importance for European states and citizens. According to the EU's own website:

> With the collapse of communism... Europeans become closer neighbours. In 1993 the Single Market is [*sic*] completed with the 'four freedoms' of: movement of goods, services, people and money. (n.d.)[2]

Scholars working in a number of disciplines commented on the impact and implications of migration in the years following the end of the Cold War. Historians David Cesarani and Mary Fulbrook's 1996 edited collection on nationality and migration in Europe allowed scholars based in a number of European nations – EU and non-EU – to consider citizenship and migration within the continent, often by focussing upon recent examples from national history. James Wertsch (1997) too has offered an approach, in this case based in anthropology and psychology, to consider the relationship between history, identity and narrative; he asserts that narratives about the past serve as a 'cultural tool' to create and recreate national – and other – identities, particularly, it might be added, in times of social and political change. Philosopher David Carr also notes how the telling and retelling of a group's story articulates its identity: 'narrative is a mode of being before it is a mode of knowing' (2001, p. 199). This has been of especial interest to scholars and media professionals in the post-Cold War decades.

A more recent, and interdisciplinary, development in this field of scholarship has been Bignell and Fickers' (2008) collection *A European Television History*, which brings together television historians and media scholars to chart the development of television in Europe. In a similar manner, this collection brings historians, media and cultural studies scholars together to consider the related field of the representation of history on the small screen, and like the Bignell and Fickers volume, our collection too allows scholars to present case studies of programmes from different nations, reflecting their areas of expertise. Many of the authors explicitly or implicitly acknowledge the influence of international changes in the creation and distribution of history programming and also in academia.

Change and challenges: the television industry in Europe

Freedom of movement has been acknowledged in a number of scholarly analyses representing a range of disciplines, from history to cultural and media studies, produced from the early 1990s. Reflecting upon media and identity, media scholars Richard Collins (2002) and Jean Chalaby (2005) have considered the effects of these changes upon television in Europe. Chalaby asserts the close links, 'for much of its history', between television and national territory, although broadcasters have a long tradition of exchanging programmes and forming international associations (2005, p. 1). State broadcasters' monopolistic hold was not loosened until the 1980s, when cross-border TV channels, Chalaby suggests, became a potent source of the unravelling relationship between nation and television (2005, p. 1). Hundreds of such stations exist internationally and some air history programming. The Franco-German cultural channel ARTE, for example, began in 1998 to broadcast to francophone African nations (Mytton et al., 2005, p. 104), epitomizing Nestor Garcia Canclini's definition of de-territorialization: 'the loss of the "natural" relation of culture to geographical and social territories' (in Chalaby, 2005, p. 8).

More recently, Miyase Christensen and Nezih Erdoğan's collection *Shifting Landscapes* (2008) has highlighted the 'new opportunities and challenges' encountered since 1990. As they assert, for the almost 500 million Europeans, including those living outside the EU, 'this is a Europe radically different to the one that existed only a decade ago' (Christensen and Erdoğan, 2008, p. 1). Indeed, the shared history of many of the people of Europe – including the stateless – emphasizes both the need to consider the border-crossing of history on television in Europe, but also whose histories are, or are not, represented onscreen: this is not to suggest that there is a single European, Western or international culture due to the media, but rather that history on television, as this collection demonstrates, allows identification of areas of similarity – shared genres and common themes within programmes themselves and their production – as well as differences.

In 1989, the EU 'Television without Frontiers' directive, as Chalaby asserts, sought to remove 'the lingering national barriers to the international transmission of TV signals' (2005, p. 44).[3] In the face of the increasing challenge of commercial networks, which were to lead eventually to major changes in the types of programming broadcast, even by state broadcasters, in the following decade, 'Television without Frontiers' sought to preserve minimum standards in broadcasting based on the European Declaration of Human Rights, and effectively moderated the free market. In 1997 this was developed to include the free movement of programmes within the single market. In 1999, as part of the Amsterdam Treaty, this was amended to protect PSB, and underpin the democratic, social and cultural needs of each society in the EU: a compromise between national culture and free trade that recognized that broadcasting involves a cultural exchange as well as a financial transaction. Indeed, in 2001 the European Commission noted that the media 'are the principal vector for the transmission of our European cultural identities'.[4] This is despite Collins' assertion that the directive was unsuccessful due to 'Europeans' disinclination to consume each others' culture' (2002, p. 33), which Milly Buonanno views as cultural determinism (2003, p. 535). Further, although linguistic proximity may explain British audiences' preferences for US shows, the re-versioning of the same history programmes for different European audiences suggests that some themes, events and formats may well be shared. This collection, whilst demonstrating the broad range of genres and formats available to broadcasters in several European nations, also shows elements common to many, if not all. Indeed, Buonanno counsels against concluding that local – for example, British – viewers are 'naturally' disinclined towards other European cultures, and she suggests that this is due to a number of historical and cultural circumstances (p. 536). Collins too asserts that location is less significant than ever in limiting the 'possibilities of co-operative working relationships' internationally (2002, p. 1). This collection demonstrates the veracity of Buonanno's comments.

Whilst Collins emphasizes the plurality of European identity, and Buonanno does not deny this although she seeks to contextualize it, they do so by identifying Europeans' shared experience of the mass media. This volume too seeks to consider elements of television, one aspect of this, across the continent. Like Collins, we accept the difficulty in identifying a European cultural identity (2002, p. 33). As historian David Ellwood asserts, there are 'current tensions between the local and the global in Europe ... [in terms of] the region's audio-visual industries'. These, he believes, originated in the 1920s and in efforts to defend 'an idea of nationhood which presumed sovereignty over culture' against the perceived onslaught of American cinema and radio (Ellwood, 2009, p. 109). These strategies of cultural protectionism were developed in the following decades and, he suggests, although every European society uses the same tactics to face up to globalization, the impulse to cling to local identities 'is, if anything, getting stronger' (Ellwood, 2009, p. 109).

Taking this desire to maintain national identities into account, and history on television as our focus, this collection also finds much in common with the NHIST project. The ESF-funded 'Representations of the Past: The Writing of National Histories in Europe', or NHIST, research programme (2003–2008) brought together historians from across Europe and the multivolume edited collections produced as a result of this project compare and contrast the ways in which written accounts of the past, and particularly 'master narratives' linked to the specific conditions of their institutional production, relations of hegemony and forms of political organization in a nation, and to some degree heritage sites and cinema, have created and sustained national identities for centuries before their more recent erosion. The initiators and chairs, Professors Stefan Berger, Christoph Conrad and Guy P. Marchal, outline the significance of the project and see it as arising from 'the long and successful history of the national paradigm in history-writing; and, secondly, because of its re-emergence as a powerful political tool in the 1990s in the context of the accelerating processes of Europeanisation and globalisation'.[5] The participants' findings allow comparisons to be made between historiography and national identity in different regions of Europe, as well as acknowledging the ways in which national histories and historiographies may ignore, erase or otherwise neglect the presence of religious and cultural minorities: Jews and Muslims are key examples (see Berger, 2008, p. 14). Those involved acknowledge the potential of representations of the past in other forms such as film and heritage sites; this collection similarly offers comparative and comparable accounts of the mediation of history through television.

A further initiative in which we were invited to participate is the 'For a European TV History' workshop series held by the Istituto Parri in Bologna, enabling comparisons to be made, primarily by historians, across Western European (EU) borders about the state of factual history programming, and in future years this will be further developed by the addition of Eastern European scholars (see Cigognetti, Servetti and Sorlin, 2009). The absence of Eastern European scholars from this collection demonstrates the still nascent status of research into the representation of the past on television in former Eastern bloc nations, a situation that will hopefully be rectified in the coming years.[6]

The representation of the past on European television

It is then of crucial importance, given the scholarly, cultural and political issues highlighted in the previous sections, to consider how the past has been represented on European television over this period of change and uncertainty. The contributors to this volume consider programming dating from the post-war era, to the present day. The volume is divided into four sections. The first, 'Perspectives', gives an overview of history programming in terms of its production, construction, aesthetics and aims. John Corner's contribution opens the volume with his analysis of the ways in which documentaries open and give the viewer a sense of the historical past in the key early minutes. The following chapter by Pierre Sorlin and Luisa Cigognetti, joint convenors of the 'For a European TV History' referred to above, is very much a position piece, highlighting the much-debated nature of the representation of the past on television and the scholarship surrounding it. Their chapter gives a sense of how such documentaries are made, particularly the role of archival material. As historians and documentary makers, they are able to bring perspectives from both disciplines to their chapter. Brian Winston and Ann Gray's contributions both, in different ways, consider the contexts in which history programmes are made: Ann Gray outlines the role of media producers and commissioning editors in influencing the type of programming broadcast, albeit within certain limitations and with the requirements of audience and broadcasters in mind. She identifies the existence of a community of professionals working together, often for many years, who have been influential in creating and sustaining a boom in history programming in the UK. Brian Winston writes as a media professional of his experiences making one particular series. Erin Bell's contribution charts the development of oral testimony in history programming since the 1960s, considering continuity and change in the representation of this particular onscreen historical source.

'Televised history and national identity' brings together the work of a range of scholars who consider explicitly the links between history programming and national identity. Isabelle Veyrat-Masson, seeking a long-range perspective, considers the particular use of Napoleon Bonaparte as a historical figure, used in differing ways in different periods, but almost always to reflect upon French national identity. Emma Hanna considers British identity, but in this case the history series that have identified the role of other landscapes – in France or Belgium – in evoking a sense of identity through the battlefields of the Great War. Sira Hernández Corchete considers more recent events – the 'Transicion' from autocratic to democratic government in Spain in the late 1970s and early 1980s – and the ways in which Spaniards more recently have reflected on these events, and their national and European identities.

In 'Televised history, memory and identity', scholars consider the representation of minority, religious, cultural or ethnic identities. Sonja de Leeuw's analysis of several Dutch fictional series allows insight into the still sensitive and significant topic of the murder of the majority of Jewish Dutch citizens in the Second World War, and the ways in which this has been remembered, or forgotten, in later years. Aileen Blaney similarly considers the way in which memories of more recent events, the 'Troubles' in Northern Ireland, have been represented in recent series, although, as her account suggests, such memories cannot yet be set aside and are still raw and troubling. Margit Rohringer's consideration of documentary representations of the Balkan conflict, particularly of the abuse of women, draws attention to the international debate surrounding war crimes, and the ways in feminist scholars in other nations have identified with the conflict and its victims. A position piece, it highlights the ways in which contentious aspects of the past have been represented onscreen and continue to prove significant in ongoing international debates. Finally, Alexander Dhoest's contribution considers dramatized representations of the rural Flemish past in Belgium, but also its relationship to the nascent Flemish-language and cultural community that later developed effectively into a (sub)nation.

In the final section, 'History programming: form, genre and technique', the contributors consider a range of genres of history programming. Jerome de Groot considers the recent phenomenon of diet-related reality history, and the ways in which this may offer opportunities for viewers and participants to see or experience the embodiment of the past whilst reaching present-day goals relating to appearance. Tobias Ebbrecht's chapter considers the more commonly considered genre of dramadoc/docudrama, and he analyses several German-language examples from the 1970s to the present day, allowing him to suggest the way in which the genre can open up a narrative, avoid a passive viewing experience, and ultimately problematize ideas of historical knowledge and its representation. Iris Kleinecke-Bates' chapter on daytime programming and the representation of the past offers insights into the ways in which history and historical objects are used in programming based around the selling of (often) inherited objects in order, as in the series de Groot considers, to attain a goal in the present. This employment of 'daytime' and 'lifestyle' genres is amongst those seen by BBC2 Controller Janice Hadlow (2009) as demonstrating that representations of the past have seeped into programming across genres and the schedule. Amy Holdsworth considers how the past is re-enacted to some degree in the extremely significant, and now international, series *Who Do You Think You Are?* and provides an overview of some of its key elements whilst alerting us, as all the chapters in this section do to some extent, to its significance as an alternative means of representing the past.

When introducing this collection, then, it has been important to emphasize the range of national televisions' output, of genres and of scholarly approaches to them. However, as this overview demonstrates, there are considerable opportunities for the contributions to be used towards comparative research into the representation of the past on television. If this is achieved, many of the original goals of the editors in bringing the collection together will have been attained.

Notes

1. See the Special Issue, 'Televising History', of the *European Journal of Cultural Studies* 10.1 February 2007, guest edited by Erin Bell.
2. The History of the European Union (English version) (n.d.) *Europa*: http://europa. eu/abc/history/index_en.htm. Accessed 20 June 2009.
3. See the Television without Frontiers directive (n.d.) *Europa*: http://ec.europa. eu/avpolicy/reg/tvwf/index_en.htm and amended in 1997: http://eur-lex.europa. eu/LexUriServ/site/en/consleg/1989/L/01989L0552-19970730-en.pdf. Accessed 20 June 2009.
4. Commission Staff Working Paper on certain legal aspects relating to cinematographic and other audiovisual works SEC (2001) 619 11 April2001 (p. 3): http:// www.docstoc.com/docs/969417/Commission-staff-working-document-Films-andfilming-industry. Accessed 20 June 2009.
5. See www.esf.org for further details.
6. See, for example, Aune Unt's work on Estonian television presented at the 'Narrating the Nation' conference in Reus, Spain, 4–5 October 2007.

Bibliography

Berger, S. (2008) *Writing the Nation: A Global Perspective* (London: Palgrave MacMillan).
Bignell, J. and A. Fickers (eds) (2008) *European Television History* (London: Blackwell).
Buonanno, M. (2003) Book review, R. Collins, *Media and Identity, European Journal of Communication* 18.4, 534–6.
Cannadine, D. (ed.) (2004) *History and the Media* (London: Palgrave MacMillan).
Carr, D. (2001) 'Getting the story straight: narrative and historical knowledge', in G. Roberts (ed.), *The History and Narrative Reader* (London: Routledge).
Castelló, E., Dhoest, A. and O'Donnell, H. (eds) *The Nation on Screen: Discourses of the National on Global Television* (Newcastle: Cambridge Scholars).
Cesarani, D. and M. Fulbrook (eds) (1996) *Citizenship, Nationality and Migration in Europe* (London: Routledge).
Chalaby, J.K. (ed.) (2005) *Transnational Television Worldwide* (London: I.B. Tauris).
Christensen, M. and N. Erdoğan (2008) 'Introduction: the many faces of film and media in Europe', in M. Christensen and N. Erdoğan (eds), *Shifting Landscapes: Film and Media in European Context* (Newcastle: Cambridge Scholars).
Cigognetti, L., L. Servetti and P. Sorlin (eds) (2009) *Media e cultura comunitaria: per una storia televisiva dell'Europa* (Bologna: Regione Emilia-Romagna Assemblea legislativa).
Clack, T. and M. Brittain (eds) (2007) *Archaeology and the Mmedia* (Walnut Creek, CA: Left Coast Press).
Collins, R. (2002) *Media and Identity in Contemporary Europe* (Portland, OR: Intellect).
Feil, G. (1974) *Zeitgeschichte im Deutschen Fernsehen* (Osnabruck: Fromm).
Georgiou, M. (2008) 'Shifting cultural landscapes, shifting boundaries: disaporic media in Europe', in M. Christensen and N. Erdoğan (eds), *Shifting Landscapes: Film and Media in European Context* (Newcastle: Cambridge Scholars).
Hadlow, J. (2009) 'The future of history programming on TV' presentation at the 'Televising History 2009' conference, University of Lincoln, 22–25 July.
Korte, B. and S. Paletschek (eds) (2009) *History Hoes Pop: zur Repräsentation von Geschichte in populären Medien und Genres* (Bielefeld: transcript).
Knopp, G. and S. Quandt (eds) (1988) *Geschichte im Fernsehen* (Darmstadt: Wissenschaftliche Buchgesellschaft).

Kuehl, J. (1976) 'History on the public screen II', in P. Smith (ed.) *The Historian and Film* (Cambridge: Cambridge University Press).

Mak, G. (2007 [2004]) *In Europe: Travels through the Twentieth Century* (London: Harvill Secker).

McArthur, C. (1978) *Television and History* (London: BFI).

Mytton, G., R. Teer-Tomaselli and A.-J. Tudesq (2005) 'Transnational television in sub-Saharan Africa', in J.K. Chalaby (ed.) (2005) *Transnational Television Worldwide* (New York: I.B. Tauris).

Reimers, K.F. and H. Friedrich (eds) (1982) *Zeitgeschichte im film und fernsehen* (Munich: Olschlager).

Roberts, G. and P.M. Taylor (eds) (2001) *The Historian, Television and Television History*. Luton: University of Luton Press.

Watt, P. (1976) 'History on the public screen I', in P. Smith (ed.) *The Historian and Film* (Cambridge: Cambridge University Press).

Wertsch, J. (1997) 'Narrative tools of history and identity', *Culture and Psychology*, 3.1, 5–20.

Part I
Perspectives

1

'Once Upon a Time...'

Visual Design and Documentary Openings

John Corner

In this chapter, I shall explore aspects of documentary design, particularly visual design, in relation to depictions of the historical. The broad issue of how varieties of documentary television treat historical topics has recently become the subject of lively discussion, as this volume amply indicates (for other examples, see Champion, 2003; Cannadine, 2004; and Bell, 2007). I want to provide focus and originality for my own account not only by my choice of examples but also by the way I use them to concentrate on how documentary accounts *start* and on the way they establish their connections with 'the past', mostly by variously locating viewers within their material and subjective settings. Before I do this, it might be useful for me to make some brief points of a more general kind about the relation of documentary visual design to historical themes. These points will connect, and at points overlap, with discussions and typologies put forward in other chapters.

The 'visual challenge' and the modes of television history

Historical subjects, with the constraints they introduce on what can be seen, and on what is available to show, present documentary film with a challenge to its strategies of picturing. Unlike engagement with the contemporary, where a variety of methods can be used to obtain a strong 'visual offer' of people, places, circumstances and events relevant to (if not always literally depicting) the subject-field, historical portrayal frequently has to work more indirectly. As the available filmic and photographic record – the accessible archive – becomes fragmented and reduces to zero in relation to a particular topic and its historical distance, this indirectness of engagement is forced into greater ingenuity and, indeed, faces greater challenges in respect of programme integrity.

I think we can usefully identify four basic modes of portrayal for films and programmes with a primary interest in historical material. Other contributors to this book will connect with them variously, according to their analytic focus and conceptual agenda. Each mode has different implications for the deployment of images, but each is capable of being used in different combinations with the others.

1. Commentary mode

Here, the experience of viewing is largely if not wholly organized in terms of the speech of a voiceover account that may be continuous but also can be regularly interrupted so as to allow more direct engagement with forms of visual portrayal or with a section of on-screen speech. The advantage of commentary mode is that it allows greater scope for the compilation of pictures from widely different sources, including archives, and it is therefore not surprising that it is the form in which many historical series are grounded, although often they include work in other modes too. It also provides strong narrative shaping, since the spoken exposition can take the form of a story with varying degrees of emphasis and approximation to fictional models, and it can use its spoken account economically and effectively to embed shorter stories within the broader one. The exposition can operate at a very general level, using the images over which it is placed merely as indicative and generic, whatever their specific origin. On the other hand, the material and the approach may permit a move down to a lower level, one where the commentary articulates both temporal and physical particularities in alignment with what is depicted visually (e.g., *this* street, *this* man, *this* boat, *this* storm at sea, *this* day in *this* year).

There has been suspicion of the way voiceover commentary in historical documentary can foreclose on viewer engagement with the images and perform an unacceptable degree of closure on what viewers understand about what they see. In his brilliantly original short monograph on television and history, Colin McArthur (1978) examines some instances of this as part of his wider exploration of word–image relations. However, for many projects commentary has been judged as indispensable given the continuity and descriptive detail it provides (often using an actor to bring out the best from the script), and it is likely to remain a strong option for historical television, used increasingly in combination with other modes rather than as the sole approach. Classical examples of work using this mode would be *Victory at Sea* (NBC, 1952) and *The Great War* (BBC, 1964), the latter also incorporating extensive interviews with surviving soldiers.

2. Presenter mode

Presenter mode is a form with an extensive and varied lineage, but also one that has been extensively used in television over the last decade, especially in the format of big-budget historical series, where it has made inroads on the dominance of commentary formats using an unseen narrator. The impact of 'reality television' on historical programming has clearly worked to increase the premium placed on work that is 'personalized', and a presenter address achieves this more directly and perhaps more effectively than any of the other modes. Work in this mode may, of course, use voiceover commentary for sequences, but even these sequences then take on a different identity as a result of the voice being that of an identified person who at points appears on screen and is the notional *author* of the words he or she speaks in a manner quite unlike that of most work organized by commentary alone.

A pictorial requirement of this mode is that there are shots of the presenter in a historically significant context, whether outdoors or indoors. The presentation may thereby often be offered partly from 'within' the relevant historical frame, allowing for imaginative extension, or at least in close material proximity to its traces. This provides a very different affective quality to the presentation from that obtained by speech from a study or library (sequences of which might also be included to reinforce the academic or research dimensions of the account). In programmes that include extensive presentation from location settings, it follows that quite elaborate strategies of composition and movement may be devised. These enable the speech to be delivered within pictorially 'strong' framings, where the following of the presenter's own movements and gaze is efficient for the evocativeness of the visual display, for the cogency of the spoken account and also for the production of a more general historical *feeling* in the audience. There are countless examples employing this extremely popular mode as the main approach, including Simon Schama's major series, *A History of Britain* (BBC, 2000–2).

3. Testimony mode and interviews

One of the strongest developments in documentary history on television has been the use made of oral testimony in contexts where the period under scrutiny makes this possible. Unlike the interviews of news and current-affairs programmes, the speech here will most frequently consist of long stretches of reflection, sometimes strongly subjective in character, delivered as if without prompting and certainly without following the tight agenda of an interviewer. The use of testimony interviews in historical films and programmes will tend to differ from usage in a broader range of social issue documentaries in respect of the emphasis on memory, often supported by physical contexts within which particular acts of recall are given amplified significance as both forms of 'inner speech' and forms of public communication. It is significant for my overall theme in this chapter that testimony often provides a powerful watching, not just listening, experience for the viewer. It may do this partly because of the physical location of the speaker. However, the visual and dramatic interest of a person, and particularly a face, in an act of recollection, is an important factor in the semiotics and the power of testimony.

In many instances, testimony begun in-shot is carried across as voiceover film, where it performs a role similar to commentary except that it is likely to read as being located, at least partly, within the event-world being portrayed on screen rather than being external to it. So the affective character of such sequences, as well as the nature of the information being offered, will be different from that of conventional commentary, setting up more experiential and subjectively deep viewing alignments with the past.

Interviews with historians and various 'experts' really constitute a separate mode, although interviews can be included in programmes designed primarily to work with testimony, just as they are to be found in commentary and presenter structures. In a programme driven by commentary, different interview positions can be subsumed within it to reflect variant interpretations and perhaps interpretive conflict (just how the commentary account relates to the interplay of interview accounts would then be a key issue). In the case of interview speech primarily presented in-shot, the historical interpretation of the presenter can be brought into a sharper and more personalized confrontation with those of other specialists, often within interviews portrayed as personal encounters consisting of dialogue rather than discrete sequences of 'input'. Although interviews with those professionally concerned with producing historical knowledge offer an obvious route to getting depth of detail, context and debate into a programme, the sense of distance they introduce and the possibilities for reduced appeal they can bring (lowered visual interest, preference for the complex over the simple in relation to both explanatory schemes and language) has resulted in them being treated warily within much recent television. One clear option has been the personable historian presenter as discussed earlier, anchoring the programme throughout within visually engaging settings and requiring little further academic supplement, thereby avoiding the risks this can bring to design and pacing.

Examples of testimony mode can be found in classic work like *World at War* (Thames/ITV, 1973) and in a wide range of more recent television where techniques of oral history can be applied. A 'casual' rather than formal use of specialist input (i.e., through conversational encounters rather than discrete sections) is to be found in a current series, *Who Do You Think You Are?* (Wall to Wall/ BBC, 2004–) where the person tracing his or her family tree frequently receives guidance from archivists and historians. Many current one-off and series-form history documentaries bring in elicited comments from historians to develop a specialist point, either by interview exchange with a presenter or by a straight insertion into the programme flow, introduced by the commentary. An example would be the widely popular *Timewatch* series, currently shown in weekly editions on BBC2 since 2002. Using interview and/or testimony as the sole mode, thereby giving up both on commentary and presentation, requires the right topic, 'strong' participant talk and very careful design, almost always at points including speech from the participants used as voiceover in order to open out the narrative space across images other than those of people speaking. One of my examples discussed below, Michael Grigsby's *Rehearsals* (Channel 5, 2005), uses this approach.

4. Re-enactment mode

Re-enactment has caused dispute about integrity not only between documentary producers and historians but also amongst documentary makers themselves, some of whom have declined to use it while others have made it a key feature. Re-enactment offers itself as an answer to the central problem of historical documentary referred to earlier, that is to say the fact that 'history' is often more a matter of absences than presences. However evocative the portrayal of places and objects can be, together with descriptions from various sources of the circumstances and events in which they were involved, the showing of historical persons and historical action through dramatization has been a tempting option, especially for those seeking a popular audience within a television economy increasingly weighted towards entertainment. Jerome de Groot (2008) provides a thorough survey of history as popular culture that includes those 'reality show' re-enactments in which 'ordinary people' perform historical roles as part of their own, as well as the audience's, route to a deeper understanding of the past.

The scale of dramatization across the range of historical documentary production varies from minimalist usage in which indications of action (a swung sword, a coach arriving at a castle, a body falling into the river) are offered for a brief shot or two in order to give strong visual projection, through to work in which dramatic portrayal is sustained and elaborate, aligning the work more closely with feature fiction.

A key issue in historical re-enactment, as in all drama-documentary production, is the extent to which what is portrayed is underpinned by evidence or is an exercise in creative licence, taking its cue from only the most general and perhaps questionable of historical sources, if any at all. Dramatization is perhaps a better term than re-enactment to cover the entire range of practices under this heading, given the real obstacles to obtaining clear and precise data on the initial 'enactment'. However, the availability of recorded speech and film from more recent periods has sometimes allowed a high degree of fidelity to be achieved, at least for brief sequences and for longer in cases where transcripts from the original event can be sourced.

Dramatization is now extensive in history television, sometimes as a component, less frequently as the main or even exclusive mode. *Culloden* (BBC, 1964) is discussed further below, but another classic example would be *Invasion* (Granada, 1980), reconstructing the events of the Soviet invasion of Czechoslovakia in 1968. A more recent, and very powerful, example would be *Witchcraze* (BBC, 2003) concerning the persecution of suspected witches in late sixteenth-century Scotland.

History lessons

I want to look now at four brief examples of historical styling in documentaries. Although they display no more than a selection of the range of approaches and techniques that have been employed by production teams, each attempts to engage innovatively with the practical business of generating both knowledge and feelings in the viewer. Each also displays at least one of the modes discussed above, although there is inventiveness and combination too, and therefore no straight, illustrative relationship between the sequence of the basic modes as outlined and the sequence of the examples. Together, the examples run across different periods in the technological, aesthetic and economic development of the documentary and my inclusion of a first instance from cinema rather than television is, I hope, provocative and revealing rather than digressive. Jennings' historical portrait from 1951 was addressed to a popular national audience just at the time when television was establishing itself as a major medium of knowledge and entertainment, and would do so with increasing pace around the Coronation of 1953, After the strongly English-oriented emphasis provided by Jennings, my other examples work rhetorically with Scottish, Welsh and Northern Irish themes.

Family Portrait (Wessex Films, 1951)

This film was written and directed by the influential documentarian Humphrey Jennings (and produced by Ian Dalrymple) for the Festival of Britain in 1951. It is subtitled 'A Film on the Theme of the Festival of Britain' and is essentially a commentary film:

> Perhaps because we in Britain live on a group of small islands, we like to think of ourselves as a family. And of course, with the unspoken affection and outspoken words that all families have. And so the Festival of Britain is a kind of family reunion . . . . .
>
> And so let's take a look at ourselves . . . . .
>
> *(The above is spoken over a sequence of 7 still shots angled in the frame as a hand turns over the pages of a 'family album' in which they are placed. The images are of family groups on the beach in Summer, scenes of the blitz, scenes at a christening and at Christmas).*
>
> **Where to Begin?**
>
> Here, this is Beachy Head. *(cliffs: camera tilts down to lighthouse on rocks below and then pans, and then cuts to other objects)*. There's the Channel joining and dividing. That's the remains of a Radar Station here during the war. Air Ministry property – Keep Out.
>
> *(Portrait of Sir Francis Drake, a pan across a painting of the Armada, fading into real sea and cliffs again). Music begins: soft strings.*

When Drake was fighting the Armada – and this is part of Family History – the Spaniards said he had a magic mirror in his cabin which revealed enemy ships to him. What we should call marine radar. You could have seen the Armada from here, and the Normans too over there, the other side of Eastbourne. And the Romans.

The fact is our Ancestors nearly all came as invaders. (*Stone circles*) And they had to be enterprising chaps and good sailors to do it. Early Bronze Age, Late Bronze Age, different layers of Celts, shiploads of Jutes, Viking and Saxons. Remember Kipling? 'Where the Long Man of Wilmington Looks Naked to the Shires' (*picture of this landmark carving*). Saxon probably. *Music: rhythmic and faster in tempo but still soft.*

A very mixed family as you see. But who together have resisted further invasion for nearly a thousand years.

And then the extraordinary diversity of nature in this small space. The variety of land structure.... The rapid exchanges in the weather above.... All, somehow, match the diversity of the people. (*Landscape and sky shots; scenes in a mine*). *Music: strings increasing in melodic development and volume.*

You can see it in Shakespeare. (*London dock scene*) Today it's all wharfs, cranes, warehouses, imports, exports. But the place is still called Bankside (*street sign*). It was here that Shakespeare created Hamlet and Lady Macbeth and Falstaff... 'To hold, as twere, the Mirror up to Nature'. (*Portly man drinking from beer glass in crowded pub*). Nor classical gods or heroic figures. But individual people, with souls of their own. And the small parts, the comics and hangers-on. (*Barrel organ player in exterior shot; interior of pub, trio of men miming to music; man finishes his glass of beer*). All different from each other, as we feel ourselves to be...

The rhetoric of this opening is, characteristically for Jennings, a quiet one. Indeed, the commentary, although it controls the entire sequence, is understated, conversationalized, to a point which can now appear comic in its wish to work with certain assumptions about the casual, taken-for-granted equality existing between speaker and audience and between audience and the diverse parts of the nation. Nothing needs asserting over the pictures; a 'mention', a 'reminder' is enough. It is, of course, the framing conceit of 'nation as family' that underpins this spoken address, a conceit that is aspirational (and ideological) as much as descriptive. The commentary presents us with a sense of place that develops into a sense of time and then of value. Our visual access to Beachy Head and the Thames-side setting achieve their magnitude of interconnected meaning as a result of the phrasings placed across them, the national story which they help 'illustrate'. This is a story in which diversity is built into the making of the nation not simply identified as a contemporary social feature. The historical orientation achieved by the visuals is not period specific but a series of connections, with the heritage of national place, national person and national character given continuity by landscape, weather, commerce and a Shakespearean sense of the richness and pathos of the mundane. This is the past not as 'distant' but as formative and active, so that the Armada and the coastal defences of the Second World War show continuity around the idea of 'invasion' that is both topographical and political. We can read the past by looking at the present, and the commentary guides us in doing this.

Culloden (BBC, 1964)

Peter Watkins' *Culloden* is one of the most powerful and innovative history programmes ever to be shown on British television. It is a dramatic re-enactment of this crucial battle of 1746 (in which an English army put down the Jacobite 'rebellion'), but its brilliance of impact is achieved by the idea of portraying events as if they were being filmed by a modern television current-affairs documentary team (the style and mode of address of the Granada series *World in Action* was a particular influence, as it was in Watkins' later and perhaps even more famous programme, *The War Game* (1965)). This conceit reframes the historical events in an 'as if' contemporary way, modifying audience perception both of the physical action and of the motives and experiences of the participants so as to intensify our sense of what is happening and our emotional involvement with it. After a pre-title sequence, rendered through commentary and interview exchange, the film provides a sustained scrutiny of the Jacobite army gathered on the moors:

> *To the music of pipes, faces of men and boys gathered in line are slowly panned across; they look at the camera, some blankly and some with evident self-consciousness and awkwardness. The commentary describes them:*
>
> James MacDonald, taxman, senior officer in a ruthless clan system who has brought with him on to the moor men whose land he controls.
>
> Alistair McVurrich, subtenant of a taxman, owns one eighth of an acre of soggy ground and two cows.
>
> Alan McColl, sub-tenant of a sub-tenant. Owns half share in a small potato patch measuring 30 feet.
>
> Angus Macdonald servant of a sub-tenant. He owns nothing. Lowest in the clan structure, he is called a cotter. This man is totally dependent on the men above him in the clan system, they in their turn on the taxmen, they in their turn on this one man, the man who has brought them all on to the moor. Alexander MacDonald, called in Gaelic, MacDhomhnuill, Chief of the McDonalds of Keppoch. The owner of all his tenants' land, the rent he has charged them is to fight with him as clan warriors whenever he decrees. This is the system of the Highland clan – human rent.
>
> *There follow brief comments from some of the men in direct address to the camera, medium close-up. The first is in English from the 'taxman' noted above:*
>
> 'I hold my land from MacDhomhnuill as my father did by bringing him 20 fighting men from among my tenants – these I have brought.'

There then follow statements in Gaelic from other men, translated into English afterwards. The first of these speakers says:
  'I fight today because it is an honour to be with my chief, MacDhomhnuill, and because my father fought beside his father'.

The strength of this scene lies in the way in which it provides us with what sounds like a cool, schematic history lesson about the clan system at the same time as the camera concentrates on the faces of the men who are being discussed, locating them in the ranks preparing for battle. The 'coolness' of journalistic address acts as a kind of front for what is, in effect, a devastating critique of social relations and of exploitation drawing partly on modern assumptions about power and social order. As John Cook points out, in the perceptive critical commentary on the film made available as an option in the DVD release (Cook, 2003), the men look back at the camera, at times staring blankly into it, in a way that accords more with the conventions of news footage than classical observational documentary. This returned gaze, as Cook notes, works to implicate viewers in the developing events in a disquieting manner that would not occur were they to be placed 'unaware' before the camera in the styles of observational documentary and (differently) of fictional drama. The analytic distance achieved by the commentary and the uncomfortable proximity achieved by the camera are twin parts of the strategy of portrayal. A little later in the film, something similar can be seen in the way in which Watkins depicts the weaponry in use and then its effects:

A cast iron ball of 3 pounds weight, fired from open sites, this is roundshot.
  (*visuals: shot laid ready on the ground and the loading and firing of a cannon*)
  This is what it does
  Alistair McInnis, age 20, right leg severed below knee joint.
  Malcolm Angus Chisholm, age 24, disembowelled.
  Ian MacDonald, age 13, shot.
  (*visuals: cannon shots before each of these identifications, and scenes of the screaming, injured victims after each*).

Here, the sharp contrast between the dispassionately *spoken* factual details of the munitions and the roll call of the victims, on the one hand, and the suffering which is *shown*, on the other, is shocking in a way which suggests a clear intention to play off viewing relationships (distant/close) against one another and also to play off forms of knowing (abstract/particular).
  Culloden is internally framed by what I termed above the 'commentary mode' but it works essentially and powerfully within the 're-enactment' mode, within whose terms the primary design is conceived and of which it is

an outstanding, 'classic' instance. The two are fused by the fact that the presenter is projected as 'there' at the battle himself (though, in order to avoid visual anachronism, not seen), commenting and interviewing within the diegetic frame. The commentary is therefore part of the dramatization rather an adjunct to it, as might be the case in another kind of documentary design.

The Dragon Has Two Tongues (HTV: Channel 4/S4C, 1985)

This series on the history of Wales, directed by Colin Thomas, also stands as a landmark in the styling of the past for television. It is most notable for the ambitious way in which it directly engages with the nature of history as contentious knowledge, subject to variations in interpretative framework and selected detail. It starts with a pre-title sequence:

1. The TV presenter Wynford Vaughan Thomas, wearing a suit and standing at a table in a well-furnished and book-lined study, addressing students (connotations of 'college seminar').

When I first went up to Oxford in 1927 my college tutor said to me 'Ah my dear fellow so you're going to read history. Fascinating subject. After all what is history? Divine gossip about the past among gentlemen. Have another glass of port.' *He picks up a glass from the table and drinks.*

2. Labour historian Professor Gwyn Williams surrounded by a group of workers in an exterior industrial setting. The context is suggestive of a work meeting and his speech is powerfully delivered. It runs across a few seconds of silent visuals from the preceding, 'Oxford', scene before the visual shift:

History is more than a page in a book. History is the buckle that bites your back. History is the sweat that's hanging over your eyes. History is the fear crawling in your belly.

The programme then moves through its title sequence, run underneath a lyrical score, including the use of traditional instruments. A Welsh flag unfurls, a dragon snarls and breathes fire. Shots in succession contrastively show 'snapshots' from ancient to modern (e.g., stone circles and castles to mines and steel works) ending in a museum gallery and its marble statues.

Series Title: 'A History of the Welsh'

Two inset screens, side by side. In one, Vaughan-Thomas in a smart raincoat walks across a field. In the other, Gwyn Williams, in working clothing, is with the group of men. The two presenters are placed in a relationship both of marked difference and implied antagonism (through both their positioning and their movement within their inset frames).

Edition title: 1. Where to Begin?

OPENING SCENE 1. *A rough sea on the Gower peninsula, near Swansea. Shots from the side and from above and below. Vaughan-Thomas, in walking clothes, booted and carrying a rucksack, makes his way up across steep rocks. He approaches the camera point and lifts up his face in direct address:*

The history of Wales. Where does it start? Well, I reckon it starts right here on the wild cliffs of Paviland in the Gower peninsula, 15 miles west of Swansea. And the reason that I've chosen this point? Quite simple. Just around the corner from here, on a rather slippery rock traverse which I hope I can negotiate, they found in the Paviland caves, the remains of the very first human being, I didn't call him the first Welshman, whom we can recognise in our history. They dug him up and they discovered he was the remains of a young man who lived 17,500 years ago.

OPENING SCENE 2: *Williams, wearing a miner's helmet and overalls, is shut into a colliery cage, which goes down the shaft. As it noisily descends, he addresses the camera:*

I want to begin the history of Wales with this particular journey into a Welsh past at Blaenafon Big Pit in Gwent. For years, 1 Welshman in every 4 made this journey every day of his working life and thousands of Welsh women worked alongside them. 60 years ago nearly half the population of Wales lived from this hard and dangerous work underground. Of course, human beings have lived in these two western peninsulas of Britain for thousands of years, it's over the last 1,500 years that these people have lived here as Welsh people. Today, it looks as if the Welsh people have been declared redundant, as redundant as this pit, which after 200 years is now a museum. This is a museum. Wales is being turned into a land of museums. Now what is shovelling us into these folk museums? History, they say, History. What is History?

OPENING SCENE 1 *continued*

Vaughan Thomas continues climbing above a heavy sea until he reaches the ledge and the cave.

And here's the cave. And in there surrounded by bones of prehistoric animals lay this broken skeleton. Beside it a few precious possessions (*shot of bones and ornaments as removed and displayed in a museum*). And his bones stained in red ochre (*shot of skeleton*), in a pathetic attempt to bring the lad back to life (*shot of cave mouth from within*). Here's the start of our long journey through the ages, in which we will also try to bring Welsh history back to vivid life.

OPENING SCENE 2 *continued*

Gwyn Williams, still in descending cage:

'History isn't something you can bring to life. History isn't a story, it's an inquiry (*the cage reaches the mine floor. A man opens the gate, Williams gets out and walks across to address the camera.*) The past is chaos. We in the present make sense of that past by manufacturing a history out of it. We do that by putting questions to it and the kind of questions you put depend on who you are, what you are and when you are. We won't ask the same questions as our grandparents, a collier won't ask the same questions as a merchant banker, a wife as a husband, a Welsh speaker as an English speaker...

The bold, innovative design of this programme is an integral feature of its visual styling. The conflicting accounts are given by presenters, both Welsh, who contrast strongly in appearance and demeanour as well as mode of address and who draw upon different examples by which to *particularize and exemplify* history and to develop and interpret the historical narrative. The idea of the dual, and dialogic approach (neatly captured in the series title) is immediately set in train by the pre-title scenes. It is part of the series' brilliance that it then develops this by location sequences in which the space from which the presenters speak, the little journeys they make (to the cave and down the shaft) are as much a part of the meaning as what they *say*. Both accounts have a strongly *performative* dimension, insofar as both presenters consciously articulate and embody a personalized version of the historical perspective they seek to develop. Part of the skill of the programme is in sustaining a degree of balance between both accounts, particularly in respect of their pictorialization. The class-conscious analytic robustness of Williams is deliberately set up to undercut the romantic and conservative narrative favoured by Vaughan-Thomas, although it is important that this play-off does not become too 'easy'. The directness of address to the problem of defining history itself and of pursuing historical understanding from diverse resources is at the heart of the programme's originality and conceptual vigour.

Rehearsals (Channel 5, Northern Irish Film Council, 2005)

Rehearsals is a recent documentary by the veteran documentary maker Michael Grigsby. Here, the opening visual design is put to work alongside testimony in order to establish viewing connections with the topic – the city of Belfast in the context of the Northern Irish conflict. Unlike the previous examples, the topic is recent history, history as part of living memory and manifestly at work within the present. The programme essentially offers a series of reflections on a past that is *negatively active*, both objectively and subjectively.

The opening sequence, taken at night, is a long shot (over 1 minute 30 seconds) taken from the side window of a moving car on a road overlooking the city and at some distance from it. Initially trees and hedges block the view but gradually a pattern of lights appears below. Traffic occasionally passes in front of the camera and the view changes as hedges, trees and telegraph poles variously frame what can be seen. Belfast becomes the object of sustained viewing contemplation in both its immediate physicality as lit urban space and as the site of recent political conflict. A female voice begins to speak:

This is a beautiful picture of Belfast, the most beautiful picture you'll probably see. And when you look down on the houses and the spaces it make your realize how small it is and how ... it makes you wonder how its possible there could be so much hatred down there in that small space. Where people are living so closely together yet so separately, so widely apart in their ideas and their, their minds. It's a strange thing, yet this is a beautiful place ... it's just a pity.

An acoustic guitar playing a rap rhythm is heard; the scene cuts to a small, domestic room where three young men are performing a tune, with a standing singer reading from notes. The lyrics are about the city and its troubled past. They include the lines:

> I'm troubled and puzzled
> Too many beers that I've guzzled
> We've all stumbled and fumbled, now make it clear
> That we've struggled
> To find the truth of the sins of the past ...

The music fades and there is a return to the city lights, now getting closer. The female voice resumes:

Two bombs had gone off, there was 150 people injured and we were actually basically shovelling people into plastic bags that day. After my husband had been murdered I just thought this place is nuts, this place is so entrenched in bitterness.

A male voice is heard:

Anything could happen at any time of the day. It could just spark up, you know, within a minute and things are back to as they used to be.

The voice changes and a male voice *then begins* speaking the lines of a poem, first over the image of the city and then within a shot *of a face in* medium closeup. The poem includes the lines:

> *Belfast*
> The music of musical priests and cliché rap and semtex
> The music of protest against protest and strike against strike
> The music of ricocheted rumours of insurrection
> The music of rosary beads and whispers of civil rights ...

The voice fades and we are returned to the city, where the car is now entering its outskirts, passing houses, pubs and shops. Over this sequence, past voices (from the news archive) are heard, of politicians making statements about the IRA ceasefire of 1994.

Among the fragmented comments are these (the speakers are not identified but are recognizable through voice as well as speech content):

> *Gerry Adams* I want to salute the courage of the IRA leadership and the decisive initiative that they have taken and which they announced this morning
>
> *John Major* The statement is very welcome, very welcome indeed and they may mean by it that violence is over for good. But it doesn't actually say that
>
> *John Hume* The complete cessation is what the statement says. A complete cessation. And I'm afraid I'm amazed
>
> *John Major* What I want is the unambiguous statement that violence is over for good
>
> *Ian Paisley* We say never, never never never

This way of 'entering' history has, first of all, a remarkably literal dimension insofar as the view from the car first identifies the city from afar and then moves into its suburbs and centre. The movement towards engagement with the objective Belfast, the space of historical conflict and of political divide, is accompanied by a range of subjective commentaries in which testimony, song and poetry make connections across past, present and future. The past speaks directly too, as the voices of political leaders are heard taking up different, and conflicting, positions on the 'historic' moment of the ceasefire, which led to the Good Friday Agreement some 3 years later. This opening presents the viewer with a sense of the obstacles to the 'solution' of the problems of Northern Ireland, of the continuing legacy of the 'troubles', as well as attempts to engage with, and work beyond, the defining terms of the past. To a degree unusual in television documentary, emphasis is placed on a gradually unfolding visual experience becoming a listening experience too, a picking up of moods and tones, the building of a sense of place, people and orientations out of diverse elements. This is very clearly 'slow television', encouraging the viewer to participate in the construction of an historical frame within which understanding can occur. Along with the visual confidence of its sustained images of the road journey, its inclusion of the speech of poetry and song signals a very distinctive way of styling a televisual confrontation with history.

A Brief Summary

It is clear that television now has a very wide array of formal possibilities for relating viewers to the historical. These involve engagement with the *materiality* of the past – the things of the past, the places of the past – depicted in ways that encourage a more general, imaginative apprehension. They also involve connection with the moods and subjectivities of the past, perhaps as indicated by archive speech, the voicing of contemporary writing or by re-enactment, but often, also, by the phrasings and tone of the commentary or presenter's speech. The combination of 'distant' materiality and forms of subjectivity at once both alien and familiar (the relative emphasis being variable) is one that television has been able to articulate more powerfully than any other medium. The positioning of television as essentially a domestic device of casual sociability and intimacy is an important factor here. Across its many formal options for providing a *sense* of the past, television has made significant achievements towards providing viewers with historical orientation and historical knowledge. My approach only makes partial contact with the full range of documentary's historical scope, but it catches films and programmes at a point where they are working hard to serious purpose, revealing in so doing their qualities of aesthetic design.

A Note on Availability

Family Portrait and *Culloden* are available on DVDs released by the British Film Institute (BFI) and can also be viewed in extract on the BFI Screeononline website by users who have institutional access to this facility. *The Great War* and *A History of Britain* are available on BBC DVDs. *Who Do You Think You Are?*, series 1–4, is available on DVD through Acorn Media. *The World at War* is available on DVD through Fremantle Home Entertainment and *Victory at Sea* is available through Oracle Home Entertainment. There are plans to release *Rehearsals* on DVD, through the BFI. *Witchcraze* is not available on DVD, and regrettably, at the moment, a DVD or VHS version of *The Dragon Has Two Tongues* is not available.

Bibliography

Bell, E. (ed.) (2007) *European Journal of Cultural Studies*, 10.1 Special Issue: 'Televising History'.
Cannadine, D. (ed.) (2004) *History and the Media* (London: Palgrave).
Champion, J. (2003) 'Seeing the Past: Simon Schama's "A History of Britain" and Public History', *History Workshop Journal*, 56, 153–74.
Cook, J. (2003) commentary to BBC/BFI DVD release of *Culloden*.
de Groot, J. (2008) *Consuming History* (London: Routledge).
McArthur, C. (1978) *Television and History* (London: British Film Institute).

2
History on Television

The Problem of Sources

Luisa Cigognetti and Pierre Sorlin

Historians try to understand aspects of former times and give them meaning. It is their job to interpret what happened, to explain how people lived in the past and to account for their beliefs, passions and hopes. Their reading is necessarily subjective, biased by their personal opinions and by the attitudes of mind and by the ways of thinking characteristic of their own epoch. Their only safeguard is the trace left by previous generations. The quest for sources, critical examinations of the documents, comparison and confrontation are the first steps of historical investigation. Records are never self-evident; historians must decipher them, then make inferences and, by reasoning, draw logical conclusions. But they can neither invent what is not attested, nor distort what they have found in archives or archaeological remains.

What kind of history?

All we have just said is obvious, elementary – but applying such rules to television history is not easy. Both authors graduated in history, and have made history documentaries for television or educational institutions[1] and experienced the problems history filmmakers have to face. Moreover, carrying out a current research project into television history in the European Union,[2] we have seen that the question of sources, seldom mentioned, keeps recurring. In this chapter, we shall not take into account docudramas, costume dramas or historical re-enactments because such works adroitly bypass this obstacle. They are usually based on accredited facts but can give free rein to imagination in the picture of characters and places. Let us look at an example. For the 15th anniversary of the attempt on Hitler's life on 20 July 1944, the German public channel ARD broadcast a biography of the main conspirator, Colonel Stauffenberg, the eponymous lead character of the film. A three-line document tells that, in 1933, Stauffenberg, then a young officer, invited to a concert attended by Hitler, arrived late but could enter the hall and see the Fuehrer. The film opens with a couple, he in uniform, she in a silk gown, running through empty corridors, talking with ushers, convincing them to open a side door, finally looking at Hitler from afar and, enthralled, kissing each other full on the lips. It may or may not have happened this way; nobody is in a position to confirm or refute such an interpretation. The scene, ideal for a beginning, provided the director with a good starting point for the journey that led a German regular officer from blind adhesion to intransigent opposition and introduced a sentimental hint in the film. Some docudramas are of outstanding quality, but it is difficult to tell what is based on factual evidence and what is pure invention. On the other hand, documentaries based exclusively on archives or contemporary testimonies do not 'play' with the images; they are hampered by their immutable contents.

Bustle and hustle in archives

Written sources do not pose problems; newspapers, posters or pages taken from a book put viewers in direct contact with the kind of material used by specialists. Experience has led to some general principles for the presentation of such pieces: the most important facts or opinions are underlined or reproduced in bold characters and the documents remain visible long enough for the public to read them. Things are much different where audiovisual evidence is concerned. It has been a long time since film directors first began to use archival footage when shooting history programmes. In the early years of TV broadcasting a limited budget did not allow in-depth investigations, and history films were lectures clumsily illustrated by extracts from newsreels which, quite often, did not match the talk. This led channels to modify their approach; it was decided to spend money for thorough research and to produce series likely to be sold abroad. For that reason previously unsuspected resources have been dug out in industrial companies, schools, ministries, tourist offices and hospitals. The fund is far from exhausted, much more is still to come, and the unknown material is so rich that, after broadcasting *The Great War* (1964), a series filled with firsthand pictures, the BBC, together with the American PBS, could put on the air, three decades later (1997), a new original series, *The Great War and the Shaping of the 20th Century*.

Here, most of our examples will bear relation to the Spanish Civil War that lasted from July 1936 until March 1939. The main reason for this choice is the prodigious wealth of documents dealing with the event.[3] In an unsettled Europe most countries were directly or indirectly involved in a conflict that, opposing Fascism and democracy, anticipated the coming world war in which the same forces would soon be caught up. The public was anxious to get information and journalists, photographers and cameramen rushed towards the Iberian Peninsula. Initially, newsreels were the main source used to illustrate the conflict but, in the last decades of the twentieth century, a huge amount of unknown pictures was found in Moscow and Berlin film archives and in private collections. Despite hard work, the Spanish Film

Archive has not yet finished the inventory of the pictures shot during the period, and they think that only half of the available material has been listed in their enormous catalogue (del Amo and Ferradas, 1996). This is a fascinating case of a constantly changing historiography.

Is such overabundance of visual material good news for historians? Yes and no. Yes, because no individual would have been able to collect the miles of fresh images television has found and made known. Visual documentation, which looked scarce and rather poor until the late 1960s, has turned out to be one of the main sources of information about the twentieth century. But, at the same time, since any small bit of film is potential gold, prices have soared. Small archives or private collections, which let their pictures for nothing in the 1960s, now charge exorbitant sums. Film companies, intent on obtaining a benefit from their archives, often stick whatever comes to hand in hastily made programmes and sell them to TV channels so that, on television screens, excellent original works alternate with compilations of less value.

The Great War innovated by asking veterans to recall memories of their personal experience. Up to that moment politicians or generals were often interviewed, whereas ordinary people were not considered to have interesting opinions. The accounts of survivors, who told straightforwardly what they had suffered, enlivened the narration of the BBC series and reinforced the appeal of the programme. Such achievement was not lost on production companies. Interviews do not cost anything and witnesses, provided they are entertaining, appeal directly to the audience. Oral history has become a new, unavoidable historical source. At times, history broadcasting is nothing but a sequence of chats about former times, and even the most serious programmes have recourse to individuals who, directly or indirectly, were involved in past events.[4]

The importance given to testimonies is part of what has been called 'the privatization of public life' – the fact that, to form an idea about a past epoch, situations affecting only a particular person are considered as revealing as affairs involving a large community. Amateur films fall in the same category. They were often judged a boring depiction of family gatherings, but the attention paid to private life has led to a revaluation of them. However awkward they are, pictures taken by soldiers during a military campaign, by immigrants trying to settle in a foreign country, by workers intent on displaying their craft, by travellers or explorers provide information that cannot be found from other sources. Let us add that nonprofessional cameramen, all too happy to be taken seriously, usually give their reels for free.

Handling audiovisual sources: a tricky job

For centuries, history telling was based on paper; specialists found the data needed for their analysis in manuscripts, printed works, maps and drawings. TV channels have substantially widened the range of sources, and proved that a wealth of lively documents can be discovered outside traditional archives or libraries. Yet, despite the abundance and variety of oral and visual records, little has changed in the reconstruction of past events. It is not our job here to explain why trained historians seldom exploit films or videotapes; we are only concerned with the activities of television professionals.

Unlike historians, who feel relatively independent when they write a book,[5] TV filmmakers are accountable to their producers. Being obliged to keep a balance between price and quality, they are often tempted to buy a cheap, prosaic sequence rather than an original, expensive one. Bearing in mind the necessity of entertaining viewers, they often select the most riveting pictures. If they have to decide between an ordinary, unemotional, but topical image and a good, entrancing but uncharacteristic one, they will probably choose the latter.[6] Similarly, when editing their images, they will try to arouse surprise, interest and emotion, even if some assemblages are irrelevant with regard to the situation that they represent. Accuracy and reliability are not the main concern of those who work in TV channels because it is not what their sponsors, be they public authorities or advertisers, seek. We are not claiming that television history is necessarily more biased than written history. All we are saying is that, in the matter of sources, historians' requirements do not tally with filmmakers' obligations.

We must point out that dealing with films, videotapes or video interviews is not as simple as working with texts. When cinema was invented, at the end of the nineteenth century, many thought that movies would supply a fair, indisputable and all-encompassing chronicle of what had happened. Oskar Messter, a German constructor of cameras, affirmed, in his 1898 catalogue: 'Thanks to cinema, historical facts will leave a trace in the future, it will be possible to reconstruct them genuinely, not only in their own time, but also for the following generations' (Messter, 1898). It is long since specialists have given up Messter's illusions. It is true that the pictures taken by a cameraman are perfectly objective; they are the mere imprint on gelatino-bromide, or the digital scanning, of something that was really, physically in front of the camera; they reflect aspects of a place, a persona, a state of affairs, and if the cameraman was, maybe, prejudiced, the machine was not. At the same time, the cinematic images are flat and two-dimensional; they are partial and show only one side of things. The framing of an object or a person is in itself a manipulation and many factors can distort the shooting, or at least adjust it to specified needs. A picture will tell more or less according to the disposition of the image, the depth of field, the importance given to the surroundings and the lighting. A film does not 'catch' the outer world, but is, at best, a 'processing' of reality. Such is *the first paradox* of films: they are reliable because they are factual, exact, but they are untrustworthy because they apprehend a limited fraction of happenings.

It can rightly be argued that written sources are not as rigorous as photographs. We are free to imagine how Caesar was murdered because the chroniclers who inform us, Plutarch and Sallust, leave many details in the dark: where was he seated, how did the conspirators surround him, did he get up, how did his fellows react? On the other hand, the place and circumstances of Kennedy's assassination have been definitively fixed on film. There is no room for our speculation: we are confined within the limits of what was then recorded, so that to try to narrate his death is hopeless; the sole issue is to present the images. The filmmakers who deal with the event must be self-effacing; they have no other solution than to let the films pass. Sometimes they will describe the pictures, but pointlessly since spectators are able to see what is on the screen. *The second paradox* of audiovisual documents is that they block inventiveness and do not give way to personal intervention. It is relatively easy to 'sort out' a written document by selecting or rephrasing some passages, by introducing commentaries, queries or hypothesis inside the text. A picture is a spatial structure; it is possible to falsify it, not to 'recast' it in order to support an interpretation. Pictures are much closer than written texts to the way happenings or people came into sight, but they are rigid and do not lend themselves to adjustments. Today, thanks to light cameras and telephones, few incidents pass unnoticed; almost everything that occurs somewhere in the world is filmed by different people and at different stages. Yet abundance does not take us out of the quandary: ten pictures of the same occurrence are only ten limited and unchangeable aspects of an event that none of them exposes fully.

There is even *a third paradox*: cinematic documents, most of the time, are 'peripheral'. They have been shot in precise circumstances, but have seldom been taken at the core of the events. This is easily comprehensible where unpredictable facts are concerned. A myriad of operators attended Robert Kennedy's last speech in Los Angeles; when he left the meeting room all thought that the press conference was over and done with, so that none was present when he was murdered. Today, professional and amateur cameramen record everything that seems of interest; as soon as an accident or a bomb attack are signalled thousands run to film it. The first pictures of a plane striking the second tower of the World Trade Center, on 11 September 2001, were taken by a passer-by; after the London bombing, the BBC received thirty videos filmed by laymen. But these movies are usually shot *after;* there are miles of images related to terrorist activities, but all they show is the result, not the attack itself. If, by chance, someone filmed the events, emotion, distance, panic blurred the images. On 11 March 2004, when a bomb exploded in the Madrid train station, electronic cameras were turned on. What do we see? People going towards the trains, smoke, people fleeing, yet nothing to inform us of what was happening. The only interesting clue is the convulsive zooming in out, evidencing the hysteria of a guard, unable to register what was happening.[7]

Reporters have always boasted about their unremitting effort to take revealing pictures that disclose the hidden sides of politics. It is true that they go to great lengths and lay themselves open to danger, but there are limits they will never overstep. Censorship has long been effective. Right from the beginning of the twentieth century, during the Boer War and the Italian–Turkish hostilities, operators filmed strictly what was permitted. The severe rules imposed for the First World War were then strengthened until, eventually, military authorities took in hand the supply of audiovisual information. There are huge amounts of films dealing with contemporary conflicts, but they document more rear drills than real battles. In the same way cameramen do not have access to places where resolutions are adopted; they are allowed to snap before or after the meeting of decision-makers, but all they register are official announcements. A choice has been made, but who supported it, who opposed it, how was a solution reached? Images cannot answer.

It is because they do not find any response in film archives that filmmakers have recourse to witnesses. With the passing of the years, secrets look less important; new developments may even make them appear insignificant; witnesses do not hesitate to talk, and their presence brings onto the screen something concrete and alive. Yet, their statements are not unproblematic. They may have forgotten relevant details or arranged the facts to emphasize their role or lessen their responsibility. They may also be influenced by the spirit of the time. Immediately after the Second World War, few expressed doubts about the unity of the British during the hostilities, but, later, uncertainty rose and the same people who had celebrated national unity proved more circumspect (Connelly, 2004). There is no reason to cast doubt on their good faith, but human memory is inconstant and sensitive to the latest trends in the interpretation of the past.

Historians come up against the same difficulty when they read a written testimony, but they can easily signal, between brackets, or in footnotes, the contradictions, the liberties taken with the facts, the changes of approach. There is no critical apparatus on television. What witnesses say sounds like lived history. In fact it is only *their* verity, told from *their own* point of view, but while they are occupying the screen and directly addressing the public, their discourse seems unquestionable – it rings true. The filmmaker or the historian who was keen on presenting a comprehensive panorama of a state of affairs is relegated to a position of secondary importance, while an individual perspective, intensely experienced but limited, condenses and explains a complicated situation.

A short example will help to evaluate the difficulties a director has to overcome when making a modest short using newsreels and testimonies as sources. On 9 October 1934, King Alexander I of Yugoslavia disembarked in Marseilles. He had been invited to prepare a defence treaty with France, but he was assassinated by a Croatian freedom fighter. Georges Méjean, French cameraman for Fox Movietone News, filmed the scene. A few decades later, the drama was commemorated in a television programme.[8] Méjean's original footage was available at the Library of Congress, and the filmmaker could record an interview in which the operator explained how he had worked and what he had been able to shoot. Seen from a political angle, the details of the murder mattered less than the killing of a sovereign who, worried about the aggressive policy of Fascist Italy, was seeking the support of democracies. The assassination was a watershed since it put an end to any project of military cooperation between Yugoslavia and France. This historical background was, of course, absent from Méjean's images. Had he desired to expose it, the filmmaker would have been obliged to give a lecture – but there would have been no pictures to illustrate it. Therefore, abandoning all thought of contextualization, he put the emphasis on the attack. Alexander I was killed because nothing had been done to prevent an aggression; the port was in utter chaos when the king got into a car to reach the train station. Méjean managed to shoot a few glimpses of the sovereign and his suite, but, pushed away by bystanders, he filmed at random the crowd and the escort. The firing of a gun caused a stampede. The operator had the presence of mind to film an armed silhouette moving away (but it was not the murderer, who already had been caught by the police), then to come up to the car and film the corpse. Shot without any break, the film may give an innocent eye the impression that it matches perfectly the course of events: there is movement, comings and goings, much confusion, and panic – but nothing at the instant when the murderer discharged his gun.

Our chapter focuses on sources and this brief survey brings us to a simple conclusion: the available material has trapped the filmmaker. It is fair to add that he had not much room to manoeuvre; all he could do was select Méjean's best shots and assemble them. Breaking the continuity of the shooting, editing brief images, he produced an impression of great disturbance and uncertainty; viewers learn more about the negligence of the French police than about the death of Alexander I. The documentary could have been focused on that question. On the one hand, it would have shown that, in the first half of the twentieth century, the security of VIPs was not a cause for concern. On the other hand, it could have suggested that, after the violent riots of February 1934, France had entered a period of disorder that would lead to her 1940 disaster. But the second source, Méjean's testimony, did not allow expansion on the historical circumstances; added to the film in voice over, in order to comment on the making of the images, the interview reduced the murder to a sad news item.

With one's back to the wall

Sources should be tackled in the same manner, be it for a history book or a historical documentary. In both cases it is necessary to know the date and the places described or filmed, to identify the writer or the cameramen, to make sure that they were in the right observation position at the right moment and, when that is possible, to confront various documents on the same event. It is the architecture of the final product that makes the difference. Words lend themselves to various presentations, and a more convenient one can substitute any term. Pictures are rigid and it is not easy to twist them. A case study will help us to spot the difficulties filmmakers have to face and to explain how they try to solve them.

We have chosen *La guerra di Spagna,* an Italian broadcast dealing with the Spanish Civil War. Given what was said previously about the films shot during that conflict, making a documentary on this topic seems especially easy. At the same time, given the impact of the conflict, viewers are usually interested in a historical account based on primary sources. The television programme we have selected was aired as part of a highly popular series, *La grande storia in prima serata* [*Great History in Prime Time*] broadcast by the Italian public channel RAI 3. We shall neither expound the ideological bias of the film, nor discuss the way the theme has been treated. All we consider is how the filmmakers grappled with an extremely rich and varied documentation.

The programme was divided into two parts of 52 minutes each. The first part opened with a long sequence (8 minutes) on the end of the conflict. Then it described Spain before the hostilities (20 minutes), the beginning of the war with special reference to foreign interference (16 minutes), the situation of Madrid and the impact of bombings on civilians (8 minutes). The second part stressed the international aspects of the war (20 minutes), emphasized the Italian participation (12 minutes), evoked the dramatic problems the locals had to face (9 minutes) and closed with the end of the hostilities (11 minutes). Most documents were taken from the archives of the Istituto Luce, a public institution, which under Fascism had been granted the monopoly on newsreels and produced weekly informative films of outstanding technical quality. Additional material came from the archive of the RAI and from the Moscow archive. The producers, obviously concerned about money, tried to use only pictures available in the country, at bargain prices. Moscow was the only exception because neglecting its film stock would have looked shocking: in the summer of 1936 the Soviets had sent to Spain operators who, using light cameras, shot remarkable pictures, so famous that it was impossible to ignore them – but the producers made do with very few bits of that material.

Newsreels in the 1930s lined up short, disparate items dedicated to sport competitions, fashion, society life, folk traditions, daring undertakings and, thanks to exchanges with foreign countries, to the same activities developed abroad. Since spectators belonged to all social strata and had different, often contrasting opinions, newsreel companies were keen on avoiding debated issues and political controversies. Luce films were not different from the other movies, except for the unfailing attention paid to Fascist ceremonies and to Mussolini's speeches or travels. Italy's early commitment on the nationalist side interrupted the relationships with the Soviet Union and prevented Luce operators from filming in loyalist territory; it is only after Franco's victory that some republican footage was sent to Italy. The Luce archive was therefore rather one-sided; it kept in store important material about the Italian task force, pictures taken often at random in the nationalist part of Spain, a selection of images given by the Germans, and a few documents about republican Spain or democratic countries.

As we have noted, much space – nearly a quarter of the programmes – is dedicated to international affairs and foreign interference in the war. Having little material to represent such topics on screen, the producers had recourse to clumsy expedients. The second part begins with the protocol of noninterference advanced by France and warmly supported by Britain. The commentary, read in voice over, is illustrated by a *can-can* in a French theatre, by a long sequence (90 seconds) dedicated to the French singer Maurice Chevalier, and by a military parade in Paris. Such handling is not only absurd (what is the relation between the singer and the civil war?), it is also, at times, contradictory, for instance when a demonstration of the French army underlines a text explaining that France did not want to be involved in a conflict. The pictures used for Britain are worse. They show first the commotion provoked by King Edward VIII's desire to marry a divorced American, then the coronation of his brother George VI. What is shocking here, more that the inappropriateness of the images, is the fact that, in this programme, the British seem to have neglected Spain because they were obsessed by the scandal in Westminster.

Inaccurate pictures were often preferred to pertinent ones because it would have been necessary to buy the latter abroad. However far they were from the core of the subject, some images were introduced into the film for the sole reason that they were at hand. A student-fest, with gowns and music, breaks into the evocation of the Spanish pre-war political life, under the pretext that Azaña, first prime minister of the republic, had been a university rector. The motive given for the introduction of a bullfight in Pamplona is that Mola, one of the rebel generals, commanded the military academy of the town. Another bullfight accompanies, this time inexplicably, information about the founding of the *Falange*, the right-wing movement hostile to the republic. The proclamation of the republic and the subsequent demonstrations of joy are underlined by the election of Miss Spain, followed by another bullfight. The connection between such traditional events and the change of regime is so weak that the commentator finds it necessary to warn us: 'Smile seems to be the emblem of the country.'

Ill-fitting or out-of-place documents are less harmful than those pictures that may induce arguable, and at times somewhat misleading, interpretations. Bruno Mussolini, son of *Il Duce*, was often filmed piloting a bomber in Spain; his lack of discipline irritated the Spaniards who did not hide their anger. The film exploits at length the pictures of the young man, because they were free, and alleges that the boy's behaviour damaged the relationship between Franco and Mussolini. It is true that the two men disagreed on some points, but not on a trifle, which would not have been mentioned if it had not enabled the filmmaker to fill in 1 minute. In the summer of 1937 Franco launched an offensive against the Basque provinces. Mussolini was then visiting Sicily and, as usual, Luce operators followed him step-by-step. Mixing up views of landscapes, images of Mussolini bathing in the sea, dancing or talking with Sicilians, and pictures of Basque prisoners, the 4-minutes dealing with the attack on the northern provinces produce an odd impression: here, war is reduced to the pastimes of *Il Duce*. The military attack on the Basque provinces seems to have been decided and piloted from afar by the Italian dictator; its strategic importance and its consequences for the Basques are passed over in silence. The accessible material has conditioned the structure of this passage and imposed its fallacious explication.

Given their muddled structure, newsreels encourage viewers to associate insignificant details with noteworthy data. After Hitler and Mussolini had come closer to each other and signed a military pact, Germany sent Luce a great many pictures about its domestic life and diplomacy. It was tempting to introduce them into the film, all the more so since German foreign policy, extremely active in 1938, weighed indirectly on the Spanish conflict. However, was it reasonable to project 1 minute of a ballet danced in Vienna in order to announce the annexing of Austria by Germany, or more than 4 minutes on the Munich conference that resulted in the dismembering of Czechoslovakia but had no impact on Spain? Of course not. Whatever the motives were that led him to adopt such an easy solution – be they lack of money, ignorance or carelessness – the filmmaker did not pay much attention to the correspondence between words and pictures; he was only concerned with filling the screen.

Another window onto the past

There have been a few outstanding history programmes on television; *La guerra di Spagna* is not especially bad, just average. Television filmmakers are all confronted with the same hardships. To begin with, theirs is not a historical approach; being storytellers more than analysts, they are chiefly preoccupied with entertaining their public. On the other hand, the production company puts pressure on them to select the cheapest documents and shorten the editing time. Yet, the main handicap they have to face is the very nature of the audiovisual material: images show events, people and places; they follow actions, describe landscapes, explore crowds, single out details; but they are unable to recount, let alone to explain. The archival footage dealing with an event such as the Spanish Civil War is quantitatively extremely ample but thematically rather narrow. It is limited to the scenes operators could film after, or at the margin of, the events. The invaluable significance of pictures is peculiar: no written text, no oral testimony, however pathetic it is, will ever have the same impact as the images of civilians running towards a shelter during the bombings over Madrid and Barcelona; of exhausted, hungry prisoners; of wounded children pulled out from under the rubble of a destroyed building; of republicans fleeing through mud and snow to escape death.

Pictures have introduced a new variable in historical studies: the feelings and affects likely to influence people's behaviour or action. Words are of little use to evoke the fury of maddening mobs, the anger of jobless workers, the sudden rush of a multitude, a brutal police repression. On 23 October 1956, the first day of the anti-Soviet uprising, a huge crowd poured out into the streets of Budapest. Thanks to contemporary newspapers and radio broadcasts we know where the crowd was coming from and where it was heading towards, but words do not reveal what the protest looked like, whether the dissenters were calm or nervous, determined or irresolute. Films do not inform us about the itinerary of the march, but they show how the demonstrators behaved. The extraordinary thing is that, in a country under constant police surveillance, those who were taking part in the protest did not hesitate to look openly at photographers or operators. Fear seemed to have vanished as an unexpected groundswell of politically conscious opposition was shaking Hungary. In such a case, cinematic images do not modify what written documents chronicle about the course of the day, but they do add information that cannot be found anywhere else: the inhabitants of Budapest were resolute, so that the government and police, accustomed to having the city under their control, proved unable to react. We would probably be obliged to reconsider the historic days of the French or Russian revolutions if the same kind of evidence was available.

Words and pictures are of different quality; their properties do not tally in any way so that it might be wise and more fruitful to employ them separately. The trouble is that, for centuries, the past has been evoked with words. History is a rhetorical genre that calls attention to a problem, develops its various aspects and proposes a conclusion. Historians-to-be are instructed to mull over Thucydides' *History of the Peloponnesian War*, which is a model of the genre: why was there a conflict, how did it evolve, what were the consequences? Contemporary historians no longer stick to such standards; they do not dare say: 'We want to disclose how events happened really,' and they are content with asking: 'What do we know about what happened?' – but TV filmmakers, as well as the majority of viewers, are unaware of that mutation and long for a continuous, comprehensive narration. Therefore the bulk of history programmes are made up of discourses accompanied by images that do not match the speech – and cannot correspond to the reflections conveyed by words.

Much TV history, such as it is broadcast by most channels, is a perfect nonsense, an odd coupling of elements that do not square. The public, intent on following the thread of the lecture, has no time to linger on the pictures, the freshness and singularity of which are lost. Is that to say that films should be banned from TV history? Maybe, inasmuch as interactive digital technologies would allow the creation of hypertext linking data to analysis, and of graphs and diagrams likely to illustrate the antagonism between different forces: what would appear on the screen would be a visual-aid; additional information.

And, then, what about films? They could be broadcast separately, for the sake of their originality. They could be carefully introduced, with relevant information regarding the context, the circumstances in which the shots were taken, and preconceived cinematic forms (framing, camera motions, editing) the filmmakers used without wondering about their possible influence on viewers. Slow motion, repetition, the freezing of some images, a different editing of some sequences would help viewers to perceive what is noteworthy in the images and to engineer their own interpretation. The German–French channel Arte embarked on this with its show *Parallel Histories*. To commemorate the length of time the Second World War and the reconstruction era continued, Arte put on the air, weekly, from 1989 through 2000, newsreels shot at the same date 50 years before, confronting for instance the German and Soviet version of the fights in Russia or the American and Japanese films about the Pacific campaign. These shorts did not inform us about what was 'actually' occurring; they showed how both camps conceived of themselves, of their cause, and how opinion was informed. The comparison between the people and locations selected, the rhythm of the 'montage', the soundtrack and the comments was extraordinarily revealing. On the other hand, the duration of the programme offered viewers the opportunity to feel how long the days had seemed to contemporaries.

Is that 'history'? If the study of the past is an attempt to display, chronologically, a set of lived events, no, it is not. But specialists have become aware of the limits of such enterprises. They know that only a few aspects of former times have been preserved in texts or pictures, and that different sources allow varied reconstructions that, while being not conflicting, do not square. Films are among the traces left by previous generations; they provide evidence about some of their concerns and about their way of observing their surroundings. Television channels have the human and financial means necessary to collect the documents. They are also able to set them out, integrally, with critical scrutiny and explanations likely to make them enjoyable and instructive.

A last word: will television channels, in their historical broadcasts, ever treat films as authentic, self-sufficient marks of the past, and not as mere adornment? We are afraid that they will not. A straightforward lecture regarding an event is more reassuring than the tentative, inconclusive analysis of flying images – and television networks are intent on reassuring their public.

A Note on Availability

L'âge d'or de la presse filmée can be consulted at the archive of French TV (INA). *The Great War* and *The Great War and the Shaping of the 20th Century* are available on DVDs released by the BBC. *La guerra di Spagna* is available on a DVD released by the Luce Institute in Rome. *Stauffenberg* can be consulted at the archive of the ARD.

Notes

1. Luisa Cigognetti: *Val più la pratica della grammatica? Storia di un piccolo imprenditore* [The Italian 'miracle' seen through the story of a small entrepreneur], *Dalle paglie alle maglie* [How Carpi became a leading centre for Italian fashion], *Scene per una storia dei consumi* [Evolution of mass consumption in the twentieth century]. Pierre Sorlin: *Simonneau mort pour la loi en l'An II de la Liberté* [Social unrest during the French Revolution], *Les juifs de France et la Révolution* [French Jews and the Revolution] *La raison d'Etat: chronique de l'Affaire Dreyfus* [The reason of the state : account of the Dreyfus Affair].
2. The aim of the research, sponsored by the Italian Region Emilia-Romagna, is to map out the representation of history in fourteen European countries (Belgium, Britain, the Czech Republic, Finland, France, Germany, Hungary, Italy, Lithuania, Poland, Portugal, Rumania, Slovakia and Spain) and envisage a television history common to all members of the EU. The project began in 2007 and will last until 2011. Erin Bell and Ann Gray are considering television in Britain.
3. Our choice has also been motivated by the fact that we worked at the Madrid Filmoteca Española, for a research on the Spanish Civil War, and know rather well the available material.
4. See Erin Bell's chapter in this book.
5. But not always when they want to have it published!
6. Nicola Caracciolo, Italian journalist, an important director of history programmes on Italian television, confessed that, in one of his films, he had used a report about the wedding of the duke of Aosta, unconnected to the topic he treated, because 'it was very beautiful': Torre, 2008, p. 210.
7. The pictures can be found at www.diggersrealm.com/mt/archives/000262.html, or on a DVD, *Explosiones en Atocha 11-M, Telecinco Programa Día a Día*.
8. *L'âge d'or de la presse filmée*, Fr.3, February 2001.

Filmography

L'âge d'or de la presse filmée, Fr 3, 20 February 2001.
The Great War, BBC, April–May 1964.

The Great War and the Shaping of the 20th Century, PBS, alternative title *1914–1918*, BBC, November 1996–January 1997.
La guerra di Spagna, RAI 3, 2 October 2000.
Stauffenberg, ARD, 20 July 2004.

Bibliography

del Amo, A. and Ferradas, M.L. (eds) (1996) Filmoteca Espanola, *Catalogo General de la Guerra Civil* (Madrid: Ediciones Cátedra).
Connelly, M. (2004) *We Can Take It! Britain and the Memory of the Second World War* (Harlow: Pearson Education).
Messter, O. (1898) *Special-Catalog No. 32 über Projektions-und Aufnahme-Apparate für lebende Photographie, Films, Graphophons* (Berlin).
Torre, A. (2008) 'Conversazione con Nicola Caracciolo' in *Le carte delle immagini* (Rome: Ediesse).

3
Combatting 'A Message without a Code'

Writing the 'History' Documentary

Brian Winston

Television is not very good at history.

Of course, the moving image has unrivalled iconicity.[1] The first cinema audiences in 1895, familiar enough with the animated slide, were overwhelmed by the detailed movement on the Cinématographe's screen. Watching the Lumière reel, it was not the feeding of Auguste Lumière's baby in the garden that amazed them; the movement of spoon to mouth would have been easy enough to animate. It was the fact that the entire frame, including – most astonishingly – the fluttering of the leaves of the background tree, was full of movement too.[2] Such kinesics had never been reproduced before.

A century and more on, the cinema and its successor technologies have provided us with an archive of unparalleled vivacity documenting the minutiae of human behaviour and the physicality of the material world. This priceless richness, however, does not absolve the realist moving image, especially its manifestations in mass media such as television, from the ambiguities and limitations of all records. It is, after all, a (perhaps 'mere') reflection of surfaces. Its viability as evidence can be contested and, as Barthes taught us, we need context to understand it: 'the photographic image is…a message without a code' (Barthes, 1961, p. 17). The business of writing scripts for history programmes on television might be considered as providing such a code (or part of it). Yet, arguably, such writing is, as it were, locked in battle with the limitations of photography's 'codelessness'.

The efficacy of history on television is reduced across a number of axes.

First, there is the grievous problem that televising history is fundamentally conditioned by a discipline, but that discipline is not history. It is the discipline of programme making for television, which overwhelmingly determines outcomes. Second, there are the pressing constraints of the need to communicate effectively in, essentially, a time-based medium. This is less a matter of 'dumbing-down' because the demographic of history programmes remains solidly skewed towards the better educated and richer elements in the audience; rather, it is that television, as such a time-based medium, demands narrative; and screen-narratives, driven as they are by – in Chatman's coinage – 'chrono-logic', tend to diminish complexity and blunt nuance (Chatman, 1990, p. 9). Finally, there are the limitations imposed by the range and authenticity of the images the medium either retrieves from the archive or creates from scratch.

To explicate how these difficulties impact the business of writing words to provide the television image with a 'code', consider the specific case of the last two episodes of *Heritage: Civilization and the Jews,* a major history series produced at New York's public television station, WNET, in the early 1980s.

> From the stony heights of Sinai to the shores of the Dead Sea, from a Greek ampitheater in Delphi to the Forum of Ancient Rome, out of the ashes of concentration camps to the rebuilt cities and villages of Israel, HERITAGE brings to life the long and complex history of the Jews and their centuries-old interaction with the rest of Western civilization.
>
> (Anon, DVD box, 2004)

The documentary scholar Alan Rosenthal, who directed the last two, twentieth-century episodes of *Heritage: Civilization and the Jews*, has given an insightful personal overview of the production circumstances of this series and his part in them. (And mine too: he chose me to write the scripts for these episodes) (Rosenthal, 2000, pp. 235–59).

Heritage was a nine-part series made for the US public television network (PBS). Running for 540 minutes, it was first transmitted in 1984 between October 1 and November 19. It was primarily funded by the foundation established by cosmetics manufacturer Charles H. Revson and 44 other private donors as well as the National Endowment for the Humanities, the Corporation for Public Broadcasting and public television stations. Multiple donors are, of course, a norm in the American public service broadcasting system, but the number of funders involved with *Heritage* was exceptional. Their proliferation speaks to the protracted and surprisingly vexed circumstances in which the series was made, despite the persistence of documentaries on historical topics on the screen and the potential attractiveness of this particular subject to the American public television audience.

Heritage was to be in the tradition pioneered by Esfir Shub in Падение династии Романовых [The Fall of the Romanov Dynasty] (1929). She was the first to recycle archive film – newsreels and the Tsar's professionally made home movies in this case – to create a feature documentary. American television's first documentary hit series, made for NBC by Henry Salamon in 1952–3, was a history of the US Navy's part in World War II, *Victory at Sea*. It too was entirely reliant on the archive. The British, adding witness interviews, had achieved similar success with *The Great War* (Tony Essex, Gordon

Watson et al., 1964) and Jeremy Isaacs' *World at War* (1973); but the BBC had also pioneered the less archive-dependent, authored documentary history series with Sir Kenneth Clark's *Civilisation: A Personal View* (1966) and, 3 years later, a parallel account from the other of the two cultures, the science-inflected *Ascent of Man* presented by Jacob Bronowski.[3]

It was to take a decade before American television attempted anything similar, by which time the appetite and capacity of the American commercial networks for such sustained and expensive documentary efforts was a thing of the past; and public television was hard pressed to muster such resources either. Nevertheless, in 1980, KCET, the PBS station in Los Angeles, produced *Cosmos*, presented by astronomer Carl Sagan. With cutting-edge special effects, the series was a critical success, winning that year's Peabody Award for distinguished public television programming, a Hugo, and three Emmys for the series as well as 21 individual Emmys for the technical crew. Making it, though, had nearly bankrupted the station and demonstrated just how much the long-form documentary stretched PBS's production capacity.

Alan Rosenthal reports that long before this, in the mid-1970s, the concept of a series about Jewish history was being bandied about New York (Rosenthal, 2000, p. 236). The idea was, as we would say today, 'greenlighted' in 1979 with grants from the Revson Foundation. Abba Eban, the South African-born and Cambridge-educated sometime Israeli foreign minister who was then in opposition and lecturing at Princeton, was chosen to front the series. As a hook for the necessary solicitation of further donors this was an inspired choice, but on a practical level it brought many problems. For one thing, Eban, still an active and senior Israeli politician, might be called back to office before the series was completed. Moreover, not all countries were open to him. Nor was he, as any famous American Jewish cultural figure might have been, a neutral observer of the climax of Jewry's story and the series, that is, the re-establishment of a Jewish state in which he had played a not insignificant personal role. A solution to the first of these difficulties was to take Eban around the world and film 'stand-uppers' (pieces-to-camera) before a word of any script had been written. As Alan says: 'While this made sense in theory, it turned out to be nonsensical in practice' (Rosenthal, 2000, p. 240). Almost none of the resultant footage made it into the finished films. The exercise cost, Alan estimates, as much as $500,000.

Almost equally useless, and with even less justification, was the dispatch of a second unit to film Jewish artefacts in the world's great museums, again without scripts to hand. The results were largely ignored. In essence, it could be that a combination of, to be charitable, a vexed choice of presenter and a basic lack of appreciation for the logistics of how such a series needs to be made meant that, after 4 years of effort, with the coffers nearly empty, only two of the nine films were nearing completion. As Alan notes: 'a rumour was going round the station that because of the money difficulties, *Civilization and the Jews* might have to end abruptly in the sixteenth century. Good-bye, the modern age. Good-bye, the French Revolution, Hassidism, Enlightenment, nationalism, America, Marx, Freud, Hitler, and Israel' (Rosenthal, 2000, p.240).

An experienced commercial network television producer, John Fox, a non-Jew who had worked on NBC's *Saturday Night Live*, was brought in to establish some control. Top-up funding was secured and seasoned directors such as Alan, under Fox, took the matter in hand. The series was completed, but it is fair to say that, despite its continued vitality as an educational resource and its re-release on DVD, it was not a triumphant success. It won the Peabody but only garnered two Emmys for individual achievement. *The New York Times* TV critic, John Cory, said that: 'Overall, it has been a triumph'; yet it was a far from overwhelming one. For one rather major thing, the viewer needed, in his opinion, to: 'Forgive the series its omissions' (Cory, 1984b).

> Mr. Eban is carrying a heavy burden in this. He is the former Foreign Minister of Israel and a recognized author and scholar. He is not, however, a particularly forceful television presence, even though he must sustain the narrative drive himself. This viewer found himself wishing, respectfully, that Charlton Heston were around.
>
> (Cory (1984) (a))

The discipline that is not history

The problem with televising history is that it is television first and history second. It is television that demands compression, which is necessitated both by assumed audience tolerance and an inexorably intertwined need for illustration, for images – television's visual imperative.

Thus, even though 540 minutes is scarce time to outline a '5000-year ' (as the publicity had it) narrative, it was more than enough to exhaust available images, especially in the opening hours[4] of the series. The early millennia of those 5000 years present the voracious camera eye with little except, exactly, 'pictures of deserts, cliffs and mountain gorges'. Of course, *Time-Watch* has demonstrated that even the archaeologist's trench can be vividly televised; but not if, as in *Heritage*, it alone fills the screen with only voice-over commentary and stand-uppers by Eban to enhance it. Augmenting this footage were images of contemporary Middle Eastern urban and rural habitations of a traditional Arab kind. The former, in their confusion, are nothing like the regimented regularities of ancient mud-cities; even the people's dress seen in these shots is not time-honoured but is also ahistorical since it 'has been constantly modified' (Kaflon-Stillman, 2003, p. 10).

Heritage's problems in finding pictures could have been alleviated by compressing this early history but that option was apparently constrained by the series' 'advisory board'. Far from indicating a supervisory role, the advisory board on such series was usually more of a public relations gambit than an indication that academics were somehow in control. In fact, the advisory board is a further aspect of how television 'trumps' history or any other discipline. Such assemblages of the great and the good in the scholarship of the subject being prepared was then a necessary part of the politics of getting programmes to the US screen. Bodies such as the National Endowment of the Arts needed the imprimatur of academic opinion to justify expending public funds on television shows. PBS itself also needed a degree of academic respectability to hide behind in case of controversy. And controversy was seldom distant because, as Patricia Zimmerman has outlined, publicly funded PBS documentary series, including those on historical subjects, were becoming a major site of a deeply ideological conflict between rising neoconservative cultural power and the perceived intrinsically liberal bias of noncommercial broadcasting (Zimmerman, 2000; Winston, 2009, pp. 44–8).

It was, however, the mere existence of such a board that would serve these PR purposes. The broadcasters' right of free expression alone constrained any meaningful input from them. The interaction between these academic overseers and programme makers has scarcely ever been documented, although the relationship in the case of *Middletown*, a 1982 PBS series based on a classic of American sociology, the production of which had been instigated by academics at Ball State University, has been discussed at length by the sociologists involved (Vander Hill, 1982; Hoover, 1987b, 1993). Even though they had suggested the subject, the academics were largely ignored and a far from classic, sensationalist and idiosyncratic series was the result.

Working on *Heritage*, I never received any instructions – or a word of any kind – from the advisors, although Alan met one of them for general guidance sometime after we had determined how we would make the film. As far as I knew, the only influence the advisors supposedly had on the series was to insist on the detail of ancient Jewish history that had caused the opening episodes to be so pedantic. It is, though, just as likely that this rumour of the advisory scholars' fascination with what the sands revealed of early Jewish history gained currency within the station as an excuse to justify the unsatisfactory quality of the early hours. Certainly to say the series had a slow start is to be charitable.

The advisors on any historical topic, it might be thought, would represent a range of viewpoints that they would want represented. That this seldom happens is a measure of their impotence. For one thing, the need for clear narratives means that debate (as, say, exhibited between different schools of historical interpretation) is not easily accommodated on the screen. At one level this necessarily involves filming many talking heads with confusingly diverse opinions – basically an anathema. At another level, the current fashion for authored series implicitly and explicitly excludes those who do not agree with the presenting historian. Above all, the dominant journalistic thrust of much nonfiction narrative on television precludes nuance. This is because, overall, broadcasters are not good at complexity of argument.

For the Holocaust film, the penultimate episode of *Heritage,* the seminal text was Raul Hillberg's *The Destruction of the European Jews* (1961). There was, however, a major schism in the historiography of the Holocaust at that time between the 'intentionalists' – those who believed, with, say, Lucy Davidovitch (*Hitler's War Against the Jews,* 1975), in an inevitability to the Shoah as an end-point of modern post-1880s political anti-Semitism – and the 'functionalists', who saw the tragedy as an opportunist exploitation by the Nazis in the fog of war of what was previously for them a masturbatory Fascist fantasy. Although the intentionalists were in the majority, my script, with Alan's support, better reflected the minority functionalist opinion. Thankfully, we had the advisory services of the leading functionalist historian Yehudah Bauer, now Professor of Holocaust Studies at the Avraham Harman Institute of Contemporary Jewry at the Hebrew University of Jerusalem. Clearly, such *bona fides* were more than enough for our purposes and Alan secured his imprimatur with the one conversation he had with him reported above.

However, more than the general form of long-form history series, any historiographic explication was impossible in this instance. The subject matter – the Shoah – rendered debates about historical interpretations pathetic side-issues. In the context of the necessarily impressionist emotionalism of mainstream television, there was (and is) simply no space for such arguments.

The protection of the advisers, in any case, could only go so far. For example, Alan wanted 'to show Hitler as the supreme politician rather than just a megalomaniac rabble-rouser'; for me this ambition was, in effect, a welcome injunction to resist the 'Jews v. Nazis' (c.f. cowboys and Indians) tendency of Holocaust documentaries (and indeed the Holocaust 'industry' in general) by emphasizing the politics of totalitarianism. As far as I am concerned, the universal dangers of intolerance and bigotry are ever present. They are not merely to be found in the particularities of the Jewish tragedy in the Shoah. This was to lead us to universalize the Holocaust by, at the climax, turning the war against the Jews' into 'a war against humanity'. This point in the script was made over shots of French Christian gravestones, embossed with photographs of the dead, massacred by the Nazis without reason one day in June 1944 in the village of Oradour-sur-Glane. We emphasized the point by also referencing the destruction of the Romany and other ethnic groups, the homosexuals and the disabled in the camps, and some Jewish opinion found all this a touch too much.

The constraints imposed by unspoken ideological assumptions were ever present. I had written as part of 'the strong analysis of conditions in Weimar Germany', which Alan also had as one of his ambitions for the film, that

Einstein now joined Freud and Marx as one of the Jewish 'patriarchs' of the modern world (Rosenthal, 2000, p. 243). John Fox, somewhat sheepishly as I recall, indicated to me there was a problem with this. I started to laugh, so obvious was what was coming. He told me I would have to remove Marx because there was no mention of him in the previous hour on the nineteenth century. Fox and WNET had managed to save the series so it did not stop, as Alan once feared it might, in the sixteenth century; but nevertheless, Marx was gone from the history of the Jews.[5]

This was, of course, as nothing compared to the problem of Israel. Curiously, the foundation of the state and its nearly four decades of existence (at that point) was not accorded a programme of its own but spread between the last 2 hours on which we worked. Alan recalls:

> When I had looked at the original outline for the nine-part series, there seemed to me one glaring omission – there was no single film devoted to the rise of modern Israel. By way of contrast the story of America and its Jews not only took up film seven in its entirety, but was also slated to appear in the last film in the series *Into the Future*....I thought this was a dreadful decision both politically and creatively, one lacking all tact, sensitivity and feeling. My objections were to no avail.
>
> (Rosenthal, 2000, p. 242)

Like Eban, London-born Alan is an Oxbridge-educated Israeli. I, although having a different general stance on the issue of Israel, agreed that the omission bordered on the absurd. Episode seven was stridently entitled 'The Golden Land'. There was historic justification for this title since, during the phase of mass immigration to the US on either side of the turn of the twentieth century, the phrase was used in Yiddish; but the effect was, as Alan well understood, to make America, not Israel, Jewry's haven. Moreover, as the series was getting underway, Israel was completing her transformation from gallant victim surrounded by a sea of enemies into an aggressive, militaristic regional power. In 1982, Israel invaded Lebanon for the second time to attack the PLO. Her Christian Lebanese allies, with her connivance, massacred hundreds in the Palestinian refugee camps of Sabra and Shatila. In far-off New York, there thus could be little chance of a show in the series called 'A Land of Milk and Honey'.

The tension between Israel and the Jewish Diaspora was reflected in a tension between Alan and I on the second film we made, *Into the Future*, the last of the series. As English-born Jews, we share exactly similar backgrounds and education but he made *aliyah* ('went up') to Israel and I, like the majority of Western Jews, did not. Alan accuses me of objecting to the second film because he believes I thought it would come out as 'a simple Zionist tractate', an increasing problem for me given Lebanon and what he calls Israel's 'seemingly repressive actions in regards to the Palestinians'. He does have the good grace to acknowledge that: 'I may be wrong on this matter but that is how that's how I read his position at the time' (Rosenthal, 2000, p. 252). He is wrong. My 'doubts' about the task were not to do with contemporary Israeli actions at all. I knew well enough when agreeing to write the script that it would be Zionist in cast and, because it was for television, 'simple'. My problem was grounded in my failure to have the inconvenient truth of one major aspect of Zionism's initial project addressed. Western Jewry, despite the Holocaust, had, following Brandeis' line, rejected Zionism's 'ingathering' ambition and purpose. I wrote in the script that 'very, very few' Jews made *aliyah* from the West. This uncontroversial statement of fact was unacceptable to both Eban and Alan as members of the highly select group of Western Jews who had immigrated to Israel. Eban took out the 'very, very' – and, using a *nom de plume,* I took my name off the script.

We were, though, entirely *ad idem* on the periodization of the previous film. WNET had initially envisaged this hour covering 1933 to 1948. Alan argued that: 'To start in 1933 was to give the whole game to Hitler, and to end up in 1948 was to build in the proposition that Israel only came into existence because of Hitler, which I thought was untrue and misleading' (Rosenthal, 2000, pp. 241ff). He won this battle and we were able to provide the 'strong analysis' he wanted. We detailed the development of the early twentieth-century Jewish settlement of Palestine as a consequence of general pre-Nazi European conditions; and we ended the film in effect in 1946 and in Europe, not Palestine.

A good deal, though, could not be said because of time constraints. A reference to the assassination of Alexander I of Yugoslavia in an early draft inevitably did not, with much else, make it into the final film. Other references fell foul of assumptions about the audience's knowledge. In the *Heritage* production office on Columbus Circle around the corner from the studios, Alan told me we could not possibly get away with using a reference to *Mr Norris Changes Trains* to explicate Weimarian decadence. Nobody in the audience would know who Christopher Isherwood was. A secretary was passing. 'Who is Isherwood?' asked Alan, to prove his point. 'English novelist, born 1904', she said without hesitation. Nevertheless, Mr Norris was exiled from the script as King Alexander had been.

Compression rendered some material unusable. I found the story of a young lad who, with two friends, had held up the elders of the Jewish Council, the *Judenrat*, of the Nazi ghetto in which they were immured to get money for some guns so they could run off to join the partisans in the forest. The boy, at war's end, walked across the Carpathians making his way to Trieste to find a boat to Palestine. There he saw a man with a Star of David sown onto his jacket – but the star was not yellow, it was blue; and the jacket was the blouson of an officer of the Jewish Brigade of the British Army. Not only was this story difficult to illustrate and too long, but also Alan knew the man who had become a general in the Israeli army and did not think he would make a good interviewee. This last fact is another constraint. Broadcasting has no prejudice against any single group of people as strong as its bias against the uncharismatic and inarticulate.

Another reason for losing this story was that it required explaining the Jewish councils (*Judenräte*) the Nazis established to organize daily life and work in the ghettos. Self-censorship had caused me not even to consider drafting script on this point because it raised the vexed question of Jewish complicity, even as the contrary impulse had prompted Alan, with my enthusiastic support, to list one of his intentions as the revelation of 'the full extent of Jewish wartime resistance'. We did this last so comprehensively that one of the WNET executives was moved to ask me what authority I had for the estimated figure I cited of 40,000 Jewish resistance fighters in the forests with Soviet partisans. 'M.D.R. Foot's *Resistance*', I said firmly (Foot, 1976). But explaining the *Judenräte* was a different matter; although I did write, by way of explanation of attitudes in the ghettos, that Jewish willingness to work was based on an assumption that if the work was needed by the Nazis, then the workers would be too. Nevertheless, avoiding the *Judenräte* was a considered distorting personal decision. The Nobel Prize-winning Yiddish writer, Isaac Bashevis Singer, once said, in reply to the inevitable question about why he continued after the war to write in the language of a largely annihilated people, that Yiddish was the only tongue never to be spoken by policeman.[6] I have always thought it was the most dreadful irony that the only exception to this truth was that the *Judenräte* exercised policing powers; but they, like Marx and King Alexander I, did not find their way into the film. As I said to the executive, rightly or wrongly, our prime motivation in dealing with this topic, in the context of a mass medium, was above all to keep faith with the dead.

Chrono-Logic

The academic debate about the nature of narrative which, in formalist thinking, first depends on de-coupling 'story' (*fabula* or *histoire*) – the order of the events in the text – from 'plot' (*suzjet* or *discours*) – the order in which they are presented. Such analysis immediately expands the popular understanding of narrative, which is bound by straightforward notions of time-based causality. For Barthes, for example, also in play is 'the hermeneutic code': 'a variety of chance events which can either formulate a question or delay its answer' (Barthes, 1990, p. 17). In analogous fashion, Todorov suggests narrative's mainspring is 'transformation': the unveiling of situations that are then disrupted and finally concluded. For the audience, this involves the progressive liquidation of their initial ignorance (Todorov, 1981, pp. 41ff). Some would now go so far as to argue that narrative is nothing more than 'the play of suspense/curiosity/surprise between represented and communicative time' (Sternberg, 2003, p. 328). Formalists such as Fludernik dislodge 'the criteria of mere sequentiality and logical connectedness' from its central position in narrative, in favour of a more complex concept. For Fludernik, an audience deconstructing a text needs not only sequentiality and logic but, equally, a shared understanding of the world (i.e., social perceptions), as well as reception conventions. (1996, p. 19).

The received narrow concept of narrative has posed problems for the documentary and for documentary studies. The New York University film school, for example, crudely distinguishes between 'narrative', 'documentary' and 'experimental', where the first is simply fiction, the second nonfiction and the last anything else. This represents a traditional blind spot. Since narrative was a mark of fiction, then documentary demanded that it be not narrative (i.e., not fiction). One of the most influential of film studies textbooks, through many editions, denied that *The River* (Pare Lorenz, 1938), which essentially follows the Mississippi from the mountains to the sea and is loosely constructed in time from early settlement to the present, was a comparatively obvious narrative (Bordwell and Thompson, 1997, 3rd ed., p. 128). The supposed problem of the fictionality of narrative in documentary is meaningless because, both in its limited sense of sequentiality and logic as well as in its more expanded formalist guises, narrative is an unavoidable characteristic of all human communication. Documentaries are narratives perforce.

Nevertheless, the expanded notion of narrativity needs to be treated with great care in practice when writing for the screen. Unlike the written text, where the rate of information flow can be controlled by the reader, with film the information flow rate is controlled by the text. Leaving simple structures – the journey, the diurnal or their analogies – behind nearly always endangers audience comprehension. As Dai Vaughan points out, any such film 'works better in the head [of the filmmaker] than on the screen' (1983, p. 75).

I was writing narrative history to be delivered to the audience at the fixed pace of transmission. Chronology was the glue holding the film together. Nevertheless, in an early draft, I had attempted something less linear. Nazi anti-Semitism could be described as a progression. Medieval anti-Semites had said, in effect, 'you cannot live amongst us as Jews.' Modern political anti-Semitism said, 'you cannot live amongst us.' The Nazis said, 'you cannot live.' I thought this offered an intriguing way into illuminating both the historical context as well as the particularities of Nazi Jewish policy. I therefore attempted a script organized along these lines, but it led to chronological distortions – *Kristallnacht,* in 1938, somehow ended up before the Nuremburg Decrees, in 1935. Alan correctly pointed out this would not do. Chronology is a very hard master and I abandoned all attempts to manipulate it.

The visual imperative

Nothing better indicates the paradoxical nature of photography's codelessness than the image's ambiguities, despite its iconic richness. This is especially true of the archive. Burning buildings, filmed for *Feldzug in Polen* [The Polish Campaign] (Fritz Hippler, 1940),[7] are identified on the sound-track as the aftermath of Polish military action in Danzig. Subsequent use of the footage in an Allied newsreel clearly blamed the *Werhmacht* for the destruction. Such reversals of meaning are a commonplace. At the out-set of the recycling of archive material, Shub was concerned, in *Fall of the Romanov Dynasty,* with the implications of providing the Tsar's home movies with a meaning totally at odds with their original significance (Petric, 1984, p. 24).

Even if correctly contextualized, there are still problems. With Nazi-shot footage, the ethics of reuse are not as straightforward as we then thought. There was no difficulty for us in revisiting horror because the justification was a simple obligation to inform or remind. That we avoided the worse of the concentration camp footage was a decision we made because it had become a cliché, not because it was horrendous. But we were, in general, unquestioning about the status of the images we did use, arguing to our-selves, I suppose, that the Nazis would not have used pretend corpses, say, when they had created so many real ones. It was not until my ex-NYU stu-dent Ilan Ziv, a New York-based Israeli documentarist, interviewed me for his 1994 film, *Tango of Slaves*, about the Warsaw Ghetto, that I confronted Shub's dilemma head-on.

Ilan asked me, on camera, if I thought it was ethical to use the results of the hypothermia experiments conducted in the camps where Nazi doctors had literally frozen people to death. This was exactly a type of the activity that had led after the war to the development of the Nuremberg Protocols governing the use of human subjects in scientific experiments. As part of my work on the documentary, I had been concerned with the difficulties of squaring the ethical requirements of the Protocols with the demands of free-dom of expression (Winston, 1988; 2008, p. 244). I was therefore extremely discomforted when Ilan's follow-up asked why then did we use footage of a Nazi film about the Warsaw Ghetto, the script of which he had discovered in the German archive and which was therefore surely suspect. 'Why indeed'? was my only reply. Had I known that the film had been scripted I would certainly have argued to make this clear in my script. The point is that the archive never has clean hands, but history on television – and tele-historians who often seem quite naïve about such issues – seldom acknowledge this.

The quandaries for history that the archive poses are not only about incorrect and incomplete 'captioning' (as it were) or even complete mis-attribution – as where, famously, footage of the storming of the Winter Palace comes not from 1917 but from 1928 – from Eisenstein's reconstruc-tion of the event in his feature Октябрь: Десять дней, которые потрясли мир [October: The Ten Days That Shook the World]. Such cases, though, are quite easily spotted. The basic problem for users of the archive, rather, lies in the everyday practice of film production. Even if correctly contextualized, identified and attributed, the photographic image, especially the newsreel image, should be treated – essentially – as suspect.

The archive is also a source of problems because of the happenstance of what is in it. We had the services of Raye Farr, who had been the film researcher on *World at War* and whose knowledge of the topography of Eastern Europe was encyclopedic. She could identify a shot as being of, say, Bialystok and date it by the buildings. While much of what we found matched the draft script, some did not. I knew, for instance, of the existence of a small Yiddish-speaking film industry in Warsaw before the war and referenced this. Raye found a wonderful shot of a Yiddisher Fred Astaire look-alike in top hat and tails crooning with a line of chorines behind him. Sometimes a shot would, astonishingly, perfectly illustrate a script point. I do not know where it came from, but there was a set-up image, a virtual 'pack-shot', of Yiddish newspapers and magazines being tossed into the frame; it was a precise illustration of the point about the vibrancy of the Yiddish press in the context of secular Eastern European Jewish society's engagement with modernity between the wars. Footage of the Jewish rural settlements, the *shtetls*, was very rare. There was a professionally shot 1920s minifilm of a man, clearly an American, in the midst of a *shtetl* posing with the residents. Obviously, here was a local who had immigrated to the 'Golden Land' and had prospered enough not only to return home but also to bring a cameraman (I assume) with him to make a record of the visit for his family in the US. The material could clearly not be used as simple illustration of *shtetl* life because it raised more questions than it answered. Neither could it be ignored because of the paucity of other images. Despite the time constraint, which made the use of every word a matter of serious concern, I needed to add, 'Visitors taking home movies in the 1920s....; to the text about Jewish village life.

More significant was the impact of one of Raye's coups: actual footage of an *aktion* – a round-up of Jews. There were stills of this in circulation but no movie footage until that point. She had obtained the film from her contacts in East Berlin and it caused Alan to backtrack on one of his most compelling – as I though it – ideas for the film. Underlying his thinking was that what had become the clichés of the Holocaust movie needed to be avoided. Familiarity was blunting the message. I thought he was totally correct in this assumption and it was why we agreed, for example, that we would avoid showing 'living skeletons'.[8] Alan had suggested that, because this was the most familiar part of the story, we deal with the camps over black using a montage of voices delivering witness statements. I thought this was a brilliant way to avoid the worst emotionalism of the 'Jews v. Nazis' norms. The discovery of the *aktion* footage, however, began what was to be a dilution of this intention. Alan said moving images of an *aktion* had not been seen. I said the stills were so familiar I did not think the audience would think they were seeing anything new; but the archivist in him refused this point.

The change of direction was confirmed when Alan met a survivor and decided her, in my view somewhat poeticized, published account of both ghetto and camp be included and, necessarily, illustrated. Alan thinks her words, spoken by her, over archive and a restaged 'last journey' by train with the Polish countryside seen through a slat (as if of a cattle truck), constitute 'one of the most devastating scenes in the film' (Rosenthal, 2000, p. 246). I, on the other hand, thought her writing vividly proved the point about, if the not impossibility, then the hopelessness of art after Auschwitz, which was first proposed by Adorno. I argued against moving away from the black screen, putting to Alan his own initial position on avoiding Holocaust film clichés. He said he thought I was crazy to think we could get away with a minute of black on an American network. I was, of course, crazy – but the craziness was his brilliant idea. In any event, the survivor won, of course, and we spent more time inside the camp system than we initially envisaged; but we still avoided the most horrific images.

About a third of the film was archive, the rest being Eban stand-uppers and footage Alan shot. There is a continuum with such footage in the relationship of the image to the text. It runs from pure description merely contextualizing the iconicity of the image to the purely symbolic. The 'restaged' train journey to Auschwitz and the shots of the camp as it stood in 1984 (overgrown, not covered with 'Holocaust tourists') lies towards the iconic end. At the symbolic end was the footage used to illustrate the anti-Semitic legislation of the Third Reich in the 1930s.

As Oxford-educated lawyers, both Alan and I were interested in plotting how the Nazis suborned the Weimarian legal system systematically to deny human rights to sections of the citizenry while maintaining the outward show of the rule of law. I recall at Oxford listening to Hubert Hart's lecture on this. He began by asking us to consider an English law, passed in due form, prohibiting men wearing spotted bow-ties from entering Royal Parks after dusk. My understanding of the importance of natural justice was so vividly inculcated by this lecture that I have never forgotten it. I began to deal with this in the script by outlining, over two-and-a-half pages, the various legal stages in the 1930s by which German Jews were deprived of their civil rights. This was crucial to my sense of the story being more than just that of the consequences of unbridled bigotry. It was about more than anti-Semitism exactly because the persecution turned on this legalized abuse of natural justice. Alan, I think, agreed with this, but was moved to ask what I expected him to use for illustrations. I did not know but I told him I had faith that he, as an experienced documentary filmmaker, would come up with something. He did: he filmed contemporary German scenes. If the script said a law was passed in the 1930s forbidding Jews from entering parks or getting on a train, we saw a modern (1984) West German park or a train. This slightly worried John Fox, although he could never quite put his finger on why – and we certainly did not help articulate how this might be construed as unfair to the current German population.

There was less of a symbolic 'stretch', as it were, with the Danish material:

> We had always wanted to say something about the escape of the Danish Jews by sea to Sweden, but archive material and stills were practically non-existent.... I thought we could stage a simple scene of a small boat leaving the harbour with refugees. It would clearly be not the real thing, but it would say to the audience: 'Just try for the moment to image what it was like.'
>
> (Rosenthal, 2000, p. 245)

Alan filmed a boat clearly in the present, the occupants of which were therefore by no means 'refugees', but the footage, used symbolically, allowed us to tell the story of how the Danes saved their Jewish neighbours and also to outline, over these shots, other stories of 'righteous gentiles' – anti-deportation demonstrations in Bulgaria, visas being issued by the Swiss and the Swedes and so forth.

Of course, as vexed as the identification, attribution, ambiguities, ethics and implicit symbolism of the images one had were, even worse was the difficulty caused by the absence of images. Take the contentious issue of Jewish complicity in running the ghettos: the issue of Jewish labour had been reduced to the sentence about the need for the work being a supposed protection for the worker. I recall visiting the cutting room of Larry Solomon, a brilliant editor and another of Alan's friends who he had hired onto the film, to watch a rough cut of the hour. The reference to work in the ghetto and why the people did it was gone. I was horrified – a second main argument after the black-screen debate. I was told the script had not been followed simply because there were no images of people at work in a ghetto, although there were stills of other activities such as illegal schoolrooms. Eventually, though, two still images of people at work were found and the text restored. Upon reflection, I now feel this omission had upset me because I was guilty of having not perhaps thought through the *Judenräte* issue.

Obviously there has to be a line beyond which history becomes hopelessly compromised, but I find it very hard to systematize which of the various issues outlined above either cross that line or are of fundamental ethical importance; and which are simply the rather trivial and inevitable consequence of television's visual imperative or the general discipline of programme making. Behind the opening credits of the Holocaust episode, in a long shot of medieval Nuremburg across water, suddenly an almost invisible stone falls, causing a pleasing ripple. Did it happen to fall from the heavens, or was it tossed in for the purposes of making the shot more interesting? Tossed in by somebody well versed in the discipline of television – Alan, perhaps? Tossed in with no reason from the historical standpoint, but every justification from the televisual one.

'Out of the Ashes'

The Holocaust episode of *Heritage* was called 'Out of the Ashes'. I thought this was a pretty silly title for a slough of reasons: the film was not about what happened 'out of the ashes', but why the ashes were there in the first place. Indeed 'out of the ashes' had implications that Alan wished to avoid about linking Israel's founding monocausally to the Holocaust. It was also a cliché, and like all clichés somewhat meaningless.

After Alan suggested I might care to write the script of this episode, I had to go to Columbus Circle to meet with executive producer Marc Seigel. He asked me how I would handle the hour. I recall that I said: 'We won.' 'We won?' he queried. 'You're Jewish?' I asked. 'Yes.' 'Well, so am I. And we're not supposed to be here according to the Nazi plan. But we are. So, at a terrible price, we won.' I think that it was because he was so astonished by this that he confirmed Alan's decision to have me write the show.

Because 'we won' (as it were), I wanted to call the hour 'We Will Outlive Them' – a common Yiddish saying in the ghettos and the camps. It was not a cliché; it was not meaningless; and it described the film Alan had made. This was not, after all, another 'Jews v. Nazis' lament; and it did expose how easy it is, and how dire the consequences are, for a state to abandon justice and the rule of law. And that was the essence of the code I wanted to provide for the photographic image track of this documentary. But I didn't get the title changed.

The hour is still called 'Out of the Ashes'.

A note on availability

Most of the documentaries cited are readily available. *Heritage: Civilization and the Jews* was rereleased in 2002 by WNET as a DVD set (Region 1, North America only). *The River* is also available in this format. *The Ascent of Man, Civilisation: A Personal View, The Great War, Culloden, October* and *Shoah* are all available on DVD (Region 2, Europe). The first Lumiere reel, *Victory at Sea* and *Feldzug in Polan* can be accessed on You Tube.

Notes

1. Film studies has tended to class the image as indexical following a misreading of Peirce by Peter Wollen (1969, pp. 82ff). Within Peirce's sign system, however, the photographic sign is more appropriately classed as iconic (Winston and Tsang, 2009, pp. 458–63).
2. The better known response to this reel, that people in the first audience leapt out of the way of the screen when they saw the locomotive coming towards them, is a myth not least because the train arrives at La Ciotat station at a slant. It is not coming towards the audience head-on. Moreover, a certain resistance to the Cinématographe's automatic (as it were) superiority to the lantern was reflected in

a view that saw the full-colour richness of the slides as an advantage over cinema's unrealistic black-and-white – 'the kingdom of shadows', as Gorky called it.

3. There are other techniques for bringing history to the screen. In the year of *Civilisation*, maverick director Peter Watkins deployed the then-fresh conventions of direct cinema, and meticulous historical research, to film a fully reconstructed account of *Culloden*. Treating a battle of 1745 as a news event to be filmed with hand-held cameras had a tremendous impact, but such aggressive interventionism to illuminate the past was not to be emulated for decades: see also John Corner's chapter in this volume.
4. Actually, an 'hour' (or episode) lasted for 52 minutes.
5. But, to my astonishment, he did let me get away with 'careened' – as in the script line, 'Germany careened into defeat.'
6. He added that in Hebrew they were already fighting wars.
7. Actually the film was released before the turn of the year, but Hitler and others had it withdrawn for a slight recut, so it is conventionally dated to early 1940.
8. Much the same impulse clearly conditioned Claude Lanzmann's nine-and-a-half hours documentary *Shoah,* released in the US a year after our film was transmitted. Lanzmann, famously, did not use any archive.

Bibliography

Barthes, R. (1985 [1965]) 'The Photographic Message' in *The Responsibility of Forms: Critical Essays on Music, Art, and Representation* trans. Richard Howard (Berkeley: University of California Press).

Barthes, R. (1990) *S/Z*, trans. R. Miller (Oxford: Blackwell).

Bordwell, D. and Thompson, K. (1997) *Film Art* (New York, McGraw-Hill).

Cory, J. (1984a) 'TV Review: Heritage: Civilization and the Jews', *New York Times,* 1 October: http://www.nytimes.com/1984/10/01/arts/tv-review-civilization-and-the-jews-series-on-channel-13.html?scp=3&sq=heritage%20civilization%20and %20the%20jews&st=cse. Accessed 26 March 2009.

Cory J. (1984b) 'TV Review: The Conclusion of Civilization and the Jews', *New York Times,* 19 November: http://www.nytimes.com/1984/11/19/arts/tv-review-the-conclusion-of-civilization-and-the-jews.html?scp=15&sq=heritage%20civili-zation%20and%20the% 20jews&st=cse. Accessed 26 March 2009.

Davidovitch, L. (1986 [1975]) *Hitler's War Against the Jews* (New York: Bantam).

Fludernik, M. (1996) *Towards a 'Natural' Narratology* (London: Routledge).

Foot, M.D.R. (1976) *Resistance* (London: Eyre Methuen).

Hillberg, R. (2003 [1961]) *The Destruction of the European Jews* (New Haven, CT: Yale University Press).

Hoover, D. (1993) *The Middletown Film Project* (New York: Harwood).

Kalfon Stillman, Y (2003) *Arab Dress* (Leiden: Brill).

Petric, V. (1984) 'Esther Shub: Film as a Historical Discourse', in T. Waugh (ed.) *'Show Us Life': Toward a History and Aesthetics of Committed Documentary* (Metuchen, NJ: The Scarecrow Press).

Rosenthal, A. (2000) *Jerusalem, Take One! Memoirs of a Jewish Filmmaker* (Carbondale, IL: Southern Illinois University Press).

Sternberg, M. (2003) 'Universals of Narrative and Their Cognitivist Fortunes (1)', *Poetics Today*, 24, 297–395.

Todorov, T. (1981) *Introduction to Poetics* (Minneapolis: University of Minnesota Press).

Vander Hill, W. (1982) 'The Middletown Film Project: Reflections of an "Academic Humanist" ', *Journal of Popular Film and Culture*, 10.

Vaughan, D. (1983) *Portrait of An Invisible Man: The Working Life of Stewart McAllister, Film Editor* (London: British Film Institute).

Winston, B. (1988) 'The Tradition of the Victim in Griersonian Documentary' in Gross, L., Katz, J. and Ruby, J. (eds) *Image Ethics* (New York: Oxford University Press).

Winston, B. (1999) *Fires Were Started* (London: British Film Institute).

Winston, B. (2008) *Claiming the Real II: Documentary—Grierson & Beyond* (London: British Film Institute).

Winston, B. (2009) "'Ein Rätsel in einem Geheimnis mit siebein Siegeln": Frederick Wiseman und das öffentliche amerikanische Fernsehen in den siebziger jahren' (trans: Bert Rebhandl) in Hohenberger, E. (ed.) *Frederick Wiseman: Kino des Sozialen* (Berlin: Verlag Vorwerk 8).

Winston, B. and Tsang, H. (2009) 'The subject and the indexicality of the photograph', *Semiotica*, 173.

Wollen, P. (1969) *Signs and Meaning in the Cinema* (London: British Film Institute).

Zimmermann, P. (2000) *State of Emergency: Documentaries, Wars, Democracies* (Minneapolis: University of Minnesota Press).

4
Contexts of Production

Commissioning History

Ann Gray

What makes a good history programme for television? The answer to this question will, of course, be very different depending on the respondent's relationship to programming, either as a historian, a commissioning editor, a producer or an audience member. In the course of my research I put this question to commissioning editors and producers[1] and these were some of the responses: 'it has to have a gripping story'; 'we need good images – a visual core'; 'we have to get insight into the human condition'; 'we are always looking for a format'; 'gripping yarns – I want a page-turner in the treatment, I want to find out what happens at the end'; 'something that gives the audience an *experience* of history rather than show and tell'; 'there must be some kind of resonance for today'; 'things that are original, have more character and are provocative – that have opinion cut through them'; 'something that informs you about the present'; 'to give people an idea of what it must have been like'.

These criteria could, of course, apply to most forms of television and are evidence, if any were needed, of the prime function of television in the twenty-first century as a medium of entertainment. To entertain, in my view, is a worthy ambition requiring a high degree of creativity and skill and one that should not be dismissed as some kind of inferior cultural aim. Neither does 'entertainment' exclude *per se* those two other tenets of public service broadcasting – to inform and educate. Indeed, there are a number of examples in this collection of programming that offer a combination of affective and cognitive elements. However, the comments above are also evidence of a clear and quite consistent set of professional codes and assumptions, especially about the audience, which those responsible for history programming on television in the UK inhabit. Readers with knowledge of the UK terrestrial and some satellite channels may be able to detect identifiable nuances in tone here, but the consistency and, perhaps, predictability of their views is not surprising. However, they do raise questions about how, or more precisely under what conditions, television mediates, or indeed, constructs 'the past'. My aim in this chapter is to explore some aspects of the context of history programme production and in particular the close-knit networks of commissioners and producers who, whilst working within a highly volatile and changing television environment, both construct and practise these professional codes.

Having been neglected for some time, there is now a growing body of work within media and cultural studies that acknowledges the importance of the conditions and practices of production in what are now being called the 'creative industries'. This interest, as Simon Cottle points out, explores 'a relatively unexplored and undertheorised "middle ground" of organisational structures and work place practices' (Cottle, 2003, p. 4). The aim is to examine the structures, the practices and the ways of working within different cultural organizations and settings, and in particular the social aspects of these processes. How do individuals within the creative and media industries work across different skill bases to fashion the finished product? What are the commercial constraints and how do creative workers manage and negotiate these? What role do personal relationships and networks play in the creative process?

John Caldwell's recent study of production cultures in the Los Angeles film and television industries addresses such questions (Caldwell, 2008). Through a combination of methods he analysed trade journals, interviewed film and television workers and carried out ethnographic field observations of production spaces and professional gatherings. Caldwell sets the resulting data within an analysis of the economics of the industry. His specific aim, however, was to discover the cultural practices and belief systems of film/video production workers in Los Angeles. Caldwell's study is remarkable for many reasons and will provide an important document for further work on understanding the complex systems of production in this part of the creative industries. My study focuses on a much more bounded world of television production which can yield more nuanced understandings of the factors involved in the production of programmes that focus on a specific subject. Caroline Dover's study of television documentary producers and directors gives us insights into the impact of technological and institutional change in media organizations upon a specific group of genres, in what John Corner refers to as the post-documentary state (Corner, 2002, p. 263) and a particular group of workers. (Dover, 2004) This clearly has an impact on their working practice but also on their feeling of self-identification through their creative endeavours.

In common with Caldwell's and Dover's studies, we are dealing with a highly volatile and dynamic industry which during the time of our study, due to a combination of technological and economic pressures, has moved into a period of uncertainty especially for the US networks and UK terrestrial channels. These changes have many consequences but none more so than on the people who work in these industries. In both the US and UK context the 'nomadic labour system' (Caldwell, 2008, pp. 113–9), that is, based on freelance individuals on short-term contracts, is the norm and workers, especially those in the so-called 'independent sector', take this state of affairs for granted.

My focus on history programming from the beginning of its renaissance on British television in 1995[2] provides a prism through which the conditions of the development and expansion of this category of programming can be rendered visible, or at least its contours can be identified. This brief history is one of a dynamic proliferation of forms, genres, formats and hybrids which is interesting in itself as evidence of television's 'churn rate',[3] but also of the relationships between independents and broadcasters in a highly competitive market. Through my analysis of this period of production I will argue that the period saw the emergence of a particular 'production ecology' formed by a relatively small number of creative and innovative professionals who shared a passion for history and for whom the changes to the media landscape provided an environment that was ripe for innovation. This further allows us to ask a number of questions that are pertinent to cultural and media studies and that will be of interest to historians also as a plotting of the metamorphosis of this aspect of 'public history'.

From material drawn from interviews with professionals, the analysis of trade journals and attendance at professional gatherings I will evoke the complexity of this relatively small world of media production but one that has potentially far-reaching consequences for the kind of history we get on television. Whilst each stage of programme production, filming, editing, post-production, marketing and scheduling is important and worthy of analysis, for my purposes here I will focus on the commissioning process, a complex and often rather nebulous set of practices, which not only form the key initial stage in any production story but also can be indicative of the broader trends in history programming. Within this set of practices I wanted to find out where and how original ideas for programming are arrived at, how they are formed and what the main influences in this part of the production process are. I soon discovered the difficulties inherent in unearthing this kind of knowledge. The dealings and negotiations between commissioners and producers are often informal and inconsistent, and there are varying amounts of documentation laid down in the archive for future researchers. There are detailed records found in the BBC archives and to some extent Channel 4, but the documentation usually begins at the point of the contract, that is, the actual commission. But prior to this point a lot of meetings, discussions and negotiations have already taken place, both within independent production companies and between commissioners and producers, during which the potential programme has taken shape. This is, if you like, the back story to the commission which is a very important part of the genesis of any programme or series and is a strong influence on what eventually ends up on our screens. Furthermore, as we shall see, these encounters of exchange, dialogue, negotiation and direction provide often very fertile ground, not only for programme ideas, but also for the future direction of history programming and the generation of new practices in a rapidly changing environment. Material upon which I draw for this chapter was garnered from interviews with personnel at the key production companies involved in history output: BBC, Channel 4, Five (with some reference to ITV regional output), the History Channel and several independent companies.

Symbolic community

In her study referred to above, Caroline Dover identified what she termed a 'symbolic community' of documentary producers which 'is conceptually constructed through common practices, traditions and perceptions of genres' (Dover, 2004, p. 242). A strong element of this collective ethos was the notion of public service, with which documentary is associated, and a sense of particular genre boundaries that defined their practice. John Tunstall had already identified this phenomenon within the media industries in his study of media producers (Tunstall, 1993) in which the seven different programme genres he looked at had their own 'distinctive private world that stretches across all channels' (1993, p. 2, quoted in Dover, 2004, p. 244). Dover makes the point that documentary producers can be found in many programme areas, for example, history, science, current affairs, and so on, and, we should add, some 15 years on, across the range of providers, that is, broadcast, independents and satellite channels. However, Tunstall and Dover make important points about both the shared professional assumptions and codes and the bounded nature of groups within the industry. My own research adds a further important element to this which is a substantive area of programming and reveals, in spite of the expansion of history programming in the last decade or so, a relatively small group of professionals who form a close-knit network. These professionals have been, and continue to be, highly influential in shaping history programming on UK television. What is of equal interest are the career trajectories of the individuals concerned, and the formations of relationships, which are a complex mix of the professional and the social.

These particular kinds of synergies of personal and professional contacts are fostered, even nurtured, by industry practice and especially at the commissioner/producer level. In the words of one of the independent producers: 'there are very few commissioners of history television and, unsurprisingly they all know each other.'[4] His observation was not limited to the UK but also included the US broadcasting scene. If you add to that the relatively small number of independent companies who have made history programming part of their unique selling point, then the personal/professional network widens, but only slightly, and most individuals have moved across the sector. Some of the relationships formed at University whilst others were formed as colleagues at different stages of their careers and in different institutional settings. The institutional context is, of course, critical for any creative and professional development and, in the case of the BBC, the period when Michael Jackson was heading up the Arts Programming unit for BBC2 provided opportunities for a number of researchers and producers to work on *The Late Show*. Martin Davidson, now History Commissioning Editor at the BBC moved from publishing to work on *The Late Show* in the late 1980s because, as he described it 'there was a kind of window for people who could work across cultural politics in television where consumerism, culture and politics were coalescing in an interesting way and advertising and the media were a particularly potent intersection' though not, he added, in history which, in his words, 'was as dull as ditchwater'.

Janice Hadlow, now controller of BBC2 also moved from radio into television to produce *The Late Show*. Hadlow was referred to by everyone I spoke to as the most influential individual who had shaped history programming in the last decade in the UK, and she has clearly encouraged and inspired a number of highly creative individuals who are now in key positions as broadcasters and as independents.[5] In 1995, the BBC established its History Unit under her leadership and started work on the series *A History of Britain*, persuading Simon Schama to author and present. Since that time, and before moving back to the BBC in 2008, she has been Head of History, Art and Religion and Head of Specialist Factual at Channel 4 (where she commissioned, amongst other programmes, Niall Ferguson's *Empire* and David Starkey's *Six Wives of Henry VIII*) and Controller of BBC4. Although she now has a wider remit, as she did at BBC4,[6] Hadlow's commitment to history programming, and what she calls 'serious' programming in general is clear. At the time of my interviews she had taken a sabbatical to write a historical book and in 2007–2008 was the Professor of Broadcasting at the University of Oxford.

The strengths of the networks were revealed during my discussions with the different players involved in their recommendations for other potential interviewees and also, more subtly, when similar stories and ways of thinking were recounted. At the time of my interview with one independent their new 'living history' series was in transmission and had received critical acclaim and good ratings for BBC2. The commissioning editor I spoke to a couple of weeks later echoed the enthusiasm for the series but also produced similar explanations for its success. The close-knit 'we' of this group was clear. Other notions about the audience demographic as well as what constitutes really good history programming were clearly part of a shared understanding and ethos. There is no doubt that the key members of this symbolic community are the commissioning editors, and it is important to understand their quite powerful role in programme production.

The commissioners

Since the establishment of Channel 4 in 1982 as a 'publisher' broadcaster, commissioning editors have become key figures in the television business.

As a result, the independent sector expanded rapidly; indeed, many of the early independents had been instrumental in lobbying for the shape of the new channel.

In 2003, TRC Media[7] published its study 'Inside the Commissioners: The Culture and Practice of Commissioning at UK Broadcasters', for which they carried out 70 in-depth interviews with commissioners, mainly from factual genres, across the terrestrial and independent sectors in addition to regulators and representatives of trade bodies. Their report covers many aspects of the commissioning editor's world but makes general points about the television industry itself that are pertinent here. First, what they call the 'deep-seated tendency' within the television industry to 'prioritise individuals over processes'. This, in a way, confirms the external view of 'the media' commonly expressed as 'it's not what you know but who you know', which is important in getting a foothold as a prospective employee in the industry. However, this acknowledgement also provides insights into working practices within the industry. A number of respondents spoke about the lack of training or support, or even detailed explanation of their role. There is a widespread feeling that the job cannot be taught with an industry preference for the 'learning through experience' model. Secondly, most commissioners did not actively seek the job, the posts were rarely advertised and there was often no interviewing process.[8] Some had been approached by former colleagues who might be looking for allies on a channel and most felt that they were employed because of their creative and editorial skills, rather than their business acumen.

These offers, alliances and appointments are made on the operation of certain kinds of professional (and personal) instinct. The following quote from an interview with a senior commissioning editor who was heading for a more senior post, talking about appointing his/her replacement, is not untypical. She or he expressed 'personal knowledge of potential' having worked with the person: 'I just felt in my gut that he was creative, talented and had the right kind of instincts' (TRC, 2003). Instinct about instincts plays a large role in the way the creatives account for and justify their choices. Of course, instinct is not a naturally occurring quality but rather something which is developed and honed through years of practical professional experience and when commissioners and producers are questioned more deeply about their strategies and decision-making criteria much more critical and reflexive accounts emerge. In my view the claim to 'instinct' is a professional defence strategy in a highly competitive and risky climate where the mystery of the creative process is a hugely valuable asset and one which, arguably, should be protected. This is especially so in the increasingly managerial and market-led climate of the television industry. The TRC study also identifies the increasingly risk-averse environment of the broadcasters which in turn has an effect on the pressure placed on commissioning editors often manifest in more central control and involvement by senior management. Technological developments also influence ways of working, for example, the requirement for multiplatform commissioning and delivery both widens the involvement by senior management in specific projects and also necessitates wide consultation across different hitherto separate departments.

Commissioning Editors are obviously important 'gatekeepers' in programming ideas and commissions. They are often programme makers themselves and are responsible for the management of the large budgets for which they have fought. I asked the commissioning editor at Five whether she thought of herself as a manager or a creative. She considered herself to be both, and pointed out that producers and directors have to manage their project budgets. She did, however, identify what she called her 'corporate' responsibilities as a broadcaster, which were distinctly in the domain of the commissioning editor:

> my kind of pure broadcaster side of the job which is, you know, are we doing enough hours, are we delivering enough hours for, in religion for Ofcom and do the press have everything they need and do marketing have everything they need and have I signed off the trails is a management job – corporate I suppose. Corporate.

The 'corporate' responsibilities of commissioners have arguably expanded especially in relation to 'brand identity' and for those commissioners employed by multichannel broadcasters. Commissioning the right kind of product that will support and develop different channel identities and therefore attract the desired audience is an increasingly important part of the role.

In this risk-averse environment, commissioning editors cannot be blamed, perhaps, for playing it safe. Indeed, they tend to rely not only on a tried-and-tested formula but also on those independents with whom they have previously worked. This of course could well have the effect of excluding some, especially smaller, independents and not giving start-ups any chance at all. In addition to this, there are contradictions and tensions between going for what is comfortable and the constant need to be innovative and novel in the chase for audiences. However, some commissioners have so-called 'open days', which is a quasi public service mechanism for meeting new independents. These occasions, however, are not about gathering commissionable ideas, but rather about informing the independents what the commissioners are looking for. The commissioning editors who took part in the TRC study said that they had a limited number of suppliers, and conversely the so-called 'super indies' each have their 'own' commissioning editors. This symbiotic relationship is clearly a structural feature of the commissioning process. These unspoken but acknowledged ways of working can be confusing for less experienced independents, but also the constant changes within the broadcaster's structures lead to fluctuating spheres of influence that are equally difficult for more knowledgeable independents to negotiate.

If the broadcasters and independents are in a constant state of flux, then the people who work in the industry are similarly positioned. How do commissioning editors, producers and, further down the line directors, researchers, camera operators and editors establish some solid ground in this constantly moving landscape? The majority of people who work in the industry are on short-term freelance contracts with little or no stability, let alone employment rights (e.g., holidays, sick leave, maternity leave) so hard won in the previous century. The lifeline for creative and craft workers is work itself, but for reasons beyond the purely economic. Projects tend to be intense, short-term and all-consuming, and fertile ground for strong personal and working relationships to be established. Each worker is highly dependent on the others for the successful completion of the project to the deadline and on budget. All know that their marketability for future work depends on the success of their last project. The director, the producer, the executive producer and finally the commissioning editor form a chain of command that can either support the production unit or, as is sometimes the case, let it down. Certainly this is an environment where personal trust becomes not simply a matter of weighing up one's work colleagues in this respect, but a matter of success or failure. The results of these kinds of working practices are the emergence of loose creative and craft networks with individual portfolios and an important set of contacts. Whilst waiting for one of my interviewees in the reception area of one of the broadcasters, I witnessed the coming together of such a network. A group of around six people, men and women, gathered in reception prior to discussions with one of the commissioners. One person had convened the group, presumably the independent producer, but they had obviously all worked together at some point in their recent careers. I asked the commissioners I interviewed about their dealings with independents. All had a relatively small group of independents with whom they worked regularly and upon whom they could rely. Hanna Beckerman at Five said to me:

> ...you have production companies that you like a lot and that you trust and you know that they understand you and what you want and you like working with them because, let's face it – this is a communications business and if you're going to spend a lot of time looking at scripts, sitting in the cutting room with them you want it to be a pleasant and creative experience. So there are probably between twenty and thirty production companies who I have a historic relationship with and see a lot and talk about ideas a lot with and would be absolutely aiming to try and make programmes with.

Channel 4 has an online system through which, once registered, any independent producer can submit an idea and expect a response. Although Ralph Lee referred to regular meetings with favourite independents where 'we talk around ideas for programmes – they are people I trust and like.' Martin Davidson at the BBC described the relationship between him and the independents in this way:

> I suppose you've got these three circles: the inner circle who have a long a proven track record in history I know them all really well, the next ring out are people who have done a bit of it or are interested in it and are pretty good so its not implausible and then the third ring who are the left fielders. The actual indies the people you do business with I know most of them and they know most of us.

The Independents

The history of the 'independent' sector in Britain is a long one (Potter, 2008), but for our purposes here it is sufficient to acknowledge that a number of successful independents specialize in factual programming, including history. These include Wall to Wall (*Who Do You Think You Are? Edwardian Country House*); Flashback (*Auschwitz: The Forgotten Evidence, Battle Stations, The Lost Evidence*); Testimony Films (oral histories); Blakeway Productions (*Empire*); Lion TV (*Days that Shook the World, Secret History, Sparta*); Juniper (*The Great Plague, Brief Histories*); Dangerous Films (*D-Day, NASA, Princess Diana*); Brook-Lapping (*Death of Jugoslavia*); and MayaVision (presenter Michael Wood's production company). Each of the independent companies mentioned above has established its own identity in relation to the types of history programmes they produce and their own understanding of the broadcasters and commissioners. Of course, the independents are mostly run and staffed by former BBC and ITV personnel, who have carried their skills and understanding of the industry with them. They are also well connected with the broadcasters.

More generally, the history of independents in the UK is a story of acquisitions, the outcome being the formation of the eleven so-called 'super-indies',[9] the combined income of which in 2008 was £1bn, which represents 50 per cent of the total combined turnover for all independents. The consolidation of successful independents has involved the takeover of smaller companies, which largely retain their brand identity. Whilst this provides some security and stability in such a volatile environment, it has also resulted in very small independents being pushed out into the margins and fighting for survival. Many of these smaller independents rely on repeated commissioning of a particular product and have a lot to lose if the commission is not forthcoming. It is worth noting that the retraction of ITV from its commitment to regional programming has had a severe impact on smaller companies and particularly those based outside of London. As Barbara Sadler's research demonstrates, programmes representing a region's past have been a significant part of this output.[10]

The launch of Channel 4 in 1982 was significant for the independent sector. The channel's mission was to appeal to minority audiences, to represent diversity absent in the existing terrestrial duopoly. Channel 4 commissioned innovative history programming such as *The Dragon Has Two Tongues*[11] and its first history series *Today's History* was broadcast from 1982 to 1986 and produced jointly by *History Today* and Visnews. Its mission and approach echoed the overall ethos of the channel in attempting to deal with history in more challenging ways than had been previously seen on television, by exploding myths and by presenting 'hidden histories'. This was followed in 1991 by the one-off documentary strand, *Secret History* (C4, 1991–2004).

Channel 4's early years are spoken of with nostalgia by a number of freelance producer/directors and independents, some of whom went out of business in 2004 and many of whom find it difficult if not impossible to get commissions today. The 2003 Communications Act established new terms of trade between broadcasters and programme makers in that international media rights for programmes would stay with the production company and not, as previously, with the broadcasters. In the early part of the twenty-first century, Channel 4 reduced the number of independents with whom it did business. One company that did not survive was Uden Associates which had been one of the channel's biggest documentary suppliers in the mid-1990s (see Potter, 2008, p. 236). Following Michael Jackson's departure as controller of Channel 4, and according to Patrick Uden, the channel took the view that it should be more populist and in particular appeal to a younger audience. Uden Associates had made a series called *The Classics* (trucks, planes, homes, etc.), which had a regular slot at 8:00 PM and drew an audience of around two million viewers. Tim Gardham, who took over as controller of Channel 4 called Uden in and said, 'We're not having any more of that stuff. That's out, the Second World War is out, all of that stuff's right out of the window, we want you to think about Youth orientated programmes. We want high impact stuff' (Potter, 2008, p. 237). This is evidence of the vulnerability of independents and especially those that invest heavily in particular programme genres.

The commissioning process

The independent producers I interviewed all spoke of the complexity of the commissioning process and the importance of being plugged in to what the commissioners might want – what might be the next 'big idea'. I asked Taylor Downing of Flashback how they developed their ideas for programming:

Like most Independents of this size we have a small development team and they are doing a whole variety of things – they're following publishers to see what books are coming out, what movies are coming out, looking for matching documentaries, what tie in or links exist… looking for marketing campaigns which generate a lot of interest and so on – doing all sorts of things like that, but frankly we can come up with dozens of ideas for history programmes but if a commissioning editor tells us I'm very interested in programmes that cover X, Y, Z then that's a steer we can very much focus on because we can come up with many ideas but if that's not what they are looking for then there's no point.

Richard Bradley at Lion spoke of their strategy:

It's twofold one is you keep your ears open to the commissioners and what their passions are and where they're sort of, their broadcaster's priorities lie – you are always aware of that because actually there's no point in developing something utterly obscure if they are dead set against it so you've always got to do that and actually that can change from week to week. To be honest it is utterly at the mercy of a success… so, part of you has got to be aware of what the broadcasters demands are and if the broadcaster is looking to get a young demographic there is no point in taking them a series of esoteric films about the Normans because, or whatever. However if you only do that you'll never come up with a new thing and you'll never be able to surprise them and so what we do a lot is pursue things that just interest us in the hope that we'll drop something in and they'll go, oh never thought of that….

Richard Bradley also spoke about the very limited outlets for history programming, despite its proliferation:

We always in our development are minded of where it is going to go and there aren't that many, it is interesting actually, there's probably only three or four homes in Britain, erm or three or four individuals who commission – well maybe a few more, half a dozen, say, in America probably the same number – for the whole of American broadcasting – …. it's a really small world in the history genre and Britain has been at the forefront. But I think the commissioning… we are very subject to… were one or two of those commissioners to disappear or were… the public broadcasters to decide… you know what – *enough* history… then it would go out like that. It is a fragile flower.

Martin Davidson at the BBC expressed his relationship with independents in terms of a proactive and reactive mode of commissioning. This applied to both so-called 'in house' (BBC) and independent commissions. He estimated that 70 per cent of his commissions were reactive, that is, responding to ideas brought to him by either in-house producers or independents and that 30 per cent of commissions were proactive. He said he made himself available and that any independent could ring him to talk about history ideas:

> if I know them it helps but broadly I've done everything with indies and in house – right across the spectrum from being really prescriptive – we want a film on X to last the following number of minutes with this in it – all the way to being blown away by an idea that comes completely out of the blue. Sometimes we might have a season so we might put out a thing saying, look we're really interested in – perhaps the industrial revolution, say.

Where do the ideas come from?

The relationship between the broadcasters, independents and the academy is generally a pragmatic and project-driven one. All the people I interviewed about commissioning and programme making said that they had relationships with historians, largely as consultants, but at least two of the independents had longer-term and more formalized working relations with academic historians. However, when asked about how they came up with their ideas for programmes, it appeared to be a combination of consulting with academics and keeping their ears to the ground for ideas. Ralph Lee at Channel 4 told me:

> You know what? It's really difficult to explain why we get excited about some things. It's quite personal actually. That is one of the real privileges and pleasures of the job. We get to make quite personal decisions. I speak to historians we work with, naturally and talk to them widely about their subjects and what they do.... I have stayed in touch with some but we are not connected to the academy in any kind of formal way and in a way we are more finely attuned to Waterstones than we are to the Universities. They operate in the same kind of... they are appealing to the market so if there is a publishing phenomenon in history we are more likely to notice that than if there is a really interesting paper being written at Manchester University and that's the real truth of it.

He then expanded on his working practice:

> The core people – we know each other pretty well we pick up the phone to each other all the time. We talk abut things – we meet every couple of months at the least and we'll talk about ideas – what we're watching, what we're making and what we're interested in, what we've observed, what books are going on. They'll listen to what I'm thinking and what I'm

doing and try to read what I might do next and I'll look at what they're doing and wonder how I might bring their skills to different things. The most fruitful way of finding ideas is by getting round a table and discussing it with the smart people out there – that's how you make really good tv and that's what we do most.

The independents are also constantly looking for ideas. Richard Bradley at Lion said that they cultivate relationships with agents and publishers in order to catch strong and exciting 'stories' or 'discoveries' before publication. Another important source for Lion were professional historical authors: 'that's very very fruitful and if they trust us…and also trust that their work is not going to be plagiarised and they're not going to be taken for granted and I think that is something we put a lot of time into.'

Others spoke of their relationships with academics with whom they explore ideas, but just how they find and make contact with academics is also interesting and often referred to along the lines of 'I crossed paths with a youngish Cambridge ancient historian archaeologist' or 'I found this interesting' or 'someone put me in touch with'. What is notable is the casual nature of many of these encounters, which can result, after much discussion and negotiation, in major series such as *Ancient Worlds* – in production for the BBC at the time of writing in late 2009.

One of the most significant series in the period of our study is *A History of Britain,* and of three people who worked on it, one is now controller of BBC2 and two are in senior commissioning roles. I asked Martin Davidson, producer on the series, how the idea came about:

Michael Jackson who was then Controller of BBC2 said 'I want a History of Britain'. I remember first hearing that and thinking 'you're insane who will watch that'. And we suddenly realised that it was the elephant in the room – nobody had ever done it because the great emphasis in TV was what was a sideways look at a subject. The whole of Arts television up to that point absolutely prided itself on never being front on – it was lateral, it was hybridised. So doing something that smacked to us of…it was the worst kind of naivety just chronologically structured linkage.

I asked him if Michael Jackson explained why he wanted this kind of programme:

Yes. Curious. He was curious. He told me he had just read a book about Cromwell and said 'I just want to know…how did the Civil War fit in'? His idea was it was for a road map that would link all the moments that we knew about that nobody could put together. Events all existed in these little hermetically sealed bubbles and he was also a great one for the benefits of landmark scale.

Many of the accounts of the generation of ideas came from anecdotes and things that came up in conversation that struck the commissioners. One said, 'it is very personal', and indeed stories abound that include chance encounters with neighbours and doctors who had been through significant experiences and who had interesting stories to tell.

The importance of understanding these ways of working for our interest in history programming can, perhaps, be summed up by quoting Ralph Lee who recalled meeting an academic at a documentary film festival as follows:

> We were talking about history on TV and there was a question – why don't you do more Ancient History, or something like that. And I said well we're not obliged to do Ancient History, why should we? And one of the academics said well what do you mean you're not obliged to is there not some kind of quota that says you have to devote a certain amount of hours to various different periods of history, do you not have an over-arching scheme or ambition is there not any way in which it's regulated? And I think they were quite shocked to find that it really isn't and it really is ad hoc and that's also what makes it quite exciting!

Whilst the academic putting the questions to the commissioning editor would seem to be a tad naïve, it is certainly worth thinking about how, as it were, the curriculum for television history is compiled and just what might trigger something that eventually reaches transmission. This may account, also for some of the glaring absences in history programming, for example, women's history, black history, post-colonial history to name but a few of the neglected areas.

Why the late 1990s?

I would now like to return to the question of the period of the project which requires some explanation. Clearly there are continuities in history programming and it has been a constant staple of British broadcasting, especially for the BBC. However, in 1995 more visible signs of interest in the past could be seen within television. For example, the History Channel was launched and increased attention was given to 'historical event' television, most obviously marking the 50th anniversary of the end of the Second World War. As we have noted, 1995 also saw the establishment of the History Unit at the BBC, and Martin Davidson has confirmed our chronology. He explained that in addition to *A History of Britain*, the year 1995 saw the start of Laurence Rees' *Nazis: A warning from History*. For Davidson, these two programmes began a renaissance in history programming: 'Those two projects kickstarted what I would call a step change in the seriousness, the ambition of what history could achieve.' *A History of Britain* was on a grand scale and was a return to a kind of landmark programme such as *Civilisation* and *The Ascent of Man* – a genre that had been taken over by natural history thanks to the enthusiasms of David Attenborough. The only advice Davidson and his team received from Michael Jackson regarding the series was to 'make it bold not italic'. He continued:

> *History of Britain* answered a naïve piece of curiosity which took us all a bit aback for being such a simple proposition, but when we started transmitting in 1999/2000 it was clearly a millennial thing, and also, crucially, pre-9/11 – very definitely. What a moment to wake up and go 'well who are we – how did that all happen' and with Starkey on Channel 4 – the same – we just felt it was the moment.

Martin Davidson also spoke about the significance of Laurence Rees's programme:

> The Nazi series I think reminded the audience who had always been fascinated by the subject how extraordinary it would be – rather than just isolated bits of sort of frisson laden World War II spitfires, or concentration camps, – to have a series that put it all together and really made it deliver some kind of interpretation. What does it all mean? What are we supposed to think about this? Felt incredibly timely and Laurence's genius in all this was that actually in the figure of his series consultant Ian Kershaw Nazi historiography had moved 20 years ahead of where it was in the common imagination.

Here we have an account of a very interesting institutional and historic conjuncture. The establishment of the History Unit at the BBC coincided with major national anniversaries and the build-up to the millennium. In addition, under the directorship of John Birt, the early 1990s saw the beginning of reform and rationalization within the BBC and the key mechanism for restructuring, Producer Choice, was launched in April 1993. This effectively constructed markets within the organization and created a great amount of instability and feelings of anxiety amongst the staff (Born, 2004, p. 100). Nineteen ninety-five was also within the period of Charter review. The commissioning and production of big 'landmark' history series look in retrospect to have been a very smart move. Here, after all, was the BBC producing in *A History of Britain* a blue-chip 'high-quality' programme for the millennium, constructing a history of the nation, as only the BBC knows how. Laurence Rees had produced a number of strong history documentaries and edited the flagship series *Timewatch* for a number of years, but the production of, in television's historiographical terms, a groundbreaking interpretation of the Third Reich that challenged popular stereotypes and dominant assumptions was also staking a claim for the significance of history programming within the BBC. As Martin Davidson said, 'those two programmes I think left a very definite footprint which... really extended the job and the status that history on television could think itself capable of doing.'

This account, as we might expect, places the BBC at the centre of the renaissance of history television, but this does not entirely account for the consequent flourishing of programming across a number of networks and channels. One of my interviewees in the independent sector talked about the period as the time when the energy in factual programming was in history and argued that a lot of innovation in the last 10 years has been in the history area. He left the BBC to set up his own company at this time and suggested that 'there was a particular concentration of talent at that time who were all looking to reinvent television because a lot of the stories had been told' and that producers and directors were looking to find ways of refreshing these stories.' He also said:

> I think [...] it probably has something to do with the environments, the production business environment...you know now you had a number of independents who were all competing with each other around subject areas and one of the subject areas which had most fierce competition was history and so you have lots of people who are all in their own ways able, pushing in different directions....oral history... military history...living history...so you had an environment where you had all of these companies starting up and one of the areas, as I say, they competed around was history. And the other thing is it was the passion of the...we ended up with people in senior positions in broadcasting who 'got' history. There was Tim Gardham at Channel 4, Janice's career was on the up....Laurence was a senior figure, you know there was Adam Curtis doing his extraordinary...[*Century of the Self*] and so I think it was that and then I think people realised that actually history allows for a huge number of perspectives and different ways of telling and that's very exciting so you can approach stories, even stories which feel very familiar, in a number of different ways and, you know, it is an intensely creative industry and we do spend a lot of time thinking about how can we bring those stories alive again for another generation.

This person had left the BBC because its structures were not conducive to thinking across genres or disciplines. It was frustrating for him and others who wanted to develop ideas around, for example, reality history, drama doc or even children's history, but as a history documentary maker he was confined to that genre within a specific department.

Conclusion

This chapter has looked at one aspect of the production process which is part of the everyday working practices within the television industry. My aim has been to demonstrate the significance of the social and, to a large extent informal, aspects of these practices and the significance for our under-standing of both the workings of television and the emergence of particular kinds and modes of television programming. Relationships and networks formed by professionals in the course of their working lives are critical not only for them and the quality of their work, but also can be evidenced in the emergence of particular kinds of programming. Perhaps it is too soon to speak of a 'golden age' of history programming but we can look back to other fertile periods – for example, drama in the 1960s in the UK when the challenges from ITV to the BBC monopoly on 'serious' drama were partic-ularly productive – as evidence of a similar fertile period. It is the scholarly tendency to look at the texts and seek 'explanations' for them in the wider social and cultural environment. This is, of course, a necessary level of anal-ysis, but I argue that close attention to contexts of production provides the necessary knowledge of another important layer in our understanding of why we get the kind of television we do. Television constructs 'history' in its creative practice, but it is also rapidly becoming the main repository of 'his-tory'. As one of my respondents suggested, there is no curriculum. However, this is perhaps best conceptualized as a curriculum without an identifiable author. This, of course, leads to other questions, particularly in relation to the operation of the professional criteria with which I began this chapter and how this then translates into particular modes of historiography, dominant themes and absences in the curriculum.[12]

Notes

1. Other members of the 'Televising History, 1995–2010' project team put the same question to historians (Erin Bell) and educators (Sarah Moody).
2. Roly Keating, the first controller of BBC4, referred to this as a 'phenomenal growth unique in TV markets', which for him tapped a latent curiosity about and fascination for the past. In his words. 'You can feel the appetite which is there' (in discussion at the IHR 'History and the Media' conference, University of London, December 2002).
3. This was referred to by Wayne Garvie, then head of entertainment at the BBC, in an address at the University of Lincoln, 2004.
4. Interview, London, February 2009.
5. One such was Commissioner for Factual Programming at Five whom I interviewed in October 2008.
6. BBC4 launched in 2002 and provided more space in the schedules for history programming. Hadlow took advantage of this with some innovative program-ming and scheduling in her attempt to create what she calls 'clever pleasure' for her viewers.
7. According to their website, TRC Media is an independent charity work-ing in partnership with international and UK broadcasters, producers and agencies to provide training and research to the creative content industry: http://www.trcmedia.org. Accessed 1 July 2009.
8. This is not the case at the BBC where such posts are boarded.

9. At the time of writing these were All3Media, Shine Group, IMG Media, Endemol UK, RDF Media, Tinopolis, Shed Media, DCD Media, Ten Alps, Target Entertainment and Boomerang Plus. (Source: *Broadcast* 20.3.09.)
10. Barbara Sadler's PhD topic 'Constructions of regional identities by and through television in the UK', part of the AHRC 'Televising History 1995–2010' project.
11. See Corner in this collection.
12. See Gray, A. and E. Bell, *History on Television*, Routledge, forthcoming (2011).

Bibliography

Born, G. (2004) *Uncertain Vision; Birt, Dyke and the Reinvention of the BBC* (London: Secker and Warburg).

Caldwell, J.T. (2008) *Production Culture: Industrial Reflexivity and Critical Practice in Film and Television* (Durham, NC: Duke University Press).

Corner, J. (2002) 'Performing the Real,' *Television & New Media* 3.3: 255–70.

Cottle, S. (ed.) (2003) *Media Organization and Production* (London: Sage).

Dover, C. (2004) '"Crisis" in British documentary television: the end of a genre?' *Journal of British Cinema and Television* 1.2: 242–59.

Potter, I. (2008) *The Rise and Rise of the Independents: A Television History* (Isleworth: Guerilla Books).

TRC Media (2003) 'Inside the Commissioners: the culture and practice of commissioning at UK broadcasters': http://www.trcmedia.org. Accessed 1 July 2009.

Tunstall, J. (1993) *Television Producers* (London: Routledge).

5
Beyond the Witness

The Layering of Historical Testimonies on British Television

Erin Bell

> The French philosopher Emmanuel Levinas [suggests]...that the witness'
> speech is one that, by its very definition, transcends the witness who is
> but its medium, the medium of realization of the testimony...By virtue
> of the fact that the testimony is *addressed* to others, the witness...is
> the vehicle of an occurrence, a reality, a stance or a dimension *beyond*
> *himself* [sic].
>
> (Shoshana Felman, 1995, p. 15)

This chapter provides an account of the use of eyewitness, and other, testimony as part of the textual operations of British history programming since the 1970s, and relates it to broader issues of, and developments within, historical and personal remembrance, in particular the use of photography. As I have suggested elsewhere, presenter and eyewitness are familiar televisual tropes across many genres, although in history programming in particular, eyewitness testimony may be seen to have a form of auratic power: an eyewitness and his or her account is reproduced through a mass medium, but viewers are encouraged, and many are willing, to see those who testify as authentic, authoritative and unique (Bell, 2009, p. 197; Benjamin, 2008, p. 22). This is problematized, though, as testifiers must often bear witness for others; some of their authority derives from speaking for an entire group (Gray, 1997, p. 100), and as the opening quotation suggests, this transcends the individual witness. Furthermore, as well as acting as 'vehicles of remembering' in oral historical research, photographs are often offered to viewers alongside testimony. As historical and personal artefacts reproduced on television, their role will therefore also be considered (Humphries, 1984, pp. 3–6, 99–105; Pickering and Keightley, 2007, p. 273).

In both scholarly research and programme making, oral historical methods are used to collate the accounts of individuals involved in specific events or broader processes. Whether used to garner accounts of Holocaust survival, or of working-class women's lives (Friedländer, 1992; Roberts, 1996), oral history's scholarly, ethical and political work in returning a voice to the otherwise silenced is significant. Others, though, reject its apparent reliance upon individual and flawed memories, such as Oxford historian and media personality A.J.P. Taylor, who in the 1970s condemned the then-nascent field as 'old men drooling about their youth' (cited in Thompson, 1992 [1978], p. 70). In a more recent example, historians commenting upon post-1989 German accounts of civilian experiences of the Second World War questioned whether oral history encouraged sentiment and nostalgia whilst ignoring broader historical contexts and structures (Schmitz, 2007, pp. 5–6). Although these responses stem from ethical and scholarly concerns, less reflective criticism has been rejected by a number of scholars. Oral history methods are rarely used alone, and further, as Alessandro Portelli argues, the 'variable and partial' nature of oral testimony offers the scholar different types of knowledge (1991, p. 53). Although I do not engage directly in these debates, they do relate to changing uses and forms of testimony on-screen, particularly the use of photographs to encourage eyewitnesses to discuss their experiences, and viewers to reflect on individuals and their accounts.

Indeed, when we see a person on-screen affected by their memories, this may affect us too; their experience appears authentic, and particular to them, although they may be one of many.[1] The testifier and his or her account has also been mass reproduced, but the individual experience of both testifier and audience member is unique, a point emphasized by historians involved in the creation of oral history series, most notably Steve Humphries (2006). In addition, even if they do not share the same physical space, the testifier appears in the audience's home. Television in this domestic context, although a mass medium, is intimate, personal and participatory. Like German television's concern with 'interaction, proximity, and creation of affect' (Keilbach, 2007, p. 104), UK television may be seen as a space where 'lost storytellers, priests, wise men and elders are restored to cultural visibility and to oral primacy' (Fiske and Hartley, 2003, p. 100). In history programming they may take the form of male presenters (Bell and Gray, 2007), but also eyewitnesses, and those testifying for them.

Early examples: *The World at War* and *Timewatch*

Factual history programming has been broadcast in the UK since the 1950s. The televised lectures of A.J.P. Taylor (Oliver, 2003–2006) were joined in the 1960s by documentaries using footage and oral testimony, including the BBC's 26-part series *The Great War* (BBC, 1964). Described as 'a new benchmark for history programmes' (Hanna, 2007, p. 91), its developments in methodology, including the use of oral history, alongside the development of sync-sound recording allowing interviews to be used in documentaries, led the series' researchers to believe they were 'recording people for history' although interviews had already been included in German history series (Hanna, 2007, p. 96; Keilbach, 2007, p. 101) A decade later, *The World at War* (Thames TV, 1974) refined the format (Downing, 2004, p. 10; Darlow, 2005, p. 141). From the start of the project in April 1971, the key ingredients were 'the image and the word, newsreel and eyewitness', and if there were no images, interviews alone were used, except for one episode, 'Reckoning', which allowed historians to appear on-screen (Isaacs in Holmes, 2007, p. viii; Isaacs, 2006, pp. 157–8).

Considering in particular the episode 'Genocide', broadcast in March 1974, it is evident that the way in which eyewitness testimony is used allows the audience to perceive links to broader media coverage of the Holocaust, including war crime tribunals. For example, former Waffen-SS General Karl Wolff describes his wartime career, and we see a photograph of him with Himmler: he is identified as 'one of the cogs in the machine' (Isaacs, 2006, p. 143) – neither a thug nor a psychopath, and representative of many more. Wolff's ties to the Nazi leadership as Chief of Staff to Himmler are proven by the image shown, and indeed he had been imprisoned in the 1960s for his involvement in the deportation of Jews to Treblinka (Holmes, 2007, p. 28).

This contrasts with the way in which the testimony of Holocaust survivor Rivka Yosilevska is used: we see photographs of atrocities but none of Rivka herself. She speaks for those who cannot, and thus pictures of groups of people, rather than of Rivka as a young woman, are used. By giving testimony about the deaths of her family, Rivka is a key witness, paralleling the role of Holocaust survivors in the trials of leading Nazis, which received international coverage.[2]

Although Dori Laub (2009, p. 142) reminds us that testimony 'does not have to adhere to the rule of evidence relevant to juridical testimony', the episode's maker, Michael Darlow (2005, p. 144) confirms the influence of the Eichmann trial, which had brought new evidence and witnesses forward, including some of those in the episode. Jay Winter (2006, p. 7) suggests that such witnesses, alongside prosecutors and judges, created 'a new theatre of historical remembrance': war crime tribunals. Using his definition of historical remembrance – something that draws on both history and memory and uses both documented narratives and eyewitness accounts – it is possible to view the episode, and even the series as a whole, as forms of remembrance, in which photographs play an important role. As Marita Sturken asserts, '[i]t is extraordinary to consider the degree to which the still photograph has been so central to scholarship on memory, and the role that the photograph continues to play in concepts of memory' (2008, p. 75). Televised accounts have utilized this, alongside testimony, for at least three decades: the 'interplay of words and pictures' and the 'emotional weight borne by the talking heads' still resonates for contemporary reviewers and viewers (Moss, 2009).

The BBC series *Timewatch* (1981–2009) used testimony from its inception, and the 'event-television' episode 'Battle for Berlin' (1985), marking the 40th anniversary of VE Day, included a number of conflicting voices: German,

British, Russian; civilian and military; all of which raise questions about the relationship between historical testimony and political expediency at the time of filming. Major Anna Nikolena, for example, addresses the camera from her living room and justifies the brutality of Soviet troops, whilst a German civilian describes the rape and murder of her female neighbours. In addition, the then presenter-led format of *Timewatch* allowed journalist Charles Wheeler to act as both narrator and eyewitness, moving between a first-person memory and third-person account of the events, and making direct references to the political situation in Berlin in the present. Like *The World at War*, photographs were used, for example, to place Ludvig von Hammerstein, who had been involved in a plot to kill Hitler, in Berlin in 1945. A photograph of him as a young man in uniform is shown, and then he is seen in the present, giving testimony. Photographs were used in a similar way in newspapers of the same decade; Barbie Zelizer sees the use of contemporary photographs of an eyewitness alongside earlier images as 'accentuat[ing] the passage of time to readers' (1998, p. 177) and con-temporizing narratives about past eras especially, it might be added, as the chronological gap between 'then' and 'now' widened.

This technique grew more common in the 1990s: if, as Stella Bruzzi asserts (2000, p. 12), documentary acknowledges 'that the "document" at its heart is open to reassessment', this is borne out by developments apparent in later history series. As she suggests, reassessment is not always of the 'truth' of the documents or records shown, but may be of the 'way in which we are invited to access [them]...through representation or interpretation', includ-ing the presence, or absence, of testimony. Corelli Barnett's criticism of the 1996 BBC/KCET series *1914–1918* for its use of historians rather than eyewit-nesses (1997) suggests that by the 1990s, eyewitness testimony had become an expected and authenticating element of history series which reached its zenith with *People's Century*.

People's Century and subaltern history

As one documentary maker interviewed as part of this research asserted, tes-timony personalizes historical events, allowing them to be better understood by an audience:

> [H]istory is about people...and I think that's what television can do quite well; the identification factor. And of course the usual format now is that you zoom in to a personal story...then you can broaden. So it's always the small droplet which is a mirror of the big society.
>
> (Interview R)

This technique is used to great effect in *People's Century*, the 26-episode series broadcast in 1995–1996 on the BBC and in 1998–1999 on PBS, which included footage or photographs of the events discussed, and sometimes of the eyewitnesses interviewed. It allowed access to subaltern history, or in some cases the testimony of the oppressed. The executive producer of *People's Century* stressed that 'no pundits, no academics appear on camera', which according to the PBS website was unique and was certainly a selling point. The first episode was introduced by the narrator as 'the story of those turbulent changes, told by the people themselves'. It was also the last sustained series of testimony-based history in the UK in the 1990s, despite the success of series produced by the British 'Testimony Films' from 1992 onwards, until a recent revival (Humphries, 2008).[3] *People's Century*, heralded as part of the BBC's 'Millennium effort' (Briggs, 1997) was, like other oral history series, overshadowed soon afterwards by *A History of Britain* (BBC, 2000–2002) which epitomized a return to presenter-led history noted by those working within the industry (Humphries, 2006).

An example from *People's Century*, demonstrating the potential of such series to provide testimony of those otherwise rarely heard or seen, is Birenda Kaur's account of India in the 1940s in the episode 'Freedom Now'. The schoolgirl whose photograph we see will, we know, grow up to be the woman remembering independence, and encourages strong, affective responses (Hirsch, 2008, p. 117). Indeed, as part of a section on Indian independence that otherwise includes only a few images of individuals with a large amount of archive footage, encouraging conventional interest and attention on the part of the audience, a form of Barthes' *studium*, Birenda's photograph and personal account work as a *punctum*. According to Barthes, a photograph's *punctum* may be a poignant accident whereby a detail, such as an aspect of an individual's appearance, disturbs us and 'pierces' the distance between us and what is depicted, although we may not know why, comparable to the 'unpredictable and disruptive' bodily reactions felt in response to some photographs, identified by John Urry (Barthes, 1980, pp. 26–7, 42–3; Pickering and Keightley, 2007, p. 277; Urry, 1996, p. 50). The use of a still photograph amongst moving images and alongside a personal account of a well-known event may, then, also pierce the chronological, and other, distances between eyewitness and viewer, and give a sense of 'communication across time' (Pickering and Keightley, 2007, p. 277). This helps to grant Birenda authority when there is otherwise a lack of such testimony on television, and allows an Indian woman to be heard alongside other post-colonial voices. Her experiences dovetail with footage of Gandhi and Nehru, and as she describes staying up late to welcome in the first day of Indian independence, we can place her memories in a national, historical context.[4]

The sustained use of footage or photographs of those appearing on-screen has been seen as a key element differentiating *People's Century* from earlier series (Bruzzi, 2000, p. 34). It 'constructs a bridge between personal history...and the official history of the historical image'. Anonymous individuals in footage are reinstated into the official record, demonstrating that 'archive functions as the substantiation of memory' (Bruzzi, 2000, p. 34). Further, it has been suggested that its primetime slot necessitated the use of archive footage to 'justify its place' and gain more substantial ratings (Humphries, 2006). Although this may seem an attempt to gain a bigger audience by enlisting 'human interest', it also, importantly, emphasized the individuality of those interviewed.

Auschwitz and the spectral *punctum*

Other examinations of the use of photography in order to provoke affective responses include Petra Rau's analysis of Rachel Seiffert's novel *The Dark Room* (2001), set in Germany during and after the Second World War. Rau (2006, p. 295) identifies the 'spectral *punctum*' in the photographs described in the work: 'a subjective affect caused by something that the image does not record but that nonetheless conditions its reading as traumatic, a negative supplement signifying loss or absence'. Seiffert, she suggests, is exploring the limitations of photography, which is 'habitually entrusted with aiding our access to that past' (Rau, 2006, p. 296).

Comparable representations on television include the 2005 series *Auschwitz*, a British–US co-production to mark the 60th anniversary of liberation. One of its most significant developments is an extension of testimony to include not only accounts of the experiences of those no longer alive, as *World at War* did, but also to enable them to be distinguished from all other victims; the absence of individualism in Holocaust photographs, as they are often used, is acknowledged. As Susan Sontag suggests when looking at such images, we 'should feel obliged to think about what it means to look at them, about the capacity actually to assimilate what they show' (Sontag cited in Rau, 2006, p. 307). Perhaps in response to such comments, *Auschwitz* concludes with the testimony of Hungarian-American artist and Birkenau survivor Alice Lok Cahana. A photograph of women and children is shown, a summary of the numbers of murdered is heard, and the camera pans over one woman and her children in particular. A child holds her hand and looks directly at the camera and through it to us, the audience: our conventional attention to the subject may be pierced by the child's direct gaze. We then hear Alice's testimony:

> In this photograph I recognise my aunt, her name is Yolanda Wolstein [*camera focuses on Yolanda*] and her four little children [*on two of their faces*], Ervin, eight years old; Dory, ten years old [*pans to Dory*]; Judith, six years old, and Naomi, the little baby [*pans to the baby in Yolanda's arms*], two years old. It's such an incredible shattering feeling, [*we see Alice in her home*] to recognise somebody you love, to see how they looked minutes before they entered the crematorium.[5]

The inclusion of this photograph demonstrates the image's acute communication across time: Alice is 'shattered' by the experience. Although this takes barely a minute, it is an extremely powerful part of the episode, combining factual information with the affect described by Rau: Alice's family's movement to their deaths is unseen, but not, to us, unknown. As Bruzzi asserts of *People's Century* (2000, p. 34), *Auschwitz* too retains the notion that footage, and in this case photographs, possesses inherent meaning. Certainly, those filmed responding to images find them meaningful, and their response, as much as the images, allows the identity of previously anonymized individuals to be acknowledged. This is comparable to Marianne Hirsch's (2008, p. 112) analysis of the graphic novel *Maus*, in which Art Spiegelman reworks a well-known image of liberated prisoners in Buchenwald to include his father, making it part of his family album. Unsurprisingly, after writing and producing *Auschwitz*, Laurence Rees (2005, p. 23) noted that 'the voices I heard loudest' were those of 'the people we could not interview'.

Alternative sites of testimony: *The Trench* and *Mitchell and Kenyon*

In recent years the declining number of eyewitnesses to the major events of the twentieth century has been recognized as potentially problematic for television, not least because the presenter–historian and the 'archive and eyewitnesses' format have dominated for many years (Downing, 2004, p. 10). Increasing chronological distance from events may, as Pierre Nora notes, require 'rapprochement to counteract its effects and give it emotional resonance' The longing Nora describes for the affective and the physical – 'the feel of mud on our boots' – has led to alternative forms of testimony and of witnessing (Nora, 1996, p. 13). For example, the 2002 BBC2 series *The Trench* allowed Great War soldiers' descendants to re-enact elements of life in the trenches, whilst they also 'stood in' for their ancestors by reading out their grandfathers' and great-grandfathers' letters home. The ethical necessity of remembering traumatic events was supported by re-enactment and testimony on behalf of their ancestors (Bell, 2009).

As Alison Landsberg reminds us (1997, p. 63), Michel de Certeau asserts that in such situations, 'Memory produces in a place that does not belong to it.' Landsberg goes on to suggest that whilst the film *Schindler's List* attempts to transfer 'authentic living memory from the body of a survivor to an individual who has no "authentic" link to this particular historical past' (1997, p. 64), *The Trench* attempted to transfer the memory of those who died to volunteers with a familial and regional link to Great War soldiers. This 'alternative living memory…produced in those who did not live through the event' (1997, pp. 65–6) is necessary if events are to be remembered, and, she suggests, has the potential 'to produce empathy and social responsibility' transcending race, class and gender (1997, p. 21; Saxton, 2008, p. 45). Although some series rely on the auratic power of remaining eyewitnesses, for example, *The Last Tommy* (BBC, 2005), which claimed of those interviewed '[t]heir deaths will cut forever our last connection to the distant [archive] image', the use of re-enactment points to programme makers' aspirations to find, as veterans die, a way to achieve insight and affective connection still.

Different forms of testimony are also apparent in 'found footage' series, such as *The Lost World of Mitchell and Kenyon* (2005), which used rediscovered footage of life in Britain, filmed in the 1890s and 1900s. The series focuses both on the footage, and on descendants of those filmed, as they watch footage and then respond to it. In the episode 'Saints and Sinners', we see an advertisement placed in the *Manchester Evening News* asking for 'descendants' to contact the BBC. Later, an elderly man, Reg Jelves, describes his father George, shown on a temperance march in 1901; descendants are often shown providing information about the family members shown. They can give further details, commenting on specific attributes: Reg mentions his father's cheeky grin, as a boy, captured on film. This seems, for him, to be a form of *punctum*; the point at which an original source in history, before his time, has a disturbing resonance, and enables empathy with those living at the time, such as his father, other boys at Ardwick Industrial School, and their families. When he is shown records from the school, detailing boys' young ages, he reflects on the hard life experienced by working-class people of that generation: 'I'm glad I wasn't there.' It is possible, by triggering such memories and reflections, to approach the prosthetic memory described by Landsberg (1997; 2004). To authenticate Reg's comments, a photograph of Reg and George together completes 'their' story.

Alternative sites of testimony: the album and the encyclopaedia

Related to the layering of testimonies in programmes such as these is the developing importance of family history and testimonies to the representation of the past. A pertinent example is the hugely successful BBC (BBC2, 2004; BBC1, 2005–date) series *Who Do You Think You Are?*, seen by some media professionals as heralding a revival of oral history on television (Humphries, 2006). An innovative format discussed at greater length within this collection by Amy Holdsworth, it popularizes history by combining celebrity with family history, and with 6.5 million viewers it has gained the largest audiences for popular history programming in the UK in recent years. Undoubtedly it relies upon, in part, what Hirsch terms 'the power of the *idea* of family...forms of mutual *recognition* that define family images and narratives' and which she also recognizes in some museum displays (Hirsch, 2008, p. 113). The format has been sold to Australia, Canada, Poland and the US, and it is possible to argue that, using Friederike Eigler's account

(2005, p. 17) of surging interest in family narratives in literature, such series offer the opportunity to recapture '20th century collective and individual histories…at the beginning of a century where a more integrated Europe faces new challenges'.

Furthermore, Hirsch's recent analysis (2008, p. 103) highlights the significance of the role of the family 'as a space of transmission' to the 'second generation' after the Holocaust in particular, for whom photographs in particular act as 'a primary medium of transgenerational transmission of trauma'. As author and comedian David Baddiel remarks in the first series (BBC2, 2004), his is a 'family history of immigration and refugeeism [so] you're never entirely sure how you ended up here'. In the following scene, he and his daughter are described as 'descendants of the German Jews who fled the Nazis'. and we see him and his brothers as children, as he describes childhood visits to his grandfather, and his 'strong emotional connection to his memory'. Reminiscent of Rau's 'spectral *punctum*', he remarks that a photograph of his grandparents shows them 'when they were happy…before it all started to go very badly wrong'. We are all too aware of the crimes being planned against those pictured, and this is the spectral *punctum* for us, an audience who do not know those involved, but develop empathy for them. As Judith Keilbach notes, 'the knowledge that the viewer brings to a photograph is essential to its capacity to display the truth about its subject matter' (2009, p. 60). Unlike images of an atrocity, discussed by Hirsch and Sontag, these pictures are poignant because of what they do not show. As Irit Dekel suggests of a photographic installation at the Berlin Holocaust Memorial, such images, originally taken as part of everyday life, call for viewers to imagine those depicted '*not* behind barbed wire or in a heap of dead bodies' (2009, p. 81). Instead, we are disturbed by the 'presence of lives halted at a set moment in their duration, freed from their destiny' (Bazin in Langford, 2008, p. 28).

To begin his 'search for answers', David visits his parents and his mother shows him photographs inherited on his grandmother's death. Unlike their use in other series to provide evidence for the assertions of eyewitnesses or narrator, here photographs prompt contributions from family members appearing on-screen, and this technique is not unlike that used by oral history researchers who sometimes use photograph albums as a source of discussion and elaboration.[6] Such images, however, as David concludes, can 'raise as many questions as they answer', particularly regarding Arno, his great uncle. Seen both as an adult and a child, this (as we discover) victim of Nazism is given a place within a family, despite being one of many who did not live long enough to have children. A lack of information about Arno, David says, evokes 'a sense of poignancy', also evoked in the audience by the use of photographs. Although Arno cannot give testimony, his family can, and this lack of information testifies to the fate of millions more. A sense of dislocation and loss pervades the episode, as does the testimony of those present, on behalf of those absent. As Hirsch suggests, such photographs 'that survive massive devastation and outlive their subjects...function as ghostly revenants from an irretrievably lost past world' (2008, p. 115). Through the family's testimony, both about their own lives and the information they can bring about absent members of their family, the programme's narrator can give a more complete account. Often accompanying graphics depicting a family tree, with photographs of the individuals reproduced above their names, this provides the overall 'story', bringing together both spoken and written testimonies in order to speak of the experiences of those who did not live to tell them. Although this is done in all episodes, it is particularly poignant when those described died prematurely, within the lifetime of some of those seen on-screen.

The use of photographs in the series is hardly surprising, as family images relate the celebrities to the audience; like them, we have family snapshots, but theirs, like ours, have a place in a bigger picture. It seems, though, that in later series those involved have been more aware of the series' tropes, and perhaps the programme makers themselves were keen to develop their use of photographic material, as their comments reflect current issues of history and remembrance to a greater extent. For example, talk show host Jerry Springer is filmed with his sister Evelyn, discussing the significance of 'faded pictures' of his German Jewish family, murdered in the Holocaust. Most families preserve photographs, and albums in which they are kept have been seen by scholars as a site of 'cross-generational exchange', reorganizing the ways in which we remember (Chalfen in Langford, 2008, p. 4). Even for those who do not share their family history, his assertion that 'we *all* have these faded pictures' brings the audience into the fold, underscoring the need for awareness when only photographs survive. Removing the album 'from a private situation to the public sphere', in this case a television programme, 'does not deprive it of a context, but substitutes one set of viewing conditions for another' (Langford, 2008, p. 18). Such episodes also demonstrate how 'narrative links between photographs and lives' (Pickering and Keightley, 2007, p. 284) may be sustained in later generations.

Through family photographs, Springer speaks for a particular group, but in so doing communicates to us all. Indeed, as one viewer commented, 'When I was a child my mum worked for a lovely Jewish family who'd fled the holocuaust [*sic*] – amazing to think how close to us historically it is.'[7] Another reflected: 'It really is just mind-blowing when you can't help but have emotional transference and imag[in]e them being your own grandparents.'[8] The account of the Holocaust given in the episodes includes details of the likely fates of both men's families, and therefore the audience's response 'becomes subject to ethical scrutiny' in Vivian Sobchack's analysis (in Saxton, 2008, p. 76). Perhaps this explains the need felt by some viewers, when commenting on the series, to emphasize their distress, but also their empathy for those depicted and their own ties to the Holocaust. The spectral *punctum* is the fate the viewer's grandparents did not share, but which can still be considered. In the same conversation, Evelyn refers to their parents' refusal to discuss their experiences. Considered by scholars and survivors' families for decades, *Maus* and Gabriele Rosenthal's interviews with victims and perpetrators are landmarks, but little acknowledged on British television. To do so, on prime time BBC1, may be considered a breakthrough.[9] Indeed, when Springer is shown evidence of his mother's refugee status, he remarks: 'This is not just family history, this is world history.'

Given Vanessa Agnew's assertion (2007) that several series in Germany and the UK demonstrate a turn to 'affective history' by emphasizing individual experience and daily life, Harald Welzer's analysis of the ways individuals experience affective and cognitive memories separately, for which he uses the metaphors 'family album' and 'encyclopaedia', seems particularly appropriate (quoted in Eigler, 2005, p. 21). Both appear on the bookshelf in households, although individuals are often aware of family history, but not of how this relates to broader historical events. Both forms of memory appear in the series, which reconciles the personal, family album view of the past, often using photographs as a starting point, with broader, often traumatic, histories. This makes such events comprehensible to a wider audience, and one viewer's comments encapsulate this: 'For all of the teaching and programmes about the Holocaust, nothing ever hits home like a personal story like the one shown.'[10] It is similar, then, to developments described by scholars from European nations which acknowledge 'the historical, political, familial and individual forces that complicate or preclude facile notions of identity and continuity' (Eigler, 2005, p. 27). Television is particularly well-suited to the combination of personal, collective and national histories and memories, bringing otherwise alien and inconceivable events into viewers' living rooms.

Re-enactment as testimony; testimony as re-enactment

In 1936, the Oxford philosopher of history R.G. Collingwood asserted that to understand historical experience the historian should not conceive of the past as 'a dead past', but instead as a 'living past', and wrote of the need for a historian to perform mental re-enactment in order to fully understand this (1992, p. 158). Although this is an audacious claim, it is used by scholars such as Agnew to justify the use of physical re-enactment in series such as *The Trench* (Corner, 2003; Agnew, 2007). Despite, then, the claims of some historians that television cannot or will not 'do' complexity, re-enactment may demonstrate an alternative way of making historical meaning, and makes mental re-enactment public.

This is especially apparent in *Who Do You Think You Are?*: celebrities visit geographical sites linked to their ancestors and often demonstrate a need to empathize with them there. In one example, after learning of his

Protestant Irish ancestor Thomas Walker's role in the suppression of the United Irishmen's 1798 rebellion, presenter Graham Norton reflects on the implications this has for his sense of his own Irish identity (Series 3, 2007). He comments that when

> you discover that your ancestors were on the side that history and time has decided was the wrong side, it means that you've got to stop...and imagine what their lives were like, why they made the choices they did.

Arguably, this is mental re-enactment – an attempt to understand why someone acted as they did. Norton follows this with prosthetic memory; he seeks to give testimony about Walker's actions, from Walker's perspective:

> [A]s far as he knew he was on God's side, hopefully he was just a decent man caught in a difficult situation, who believed he was doing the right thing.

Through the use of such techniques, regional, religious and ethnic identities are contemplated, alongside their resonance in the present.

Unsurprisingly, this move from national histories, alongside the problematizing of simplistic notions of identity, led to the creation of alternative sites of shared, but disparate, memories on the internet. One such site is the weblog dedicated to Harry Lamin by his grandson Bill, who in early 2007 began to put Harry's letters from France and Italy online, in chronological order, 90 years after they were written.[11] The letters are Harry's testimony to his experiences in the Great War, and, furthermore, the comments board allows people from many nations to share their family's experiences in this or other conflicts. In another example the 'World Is Witness' project of the United States Holocaust Memorial Museum seeks international responses to testimony and photographs of current humanitarian crises.[12] Such sites transcend national boundaries and even chronology through a focus on shared experiences but also shared responses, and may form part of the 'new sociations' identified by Urry (1996, p. 59) which offer sites for identity-testing, as those contributing give voice to contemporary concerns, and to the testimony of earlier generations.

Such diverse ways of representing testimony demonstrate how changes in the representation of the past on television and in other media have arguably broadened what testimony about a historical event might conceivably include. The role of testimony as a staple ingredient in many history documentaries has led to a need, in recent years, to include written accounts by the deceased or the testimony of living descendants, those addressed by the 'first degree' testimony of parents or grandparents. Although lack of direct experience means younger generations cannot appreciate the *full* magnitude of events, the continuity of testimony through television and other media suggests that they are seeking to do so. Levinas asserted that the witness is the medium of realization of the testimony, and the related role of television as a mass medium in disseminating testimony and material such as photographs beyond national and generational boundaries is increasingly significant. The Internet, in particular, offers opportunities to identify viewers' responses, often in terms of family experiences. This suggests that, in recent years, an ancestor's experiences regionally or even globally may be used to understand national histories better, and has been reflected and encouraged by British television. Not only a pragmatic response to the increasing scarcity of eyewitnesses, this mirrors developments in wider historiography, and the search for alternative ways of understanding the past, in order to make informed decisions about the present.

A note on availability

People's Century on VHS is available from 2 Entertain Video and *The World at War* on DVD is available from Fremantle Home Entertainment. *Who Do You Think You Are?* series 1–4; *Auschwitz: The Nazis and the Final Solution;The Lost World of Mitchell and Kenyon;* and *The Great War* on DVD are available through the BBC Shop. *Timewatch* and *The Trench* are not available on DVD or VHS; for off-air recordings see www.copac.ac.uk.

Notes

1. This is unlikely to be a response to the testimony of Nazi perpetrators discussed by Keilbach (2007), which is rarely shown on UK television.
2. Transcripts are available in Holmes, 2007, pp. 322–4; for details see: http://www.jewishvirtuallibrary.org/jsource/Holocaust/WarCrimetoc.html. Accessed 13 June 2009.
3. This included the retransmission of individual episodes of *People's Century* on BBC4 in January and September 2009.
4. See also MacDonald, 1998, pp. 114–5 on the use of testimony and footage in another episode.
5. A transcript is available at: http://www.pbs.org/auschwitz/about/transcripts_6.html. Accessed 13 June 2009.
6. For example, the work of the National Life Stories: Living Memory of the Jewish Community project, recorded 1988–2000, available from the British Library: http://sounds.bl.uk/. Accessed 13 June 2009.
7. Digital Spy Forum: http://www.digitalspy.co.uk/forums/showthread.php?t=872852&page=8. Accessed 13 June 2009.
8. Digital Spy Forum: http://www.digitalspy.co.uk/forums/showthread.php?t=872852&page=9. Accessed 13 June 2009.
9. According to BARB, www.barb.co.uk, the *Jews* episode on the Holocaust, broadcast 25 June 2008, had an audience of 250,000. David Baddiel's episode of *WDYTYA?* (BBC2, 23 November 2004) reached 4.6 million; Jerry Springer's (BBC1, 27 August 2008) reached 6.5 million.

10. See http://www.digitalspy.co.uk/forums/showthread.php?t=872852&page=8. Accessed 13 June 2009.
11. http://www.wwar1.blogspot.com; see also German soldier Dieter Finzen's Kriegstagebuch as a blog: http://dieter-finzen.blogspot.com/.
12. See http://wwar1comments.blogspot.com/ and http://blogs.ushmm.org/WorldIs Witness/. Accessed 30 June 2009.

Filmography

Auschwitz: The Nazis and the Final Solution, 'Liberation and Revenge', BBC/KCET, 2005.
The Great War, BBC, 1964.
The Lost World of Mitchell and Kenyon, 'Saints and Sinners', BBC, 2005.
People's Century, 'Freedom Now', BBC/PBS, 1995.
Timewatch, 'Battle for Berlin', BBC, 1985.
The Trench, BBC2, 2002.
Who Do You Think You Are? David Baddiel, Jerry Springer and Graham Norton episodes, BBC1/2, 2004–date.
The World at War, 'Genocide', Thames TV, 1973.

Bibliography

Agnew, V. (2007) 'History's affective turn' *Rethinking History*, 11.3, 299–312.
Barnett, C. (1997) 'Oh, what a whingeing war!' *The Spectator*, 4 January.
Barthes, R. (1980) *Camera Lucida*, trans. by R. Howard (New York: Hill and Wang).
Bell, E. and A. Gray (2007) 'History on television: charisma, narrative and knowledge', *European Journal of Cultural Studies*, 10.1, 113–33.
Bell, E. (2009) 'Sharing their past with the nation: reenactment and testimony on British television', in A. Dhoest, E. Castello and H. O'Donnell (eds), *The Nation on Screen* (Newcastle: Cambridge Scholars).
Benjamin, W. (2008 [1935]) 'The work of art in the age of its technological reproducibility', in M.W. Jennings, B. Doherty and T.Y. Levin (eds) *The Work of Art in the Age of Its Technological Reproducibility* (Cambridge, MA: Harvard University Press).
Briggs, A. (1995), 'Eye-witnesses of History', *THES*, 27 October.
Bruzzi, S. (2000) *New Documentary: A Critical Introduction* (London: Routledge).
Collingwood, R.G. (1992 [1946]) *The Idea of History* (Oxford: Oxford University Press).
Corner, J. (2003) 'Finding data, reading patterns, telling stories: issues in the historiography of television', *Media, Culture & Society*, 25, 273–80.
Darlow, M. (2005) 'Baggage and responsibility: *The World at War* and the Holocaust', in T. Haggith and J. Newman (eds), *Holocaust and the Moving Image* (London: Wallflower).
Dekel, I. (2009) 'Ways of looking: observation and transformation at the Holocaust Memorial, Berlin,' *Memory Studies*, 2.1, 71–86.
Downing, T. (2004) 'Bringing the past to the small screen', in D. Cannadine (ed.), *History and the Media* (London: Palgrave MacMillan).
Eigler, F. (2005) 'Writing in the New Germany', *German Politics and Society*, 23.3, 16–41.
Felman, S. (1995) 'Education and crisis, or the vicissitudes of teaching', in C. Caruth (ed.), *Trauma: Explorations in Memory* (Baltimore: Johns Hopkins University Press).
Fiske, J. and J. Hartley (2003) *Reading Television,* second edition (London: Routledge).
Friedländer, S. (1992) 'Trauma, transference and "working through" in writing the history of the *Shoah*', *History and Memory*, 4.1: 39–55.

Gray, A. (1997) 'Learning from experience: cultural studies and feminism', in J. McGuigan (ed.), *Cultural Methodologies* (London: Sage).

Hanna, E. (2007) 'A small screen alternative to stone and bronze: *The Great War* series and British television', *European Journal of Cultural Studies*, 10.1, 89–111.

Hirsch, M. (2008) 'The generation of postmemory', *Poetics Today*, 29.1, 103–28.

Holmes, R. (2007) *The World at War: The Landmark Oral History* (London: Ebury Press).

Humphries, S. (1984) *The Handbook of Oral History: Recording Life Stories* (London: Inter Action Imprint).

Humphries, S. (2006) 'Oral history on television: a retrospective', presentation at the 'Oral history on television' seminar, British Library, 2 December, later published in 2008 in *Oral History* 36.2.

Humphries, S. (2008) 'Sex, love and the British', presentation at the 'Televising History' symposium, University of Lincoln, 29 February.

Interview R (by author, with media producer), February 2007.

Isaacs, J. (2006) *Look Me in ihe Eye: A Life in Television* (London: Little, Brown).

Keilbach, J. (2007) 'Witnessing, credibility, and female perpetrators: eyewitnesses in television documentaries about National Socialism', in V. Apfelthaler and J.B. Köhne (eds), *Gendered Memories: Transgressions in German and Israeli Film and Theatre* (Vienna: Turia + Kant).

Keilbach, J. (2009) 'Photographs, symbolic images, and the Holocaust: on the (im)possibility of depicting historical truth', *History and Theory*, 47, 54–76.

Landsberg, A. (1997) 'America, the Holocaust, and the mass culture of memory', *New German Critique*, 71, 63–86.

Landsberg, A. (2004) *Prosthetic Memory: The Transformation of American Remembrance in the Age of Mass Culture* (New York: Columbia University Press).

Langford, M. (2008) *Suspended Conversations: The Afterlife of Memory in Photographic Albums* (Montreal: McGill-Queen's University Press).

Laub, D. (2009) 'On Holocaust testimony and its "reception,"' *History and Memory*, 21.1, 127–50.

MacDonald, M. (1998) 'Politicizing the personal: women's voices in British television documentaries', in C. Carter, G. Branston and S. Allan (eds), *News, Gender and Power* (New York: Routledge).

Moss, S. (2009) 'Your next box set: *The World at War*', *Guardian* 4 September, http://www.guardian.co.uk/culture/2009/sep/04/the-world-at-war. Accessed 7 September 2009.

Nora, P. (1996) 'General introduction: between memory and history', in Nora, P. (ed.), *Realms of Memory*, volume 1 (New York: Columbia University Press).

Oliver, J. (2003-6) 'Taylor, A.J.P. (1906–1990)', *BFI Screenonline*, http://www.screenonline.org.uk/people/id/838462/index.html. Accessed 7 February 2008.

Open University (2006) '*Timewatch*, the longest-running TV history series in the world, returns to BBC Two', http://www3.open.ac.uk/media/fullstory.aspx?id=10063. Accessed 21 October 2008.

PBS website (undated), http://www.pbs.org/wgbh/peoplescentury/about/overview.html. Accessed 9 September 2008.

Pickering, M. and Keightley, E. (2007) 'Echoes and reverberations: photography and phonography as historical forms', *Media History*, 13.2/3, 273–88.

Portelli, A. (1991) *The Death of Luigi Trastulli, and Other Stories: Form and Meaning in Oral History* (New York: SUNY Press).

Rau, P. (2006) 'Beyond *punctum* and *stadium*: trauma and photography in Rachel Seiffert's *The Dark Room*', *Journal of European Studies*, 36.3, 295–325.

Rees, L. (2006 [2005]) *Auschwitz, The Nazis and the Final Solution* (London: BBC Books).

Roberts, E. (1996 [1985]) *A Woman's Place: An Oral History of Working Class Women, 1890–1940* (Oxford: Blackwell).

Rosenthal, G. (ed.) (1998) *The Holocaust in Three Generations: Families of Victims and Perpetrators of the Nazi Regime* (London: Cassell).

Saxton, L. (2008) *Haunted Images: Film, Ethics, Testimony and the Holocaust* (London: Wallflower).

Schmitz, H. (2007) 'Introduction: The return of German wartime suffering', *German Monitor* 67, 1–29.

Spiegelman, A. (2003 [1973]) *Maus: A Survivor's Tale* (London: Penguin).

Sturken, M. (2008) 'Memory, consumerism and media: reflections on the emergence of the field', *Memory Studies*, 1.1, 73–8.

Thompson, P. (1992 [1978]) *The Voice of the Past* (Oxford: Oxford University Press).

Urry, J. (1996) 'How societies remember the past', in S. MacDonald and G. Fyfe (eds), *Theorizing Museums* (Oxford: Blackwell).

Welzer, H., Moller, S. and Tschuggnall, K. (2002) *'Opa war kein Nazi'. Nationalsozialismus und Holocaust im Familiengedächtnis* (Frankfurt am Main: Fischer).

Winter, J. (2006) *Remembering War: The Great War Between Memory and History in the Twentieth Century* (New Haven: Yale University Press).

WW1: Experiences of an English soldier (2006–8): http://wwar1.blogspot.com/. Accessed 16 September 2008.

Zelizer, B. (1998) *Remembering to Forget: Holocaust Memory Through the Camera's Eye* (Chicago: University of Chicago Press).

Part II

Televised History and National Identity

6
Staging Historical Leaders on French Television

The Example of Napoleon Bonaparte

Isabelle Veyrat-Masson

According to Pierre Nora, the increased presence of historical and news programmes on television has modified our perception and understanding of history and the academic study of history: '[I]t is the method of perception of the History itself, that, encouraged by the media, has expanded substantially and has replaced memory, which rested on the legacy of its own intimacy, by the ephemeral visual image of actuality' (1984, p. xviii).

Indeed, technical changes not only modify our lifestyle but also our means of knowledge and comprehension of reality, along with our perception of our environment. They induce shifts in our centres of interest, and alter our convictions. It is not always easy to establish which interaction came first. The question of origins should not however prevent us from trying to determine in what respect these technical changes are responsible for the alterations that have occurred in the way we feel about things. This led Krystof Pomian to wonder about 'the impact of the media on people's everyday life' which 'led the historians to investigate in a new way people's approach to the past, the way it is surviving in the present, the influence it is going to have on people's behaviour, on institutions and social groups'. Indeed, he notes 'the importance given by the media to characters of the past, especially the most recent past,' and the media's capacity 'to impose some topics on public opinion and to generate controversies' (1999, p. 341). Studying the representation of the past on television enables us to uncover the way contemporaries understand their history, but also their present.

As we have seen in previous studies (e.g., Veyrat-Masson, 2000), history as depicted by television can be compared to a kind of collective memory and also to a type of modern historiographical process, a historiography that lies half-way between academic history and popular history, building something different – a public history. There are plenty of questions arising from public history; my recent book on docudrama and docufiction considers the risks of 'confusion' which relate to such forms (Veyrat-Masson, 2008).

In this chapter, I will consider the part played in the construction of French identity by the clash between a figure of the past as significant as Napoleon Bonaparte, and television, the medium of the present. Issues like the 'grandeur' of the nation, the loneliness of great men, Europe, human rights, the French left wing's destiny, independence and the future of sovereignty as opposed to globalization have all been related to this man and his representation. The values of authority and the powerfulness of the state have been evoked through the story of the Corsican general and his destiny. It is surprising to note that 'great men', as represented through new instruments of communication, have kept this role. It is always tempting with television to talk of influences: the influence of politics on the use and representation of Napoleon in the Gaullist period (1958–1969), for example, or the influence of institutional movements such as the commemoration of Bonaparte's birth in 1969; or the influence of ideological and political issues such as the construction of Europe as well as the debates over human rights. All of these aspects will be considered. Further, in more recent years (1999–2000), it has often been impossible to know how and by whom representations of Napoleon would be affected. So, is the word 'influence' the right one?

History and television is an alliance so obvious for contemporary people and yet so strange when considered further. History deals with continuation and duration, whereas television is devoted to and thrives on current events. Through reality shows, for instance, television reconstructs our experience of time. The link between the audiovisual media and their segmentation of time and the 'stable temporal and spatial framing of events' (Sobchack, 1995, p. 4) that we call history seems to be increasingly tenuous. As Vivian Sobchack notes, 'new twentieth century technologies of representation and narration – most significantly television – have increasingly collapsed the temporal distance between present, past and future that structured our previously conceived notion of the temporal dimensions of what we call History' (1995, pp. 4–5). Michel Debré, worried about the teaching of history, questioned the French Minister of Education Christian Beullac as early as 1979 about the way that the major facts and figures of our history are only known, through and because of fiction novels and television (Debré, 1979). Moreover, it is through television that the French, like the British who spend on average more than 3 hours in front of the screen per day, say they learn about historical characters and events.

This study relies, then, on a number of hypotheses, the main one relating to the representative dimension of televised content. Television, a privileged medium close to the heart of society, reflects the evolution in people's consciousness of the representation of historical figures. This phenomenon can be explained mainly by the collective nature of television production. Scriptwriting conditions in television are close to the patterns that prevailed in Hollywood in the 1930s: a collective work. The production of a television programme results from the collation of wills, desires and restraints which very frequently rely on the supposed expectations of an audience which has been previously consulted in preview sessions or by questionnaires and enquiries. We can then make the assumption that these multiple interventions, aiming at getting as close as possible to the public's feelings, and the suppression of individualism and subjectivity on the author's part, result in a manufactured product which is a sort of summary of the public's opinions at a given moment. Television plays a pivotal role in the construction of a shared national narrative and influences the nature of the relationship between the public space and the cultural sphere. As it addresses a larger public, the mass media's history programming favours a direct individual approach to history, and collective memory.

Unlike the Anglo-Saxon tradition where individualism is ancient, the study of leaders and, on a wider scale, biographies, have not always been legitimate in France. Two very strong French literary traditions are involved. The 'art in the name of art' doctrine represented by Stephane Mallarmé and Marcel Proust has been adapted by the structuralist school led by Roland Barthes. The method of the latter favours the truth, the veracity of the work rather than understanding it through the life of the author. Secondly, the 'École des Annales' and historians such as Marc Bloch and Lucien Febvre focused on structures and economy, events and politics rather than the role of individuals. Even more radical, critics of the biographical genre continued with the Braudelian branch of 'new history'. Only at the beginning of the 1980s was the biography 'taboo' toppled, since 'new History gave way to an interest in short periods and individuals' as Claude Arnaud explained (1989, p. 43). After years of structural history, 'the historians, tired of abstraction were craving for something concrete', suggests Jacques le Goff (1989, p. 48). Biography's return (although it had never left popular history) was made possible in the academic world. The success of the biography *Louis XI* (1974) by Murray Kendall marked a key turning point in the recognition of biographies. Even one of France's leading 'new historians', Jacques Le Goff, surrendered to this demand: he indulged in the 'human flesh and destiny, and published a biography of Saint Louis' (1992; 1996). According to Le Goff, biographies enable a 'magnetization' of a historical period about one personality, which is what television has been doing for years, for instance, in documentary drama.

On television, interest in the 'history of great men' has always been apparent. De Gaulle and Emperor Napoleon Bonaparte were the two figures that stand out among the numerous stories of famous personalities. It corresponds to their position in the hearts and minds of the French people,[1] a position that they hold despite the fact that both have generated a host of passionate controversies. But in the case of 'le petit caporal', as we are going to explain in this chapter, 'histories of great men' have been operated as 'tool boxes', providing opportunities to raise contemporary issues. Napoleon is one of those controversial historical leaders who, like Joan of Arc, have been constantly utilized in political debate. Thus, Nathalie Petiteau (1999, p. 395) identified a 'boost of his popularity every time France went through a political crisis'.

Who was this Napoleon, who still generates so much interest and so much fear? Few historical characters are as controversial. Of all feelings towards the emperor, a love–hate relationship was the most common for years. Chateaubriand experienced almost a religious feeling when he dared to write the first sentence of Napoleonic history. For him, Napoleon was the 'greatest man who lived in this world since Caesar'. But today, the Republican tradition carried on by Lavisse and Aulard, underlining the excesses of Napoleon, and the more Marxist approach of Georges Lefebvre (1969 [1936]) or André Soboul (1990) who considered Napoleon the 'Revolution's gravedigger' have made room for a less polarized judgement of the emperor which, with the help of Louis Madelin, André Castelot and Jacques Godechot (1967) has replaced the undisputable achievements and abuses of Napoleon in the history of the nineteenth-century revolutions (see Petiteau). Marcel Normand's and Roger Caratini's exaggerations (2002, p. 11), comparing Napoleon with Hitler, remain very unusual.

Another frontier separating those in favour and those against Napoleon is generated by the already existing division between historians on one side, and on the other side the audience and the readers who constitute a huge and invisible community, passionate about the Napoleonic era.[2] This group vows a fierce admiration for the general, whereas scholars are often more severe. We can imagine that the dominant version of the myth will be that of the audience since academic historians are not greatly involved in audio-visual media. There is suspicion on both sides. On the one hand, in the French case, historians are not familiar with television. They naturally distrust instruments of entertainment as well as relationships between fiction and history. The reasons for liking this new media were actually limited: the poor quality of the images and the lack of rigor in the representations of the past (documentaries and magazines as fictional reconstitutions) did not encourage them to get to know this new media better. But on the other hand, media professionals are not eager to have professional historians (academics or research scholars) come and work for them. However, starting in the mid-1970s, the most famous professional historians (Duby, Le Goff, Braudel) began to be given the opportunity to put some of their works on screen, but these programmes were only received with polite applause. Their experience remained limited. Historians are confined to their usual role as 'historical advisor'. Even if some of them are sometimes asked for advice as was, for instance, Jean Tulard, a professor at the Sorbonne, who became popular after participating in the series *Les Dossiers de l'écran* (A2, 1967–1991), scriptwriting, debates and productions have never really been the work of a professional historian. On the other hand, politicians too often monitored television programmes in France. Is this the reason why, following the different representations of an historical character like Napoleon, one may also identify the current dominant political ideology?

To study the evolution of Napoleon Bonaparte's representation on French television, I have consulted the database of the Inatheque,[3] the national archives that contain nearly all audiovisual broadcast since the early 1950s. From an initial quantitative study, I selected and analysed the main fiction and nonfiction programmes that dealt with Napoleon Bonaparte and his period. The quantitative results were telling.[4] Television's obvious interest in Napoleon's life, his relatives and the Empire dates from its early days in 1957. Between *La Camera explore le temps* (1957) and the series *Napoleon*[5] on France 2 (2002), I found approximately 250 works of fiction[6] or documentaries dealing with Napoleon and his time (Veyrat-Masson and Chanteranne, 2003). Despite that impressive figure, and oddly enough, a 2002 production was the first fiction covering Napoleon's whole life. And, as it was noticed by the American director David Grubin himself,[7] the first and only documentary covering Napoleon's whole life was American – his own. However, as early as 1957, the most famous historical programme on French television, *La Camera explore le temps*[8] (1957–1965), began with an episode of Napoleon's life, in particular his love story with Marie Walewska. The presentation of this film was unambiguous: 'Everywhere, those who dream of freedom have their eyes set on this man with a prestigious name: Napoleon' announced a voice over. Every year, during the programme's long reign, *La Camera* dedicated a different episode, more or less enthusiastic, to the Napoleonic era. The second most pertinent historical programme, the *Dossiers de l'écran* which began in 1967 (1967–1991) also dedicated a significant proportion of its transmission to the Emperor and his time. From 1968 to 1991, the *Dossiers de l'écran* featured more than 1000 subjects, first on a weekly basis until 1982, then monthly. Its typical show would start with a cinema movie followed by a debate that included questions from the audience. Twelve episodes were devoted to Napoleon and his time.

The commemoration in 1969 of the 200th anniversary of Napoleon's birth was a turning point of the historiography of Napoleon. French television played its part, with 46 broadcasting hours spread over 9 months.[9] On 14 April 1969, at 8.30 PM on the first French channel, André Malraux, Minister of Culture of de Gaulle's government, launched the televised commemoration. Prime Minister Georges Pompidou gave a speech on 15 August 1969, in Ajaccio (Bonaparte's place of birth), in which, he suggests, 'the parallel between Napoleon's achievements and the principles that have guided Gaullism' (Petiteau, 1999, p. 179) On television, the master of ceremonies, Roger Stephane, an admirer of de Gaulle, evidently intended to draw the same link between de Gaulle and that other general who organized a 'coup d'Etat' to restore law and order in France. For him, Napoleon was the first man to give France its true 'grandeur', the second being obviously Général de Gaulle.

A trial of Napoleon concluded the commemoration with a dramatic climax. The very idea of passing judgement on a historical event is contradictory in a discipline that is considered scientific. Passing this kind of judgement after a period of 200 years is even more questionable. However, the presence of historians in the court has resulted in the emergence of new and interesting ideas and debates (Jeanneney, 1998). Surprisingly, this trial managed to provide fruitful confrontations of ideas without falling into caricature and ridicule. Especially, with this trial, the project of an apologetic commemoration was eventually checked. The influence of the *Mai 1968* events entered, unexpectedly, into the 'Court'. These events seemed to have led to the disappearance of a traditional, nationalist France, which admired French history and the great men who built the country. With the student revolt of May 1968, the image of de Gaulle and the ideals he shared with Bonaparte were depreciated. Throughout the country, the commemoration had been criticized for its length and its zealously pro-Napoleon position. The trial was a way to give satisfaction to the criticisms of the Malraux and Roger Stéphane project. With the help of two talented socialist lawyers, Jean-Denis Bredin and the future Minister of Justice Robert Badinter, it questioned and reassessed the achievements of the Empire.

After May 1968, Napoleon almost vanished from the television screen for a decade. His 'comeback' during the 1980s and 1990s on the two main television channels raised further questions. This was still linked with current political issues but very different from the first years of television. François Mitterrand had been elected president in 1981, and the left wing inspired television programming.

The series *Guerilla ou les désastres de la guerre* (A2, 1984), about Napoleon's war in Spain, does not cast the emperor as the main character. 'How can high ideas of liberty and progress become swords, spikes and bayonets under which lies a new thrust of barbarism and domination?' were the words of the painter Francisco Goya opening each episode. This set the theme of the series: Napoleon as an arrogant and excessively dominating leader but also a strong statesman motivated by a desire to export the enlightened ideas of the French Revolution, by any means, even the most violent. It is possible to recognize here a debate spanning the 1980s, among left-wing movements close to the Communist party. Jorge Semprun and the actor Pierre Santini (Napoleon), well known for their left-wing political commitment, were, respectively, the author of the series and the main actor. For a long time, people of this conviction had thought that the flow of history is more powerful than the will of individuals, even that of great men. The fight for righteous causes and for the good of humanity justified the violation of some fundamental human rights. The series *Guerilla* is self-critical. Through their consideration of the Franco-Spanish war, the authors intended to reflect upon the failure of political voluntarism, which was also blamed for the Soviet Union's failure. The series interprets the Napoleonic epic in terms of an alleged historical development of political messianism that started with the French Revolution and ended in the dictatorships of Lenin and Stalin. During the 1980s, when the French socialist and the Communist party succeeded in gaining power, oddly enough, it used the figure of Napoleon to trigger internal disputes in its own movement.

By the beginning of the 1990s, the choice of programmes was, at last, conducted on more strictly professional criteria. Yet, once again, it was around a theme that is linked to the most immediate present – the European question – that a new important production on *Napoleon and the Empire* was scheduled. In 1991, two television channels, the Sept and FR3, asked six countries which had been invaded by Napoleon's armies to share their thoughts and impressions of the invasions. FR3 broadcast the results over seven episodes, including one on France itself, called *Napoleon et l'Europe*.[10] The perceptions of the co-operating countries appear to follow the same pattern. On the one hand, Napoleon brought the ideals of the French Revolution, and, especially for the educated class, a message of freedom. The German episode, *Berlin ou le reveil de l'Allemagne*, displays this feeling clearly. On the other hand – and the Polish episode demonstrated this clearly – the liberal thinker and liberator converted to tyranny when he waged war on the people. Then, the story goes, the Napoleonic dream of establishing a United States of Europe became instead a sequence of wars for national liberation, wars that Napoleon had not foreseen.

On 2 December 2001, Arte devoted the programme *Thema* (thematic evening) to Napoleon under the heading, 'Napoleon, Adulation and Aversion', with the unambiguous aim of deflating the myth of the Emperor Napoleon. In the programme, adulation of Napoleon the personage was ridiculed. The evening started with a fictional film that had the clear aim to dethrone Napoleon. The Franco-Polish film written and directed by Jerzy Kawalerowicz, *L'otage de l'Europe* (1988) [The Hostage of Europe] tells of the last years of Napoleon on the island of St. Helena. Historians would recognize the historical qualities of this film, its desire to be as close as possible to the facts and even to the spirit, the atmosphere that prevailed in Napoleon's last stay at Saint Helena. However, several elements in this film indicate TV desacralization. First, the choice of the topic itself: Napoleon in the middle of his decline. After 1815, the emperor cannot be compared with the romantic hero that the French people loved so much and to whom they gave so much. Bloated, petty, tyrannical and rude towards his entourage, he looks like a despot rather than the glorious general of the Arcole bridge painted by Antoine-Jean Gros (1796). Submission to historical truth or desire to demythologize? The choice of the images here speaks for itself. The emperor is played by Roland Blanche, an actor known for his interpretation of various criminals, among them Caderousse, the spineless traitor in the very popular

Monte Cristo (TF1, 1998 with Gerard Depardieu), and he is filmed in the most humiliating situations and postures: brutal sexuality, degrading illness, rudeness towards a particularly elegant Hudson Lowe, ultimate aggressive words,[11] all showing Napoleon as the very image that he was trying to fight at this time by writing *Le Mémorial de Sainte Hélène*.

The last part of the evening was dedicated to a documentary[12] with the same title as the themed evening: *Napoleon, Adulation and Aversion*. Indeed the title prepares us for the content but does not indicate the author's choice. In reality, in this succession of examples of adulation – collections of objects, constant references and blindness to his actions – sometimes moving, most frequently ridiculous – and a list of war atrocities, the sides are heard. Helped by an anachronistic distance, Napoleon is once again banished, but this time by television. After a little more than a year, 'Madame Sans-Gêne' by Philippe de Broca and Edouard Molinaro[13] is transformed into a harpy, an accuser of the person who has made her a Marshal of the Empire. Calling him 'parvenu', 'little fatty', 'tyrant' and 'vindictive Corsican', she drags the viewer into her despising of Napoleon, played by Bruno Solo, an actor of comedy sketches, an emperor of parody, who doesn't inspire the slightest respect! We do understand now that French television participates in the demythologization, which is in line with a period where desacralization of the past has become general. Therefore, what does the extraordinary investment in the production of a lavish *Napoleon* on France 2, in October 2002, mean? How can we explain the high audience figures, and how do we position it in the movement just described?

This 'imperial' production was hailed as the most expensive film in the history of French television (at 40 million Euros). The programme garnered 9 million viewers. This huge success was the result of teamwork, which is worth considering further. The idea of adapting Max Gallo's bestseller, *Napoleon*[14] (1997) for television was that of the famous actor Gerard Depardieu. Didier Decoin agreed to write the script despite his declared dislike for Napoleon. Max Gallo, who was a member of the Communist party until 1970, joined François Mitterrand and became his spokesman when Mitterrand ruled in 1983 (14 months). Disappointed by Mitterrand, he then joined a new party, Le Mouvement des citoyens, created by Jean-Pierre Chevènement, an ex-Socialist minister.[15] Jean-Pierre Guérin, the producer, also came from the Communist party. Didier Decoin is a writer and was the head of the fiction department in the second channel. The story of the film is also the story of a change of opinion. Didier Decoin declared that he discovered, with Gallo, that 'behind the black legend, a man hides, a man of good'![16]

The image of Napoleon in 2002 was comfortably 'post-modern'. The authors focused on the character behind the statesman, and in front of their camera, the familiar Napoleon was transformed into a 'housewife's emperor' (Schneidermann, 2002). It should be noted that little could have been further from historical truth than this image of the respectable husband and 'bon bourgeois' strolling down the street arm-in-arm with his wife. This production, then, provoked vastly divergent reactions. Laurent Joffrin[17] (2002) judged that 'the authors have adopted the Bonapartist legend, their angle is clear and favourable'. In the eyes of another critic, however, the same film was 'a textbook, the pages of which are turned at the pace of a charging army, and from which only emerges the image of an arrogant dictator, a megalomaniac and bloody warrior' (Belot, 2002). How can we explain this difference of opinion? Maybe the writers differed in their original point of view. The black legend of the Empire had so much impressed people's minds that a film as brutal as the former could have appeared, to left-wing partisans, moderate and sympathetic towards Napoleon. The casting of an actor best known for his comic roles was yet another and new kind of desecration of this central figure of French national history. Not only is the actor Christian Clavier famous for his interpretation (1993) of the rogue in *Jacquouille la Fripouille* [Jacquouille the Rogue[18]], but he also played the infamous thief Thenardier in Victor Hugo's *Les Miserables* (TF1, 2000), one of the most ignominious characters in the French, and even more general, imaginary pantheon.[19] The image of the Emperor had therefore been sullied twice by 2002, once through ridicule and once by moral infamy.

If the year 1968 signalled the depreciation of such values as patriotism, courage, order and national identity, the same values that Napoleon Bonaparte had come to symbolize and that, therefore, formed the foundation of his admiration, then the more recent turn is all the more significant. Bonaparte's image and its symbolic value have once again adapted adroitly to changes in the political environment, this time by the return of 'outdated' Napoleonic values. The presence in this debate of two people from the left in France, Max Gallo defending the emperor and Laurent Joffrin, are a revealing sign of this phenomenon: the drift of the Bonapartists' values from a right-wing to a left-wing point of view.

The more recent success on the political scene – the right wing this time – of two men, Dominique de Villepin and Nicolas Sarkozy, whose links to Napoleon are claimed by the writing of a book, on the one hand, and on the other hand by common traits such as the physical and moral point of view (Duhamel, 2009), seem to trigger a 're-discovery' of Napoleon and his values, in particular the place of the state and a populism that we have named 'Bonapartism'. Napoleon has divided France so much; would he have been able to reunite it in the beginning of this century? This is apparently not the case, as we have noted during the commemoration of the Battle of Austerlitz (2 December 1805). At the end of 2005, alarm over the issue of the integration of racial minorities meant that the person who had restored slavery after the French Revolution had abolished it was not celebrated. Therefore, Austerlitz was not officially commemorated, unlike the British celebration of Trafalgar.

In conclusion, this study has helped us to better understand to what extent representations of 'great men' may serve as a matrix to explain modern society. The succession of polls conducted since 1948 on 'The French and History' have revealed and confirmed how much the selection of events or figures that people believe to be the most important historically has changed over the past decades. From 1949, men and women prior to the twentieth century have progressively disappeared from our imaginary pantheon, as the polls[20] studying 'the characters of the French history that we would like to meet' show; in 1987, Napoleon Bonaparte was the only one to remain in the top three. But he only had 9 per cent of the votes, which is a real drop compared to his popularity in 1949 (32 per cent). For Jean-Pierre Rioux, the answers given to the 1987 poll raise the question of the 'overwhelming effect of the present'. Does it 'weigh too much on the past or is collective memory confined to its mediatic expression?' (Rioux, 1987, p. 75). Nonetheless he states that 'current events, as viewed by television, lasting, tampered by instant and shortsighted commentaries affect the historical vision of our contemporaries' (Rioux, 1987, p. 75) The return of interest in Napoleon observed in the 1999 poll[21] is very clear (17 per cent). How do we explain it? The series by Yves Simoneau (*Napoleon*, 2000), which marks the renewal of the mediatic interest in the emperor, is slightly later than, or at least contemporary to, the poll. It is therefore impossible to look for any kind of influence. By studying the content of the TF1 series, in order to understand other reasons to produce a series of this importance on a character this disputed, we have noticed the complexity of the values at stake in this product of mass culture, and the echo that it finds in society. Indeed, as the historian Maurice Agulhon said, 'the great man, like History, is used to teaching civics'.

A Note on Availability

Dossiers de l'écran: all the episodes referred to can be seen freely at the Centre de consultation de l'Inathèque de France, Bibliothèque Nationale, Paris: http://www.ina-entreprise.com/archives-tele-radio/universitaires/index.html.

Some can be loaded and purchased online from the Centre, especially *La Caméra explore le temps*, available at: http://boutique.ina.fr/recherche/recherche?search=la+camera+explore+le+temps&vue=Boutique_Video. *Napoleon* by Yves Simoneau is available as a 4 DVD sets (French), Éditeur: ALLIANCE, and online at http://www.renaud-bray.com/Films_Produit.aspx? id=595637&def=Napol%C3%A9on+%28fran%C3%A7ais%29+4DVD% 2CSIMONEAU+YVES%2CALFD20647042. *Napoleon* (2003), written, produced and directed by David Grubin, is available on DVD and distributed by PBS Home Video.

L'otage de l'Europe by Jerzy Kawalerowicz (1988) is distributed by Jeck Films, 5, rue René Boulanger 75010 Paris (jeckfilm@noos.fr).

Madame Sans-Gêne by Philippe de Broca and Edouard Molinaro is available on DVD from L.C.J. Editions et Productions.

Notes

1. de Gaulle is by far the most important historical figure, and polls have shown that Napoleon has (almost) never been ranked outside the three most revered figures in France.
2. See the best sellers of André Castelot, 1967 and 1968.
3. The Inatheque is part of INA, Institut National de l'Audiovisuel, a French government body created in 1974, in charge of audiovisual archives. Since the 1992 law on 'dépôt legal', researchers can have access to these archives.
4. Taking note that selected broadcasts include very long series and broadcasts that only marginally deal with Napoleon.
5. In October 2002, more than 9 million television viewers (37 per cent share) saw the first episode of the France 2 saga, *Napoleon*.
6. Counting every episode.
7. During a private meeting in 2002.
8. The authors: Alain Decaux, André Castelot, Stellio Lorenzi (also director).
9. At this time, France had only two channels, broadcasting only during lunchtime and in the late afternoon and evening.
10. This was a major project with prestigious professionals and an important budget. The main character is played by the same actor: Jean-François Stevenin, sensitive and human. He played Bonaparte the man as well as Napoleon the iconic figure.
11. Historians still debate Napoleon's last words.
12. Arte, Pierre Philippe, presentation Guillaume Durand.
13. TF1, 11 February 2002.
14. Eight hundred thousand copies were sold.
15. *Le Mouvement des citoyens* is a political party campaigning for the return of national sovereignty, against EU domination. They speak for the nation and the 'République'.
16. Didier Decoin, France 2 website.
17. Napoleon specialist and director of the *Nouvel Observateur* (a leftist magazine); author of *Les batailles de Napoleon* (2000) (Paris: Seuil).
18. In the film *Les Visiteurs,* 1993, directed by Jean-Marie Poiré.
19. According to Gérard Depardieu's account, on the France 2 website, it is by seeing Christian Clavier in this role that he thought about him for the role of Napoleon!
20. *Sondages*, 17, 1949; *Psyché*, February 1950, *L'Histoire* 100, May 1987.
21. *L'histoire*, 242, April 2000.

Bibliography

Arnaud, C. (1989) 'Le retour de la biographie: d'un tabou à l'autre', *Le Débat* 54 (March–April).
Belot, J. (2002) *Télérama*, 2 October.
Caratini, R. (2002) *Napoleon, une imposture* (Paris: l'Archipel).
Castelot, A. (1967) *Bonaparte* (Paris: Librairie académique Perrin).
Castelot, A. (1968) *Napoleon* (Paris: Librairie académique Perrin).
Debré, M. (1979) *Le Monde*, September 3.

Duhamel, A. (2009) *La marche consulaire* (Paris: Plon).

Gallo, M. (1997) *Napoleon* (4 vols) (Paris: Robert Laffont).

Godechot, J. (1967) *L'Europe et l'Amérique à l'époque Napoleonienne* (Paris: Nouvelle Clio).

Jeanneney, J.-N. (1998) *Le passé dans le prétoire. L'historien, le juge et le journaliste* (Paris: Seuil).

Joffrin, L. (2002) *Nouvel Observateur* (*TéléObs*), 3–9 October.

Kendall, M. (1974) *Louis XI* (Paris: Fayard).

Lefebvre, G. (1969 [1936]) *Napoleon* (Paris: PUF).

Le Goff, J. (1989) 'Comment écrire une biographie historique aujourd'hui?' *Le Débat* 54 (March–April).

Le Goff, J. (1992) *Esprit*, 8–9.

Le Goff, J. (1996) *Saint-Louis* (Paris: Gallimard).

Nora, P. (1984) *Les lieux de mémoire, tome I: La Republique* (Paris: Gallimard).

Petiteau, N. *Napoleon, de la mythologie à l'histoire* (Paris: Seuil).

Pomian, K. (1999) *Sur l'histoire* (Paris: Gallimard Folio histoire).

Rioux, J.-P. (1987) 'Les Français et leur histoire', *L'histoire*, mai.

Schneidermann, D. (2002) *Le Monde*, 12 October.

Sobchack, V. (1995) *The Persistence of History* (London: Routledge).

Soboul, A. (1990) *La civilisation de la France Napoleonienne* (Paris: Arthaud).

Veyrat-Masson, I. (2000) *Quand la television explore le temps: L'histoire au petit écran (1953–2000)* (Paris: Fayard).

Veyrat-Masson, I. (2008) *Télévision et histoire, la confusion des genres: Docudrama, docufiction et fictions du reel* (Bruxelles: Ina-de boeck).

Veyrat-Masson, I. and D. Chanteranne (2003) *Napoleon à l'écran,* (Paris: Nouveau Monde editions).

7
Landscape and Memory

British Televisual Representations of the Battle of the Somme

Emma Hanna

The relationship between landscape and memory is an integral part of the visual design of televisual representations of the First World War. This chapter will show how images of landscape in British television documentaries have been mediated by two levels of representation; (i) the *physical* landscape of remembrance marked by memorials and cemeteries, which act as portals to (ii) the *emotional* landscape, a place forever scarred by the events of 1914–18. The physical reminders, memorials and cemeteries, mean that the thousands of tourists that visit the former Western Front are already aware that they are visiting a site that contains the remains of the millions of men who lost their lives during the war. The place names along the former Western Front resonate with meaning and British television documentaries about the war have transferred this resonance to the small screen by utilizing accepted representations of the war's cultural inheritance to invoke a code to describe the indescribable.

Images of the Western Front dominate Britain's modern memory of 1914–18. Unlike other battlefronts in Italy, Greece, Gallipoli and the Holy Land, it is close to the British Isles, it was the decisive theatre of operations, and the majority of the British dead are buried there (Lloyd, 1998, p. 100). This is particularly pertinent to Britain's popular memory of the fighting near the River Somme. Between July and November 1916, Britain suffered approximately 420,000 casualties; the bodies of 73,412 men were never found, but they are commemorated by the memorial at Thiepval. The sacrifice of British blood in the soil of France was so significant that it led the British government to collect six barrels of earth from the Ypres Salient to fill the tomb of the Unknown Warrior in Westminster Abbey in November 1920. The fascination with the battle lies in its continual repetition in popular memory as an event that encapsulated the true texture of the First World War, a symbol of absolute horror and total futility (Connelly, 2002, pp. 21–8).

Remembrance is part of the landscape. In northern France and in Flanders, 169 cemeteries maintained by the Commonwealth War Graves Commission are contained within an area of less than 54 square miles. It has been estimated that there are hundreds of thousands of human remains outside the official military cemeteries. In the Ypres Salient alone, more than 42,000 Allied – and an equal number of German – bodies were never recovered (Macdonald, 1978, p. 239). Large areas constitute national cemeteries, the final resting place of tens of thousands of British and Commonwealth, French, Belgian and German soldiers. The first British battlefield tours to Ypres started in 1919 with the purpose of taking relatives of the deceased to the areas where their loved ones were, or were thought to be, buried. Guidebooks were widely published such as *The Pilgrim's Guide to the Ypres Salient* (1920), *The Immortal Salient* (1925) and *The Battle Book of Ypres* (1927). Britain's connections to the Western Front continued to develop in the interwar years when visitors to the battlescape assumed that at particular places it was possible to renew, recreate or capture something of the war and the experiences that defined it.

British audiences first saw moving images from the Western Front in 1916 in the wartime documentary *Battle of the Somme*. Filmed by War Office official cinematographers Geoffrey Malins and J.B. McDowell, *Battle of the Somme* was the first visual record to show British audiences scenes from the action that took place near the Somme in July 1916. The film was designed to underline the historic significance of the battle, to justify sacrifices at home, and to maintain people's support for the war. The film was put on general cinematic release by the War Office on 21 August 1916 in London and in provincial towns and cities a week later. By September 1916, it had been shown in more than 1000 cinemas and to the King and Queen at Windsor. In 1916, and to a large extent ever since, *Battle of the Somme* has offered Britons a special insight into the Western Front.

Images from *Battle of the Somme* (1916), especially the staged scenes of soldiers going 'over the top' and the explosion of a large mine at Hawthorn Ridge Redoubt, are regular staples that continue to be used in almost every modern documentary about the First World War. Indeed, the BBC's grand narrative series, *The Great War* (BBC, 1964), which was made to commemorate the 50th anniversary of the conflict, used numerous pieces of film from *Battle of the Somme* (1916) and other documentaries made during the war such as *The Battle of the Ancre and the Advance of the Tanks* (1917). *The Great War* was a huge ratings success for the BBC, and the series is still regarded as the one of the most significant history documentaries ever made. However, by the 1970s, a period of historiographical change had begun. History in the public domain began to be characterized by the stories of individual men and women (Winter and Prost, 2005, p. 20). With expanded production opportunities offered by developing camera technology and colour film, documentary makers began to produce programmes in a different style to the grand narrative approach of series like *The Great War.*

Malcolm Brown, who worked at the BBC in the 1960s and 1970s, felt that any documentary made in the wake of *The Great War* had to be different. Brown's *Battle of the Somme* (BBC, 1976) was the first British arts-style documentary to be made about the First World War, and it is significant for two reasons. Firstly, the programme did not feature veterans' testimonies but the 'voices' of men who fought on the Somme from letters, diaries and poems. Secondly, *Battle of the Somme* showed how television could utilize existing representations of the war's landscape found in well-known cultural reworkings and recordings – such as the music of Ralph Vaughan Williams and the paintings of Paul Nash – to resonate with the aural and visual impressions of Britain's modern memory of the war. Instead of providing narration in the form of a voice over, as Michael Redgrave had done for *The Great War,* it was the actor Leo McKern, best known for his lead role in *Rumpole of the Bailey* (ITV, 1978–92), who presented the programme. Brown envisaged that he was a ghostly guide appearing to battlefield tourists. He was 'the programme's lynchpin, narrating the story from the actual battlefield, the only figure in a once lethal landscape, in effect one man standing in for thousands. He wound be a kind of revenant, an ancient-mariner-figure taking the audience by the arm to explain what had happened in those haunted killing fields in the summer and autumn of 1916' (Brown, 2003, p. 42).

Figure 1   Malcolm Brown directing Leo McKern in *Battle of the Somme* (BBC, 1976) in the trenches at Vimy Ridge. Courtesy of John Goodyer and Malcolm Brown.

Figure 2   Actor Leo McKern presenting *Battle of the Somme* (BBC, 1976) in the trenches at Vimy Ridge. Courtesy of John Goodyer and Malcolm Brown.

Battle of the Somme is the televisual equivalent of John Masefield's *The Old Front Line* (1917). It is the first British television documentary about 1914–18 to show the Somme as it looked in 1976, presenting the battlefield as both a character and main feature of the story of the fighting that occurred there in 1916. *Battle of the Somme* appeared at a time when historical writing began to place greater emphasis on the experience of the ordinary man at war. In addition to Leon Wolff's *In Flanders Fields* (1957), Martin Middlebrook's *The First Day on the Somme* (1971) was used as a main inspiration, and Middlebrook worked with Brown as historical adviser on the programme. Middlebrook had published *The First Day on the Somme* (1971) after a visit to the battle-fields to France and Belgium in 1967. *The First Day on the Somme* was not a history of the High Command but the story of ordinary men who fought told in their own words.

From the 1970s, representations of the First World War on television reflected the developments of works about the war in print by mining relatively vast but disappearing seams of memory of the British Tommy at war. In 1976, *Battle of the Somme* was the first documentary to demonstrate how remembrance had become part of the physical and emotional landscape. The opening scenes remind the viewer that this area was repeatedly fought over centuries before the first wave of the British Expeditionary Force (BEF) arrived to save Belgium in the summer of 1914. McKern points out that the region of Picardy has been inextricably linked with the fortunes of the English for more than 500 years:

> If you take the train from Amiens to Arras across north-east France you will pass through a region deeply linked by emotion and history with the people of Britain. This is Picardy. Through this land in 1415 came Henry the Fifth, en route for his encounter with the French at Agincourt. And here, 501 years later, the descendants of Henry's knights and bowmen fought again – in a battle so gigantic in scale that it makes Henry's one day clash seem like a cock-fight in a barnyard.

The choice of reference to the battle of 1415 is particularly significant. The Battle of Agincourt was a victory secured by a small British force over a larger French army. It is the antithesis of the tales of tragedy on the Somme in 1916. Indeed, the ghosts of Agincourt were roused to support the British when journalist Arthur Machen wrote a story in *The Evening News* about the British Army's forced retreat from Mons in September 1914. Machen later expanded and published the story as *The Bowmen* in 1915. The poet, artist and Western Front veteran David Jones had also re-attached traditional meanings to the unprecedented actualities of war by underlining previous Anglo-French conflicts before Agincourt, including the battles of Crécy (1346) and Poitiers (1356): 'My fathers were with the Black Prinse of Wales/at the passion of the blind Bohemian king. /They served in these fields, /It is in the histories that you can read it [*sic*]' (Jones, 1963, p. 79). Placing contemporary events in the setting of a heroic past serves to root the viewers' mind in the historical as well as emotional and geographical landscape over which an industrial war of such unprecedented scale was waged. Indeed, during a visit to the forests of Lithuania, Simon Schama recognized that:

> There was, I knew, blood beneath the verdure and tombs in the deep glades of oak and fir. The fields and forests and rivers had seen war and terror [...] It is haunted land where greatcoat buttons from six generations of fallen soldiers can be discovered lying amidst the woodland ferns.
>
> (Schama, 1995, p. 24)

This viewpoint is encouraged by *Battle of the Somme*. McKern's narration describes the Somme's 'strangely evocative landscape' in that, 'You could sit on a beautiful day with the larks singing and you would realise that you were on top of someone's dead body – 70,000 were never found' (McKern, 1976, p. 3). The physical traces of the war have not completely disappeared and therefore the war remains active and alive in the public's consciousness. Indeed, the land of the former Western Front is still a dangerous place. Along some parts of where the Western Front once stood it has been calculated that there are five unexploded shells per square metre, and 5000 kilos of shrapnel per hectare. The Belgian Army now controls the recovery and disposal of weapons and concentrates its work on excavating the unexploded shells fired at the battle of Third Ypres (Passchendaele) where they harvest up to 250,000 kilos of metal each year (Derez, 1997, p. 443).

Contemporary documentaries about 1914–18 can superimpose wartime images onto footage of present-day landscapes. During the opening sequence of Richard Holmes's *Western Front* (BBC, 1999), he is sitting on a train looking out on to the same vistas as Leo McKern had in the opening scenes of *Battle of the Somme* 23 years earlier. Holmes leaves little to the audience's imagination by superimposing film images from the war on to the present-day film to show the events that were played out in that area of France. As the camera pans away from Holmes's profile, the train window is used as a projector in replaying images of 1914–1918: troops marching, artillery firing and horse-drawn wagons of supplies going up the line, the land is still haunted by a reconstructed 'ghost army'. *Western Front* also shows footage of a tank superimposed on modern-day film, which enables the ghostlike machine to roll through a village that has not seen its like since the cessation of hostilities in 1918. Today's viewers are not only told of the landscape's memory, they can watch it play upon the screen, using film techniques to re-affirm the replaying of memories and images of 1914–18.

Television documentaries about the First World War have had to develop means to impose order out of a complex historical reality. The human losses of the First World War are so great that the numbers might bypass viewers' emotional comprehension. By the conscious or subconscious act of selection, the documentary maker has to create a sense of reality for the beholder so that an incident or image stands for the whole; order is given to chaos, and a manageable symbolic image created, through which viewers may derive some sense of understanding of the larger movement of the war (Sillars, 1987, p. 88). The symbolism of the poppy carries enormous resonance in Britain's memory of 1914–18. Where the French adopted the cornflower, the *bleuet*, the red poppy is universally accepted as signalling Britain's active remembrance of its war dead since 1914. Representations of the poppy related to sleep and pain-relief had already accumulated a ripe traditional symbolism in English literature since Chaucer (Fussell, 1975, p. 243). Sold exclusively by women volunteers on November 11, the red poppy quickly became the essential element in the general symbolism of Armistice Day ritual. As a result of First World War poems such as John McCrae's 'In Flanders Fields' and Isaac Rosenberg's 'Break of Day in the Trenches', the poppy was further identified with the memory of British war dead.

Television footage of meadows and cornfields, where poppies are commonly found, have been used to great effect in documentaries about the

First World War. Even the popular comedy *Blackadder Goes Forth* (BBC, 1989) would end the series with the main characters going over the top, the script directing that 'Blackadder, Baldrick, George and Darling run on, brandishing their hand guns. They will not get far. Silence falls. Our soldiers fade away. No Man's Land turns slowly into a peaceful field of poppies. The only sound is that of a bird, singing sweetly' (Curtis and Elton, 1999, p. 452). The poppy has a sobering effect at the demise of Captain Blackadder, and when it is used in a documentary the image of the flower has attained unquestioned significance. *Battle of the Somme* gives a strong visual impulse to this theme by showing Leo McKern marching through long grass waving in the breeze; in doing so, the programme added further weight to the 'mowing down' of men who suffered the worst casualties in the first hours of the battle, many of whom were described as 'green' or 'fresh'.

Battle of the Somme also underlines the irony that the battlefields did not differ greatly in appearance from home. Of the more well-known writers, it was Masefield who wrote that the country north of the Somme 'is very like Wiltshire' and described it as 'curiously British'(Masefield, 1918, p. 21). Raymond Asquith also wrote to his wife that it was 'a rolling down country, rather like the uplands of Hampshire or Wiltshire' and Charles Carrington said of a village in the Somme valley that 'it might be Kent if it wasn't Picardy. Poppies, cornflowers, deep green lanes, wide rolling downs, all the same except that France has bluer distances and wider expanses of open country'. After the end of the Somme battle in November 1916, however, *Battle of the Somme* underlines that Private Archie Surfleet noted in his diary that the very word Somme 'conjured up a picture of miserable waste, mud and devastation'.

Battle of the Somme shows that, in addition to archived film, Britain's contemporary visual memory of the Western Front has been heavily influenced by a small number of war paintings. Paul Nash, an artist whose work did not resemble traditional mediations of the English landscape, painted the 'anti-landscape' of the Western Front as no longer a place of beauty but of death (Hynes, 1990, p. 194). McKern's voice over on Nash's 'After the Battle' and 'We Are Making a New World' admits that the war artist's interpretations of the Western Front have become significant documents of our time. Nash was just one of many official war artists despatched to the Western Front to record the war, but television has done much to exploit his particular perception of the war. An official war artist from November 1917, Nash had served as a Second Lieutenant in the Hampshire Regiment until he was wounded in March 1917. Nash turned into an angry opponent of the war's destruction, and his belief in the sanctity of landscape hastened this inner metamorphosis (Cork, 1995, p. 198).

When *Battle of the Somme* sought to evoke the reality of the destruction of war on the Western Front, it is Nash's 'We Are Making a New World' (1918) that is transposed onto film of present-day Flanders. The painting depicts the rising sun breaking into No Man's Land, a malleable landscape that is constantly reshaped by bombardment. Other wartime artists such as Percy Wyndham Lewis, Eric Kennington and C.R.W. Nevinson painted landscapes not in the more traditional style of Muirhead Bone's 'Battle of the Somme', but 'elegies for the death of landscape' (Hynes, 1990, p. 199). *Battle of the Somme* uses shots of woods around the Somme to reconnect the present-day landscape with that of the battlefields that surrounded the area during the war, in a similar way to footage of McKern walking down a tree-lined road to say that this was the road that many soldiers used to get to the frontline trenches. The straight long lines of trees could also represent an army platoon lining up for parade. This is redolent of Paul Nash's painting 'Column on the March'. By the use of dramatic perspective, a company of soldiers is depicted on a road that is flanked by tall sinister trees, accentuating a sense of oppression and confinement. The trees do not offer protection, but condemn the weary soldiers 'to trudge in an apparently unending procession on a road as monotonous and inflexible as the war itself' (Cork, 1995, p. 199).

Battle of the Somme was the first television documentary to focus on representations of nature that were already established in First World War literature. Henri Barbusse wrote in his *War Diary* of '[t]he charred skeletons of the trees', and Harold Macmillan thought 'the most extraordinary thing about the modern battlefield is the desolation and emptiness of it all. Nothing is to be seen of war or soldiers – only the split and shattered trees' (Dyer, 1994, p. 115). The appearance in documentary film of corpses and shattered woodland areas from the war enables producers to underline the parallel destruction that war has wrought both on nature and man. *Battle of the Somme* comments that the Western Front 'seemed to belong to another world. Every sign of humanity had been swept away'. The landscapes seen by soldiers on the front line were often altered by the presence of death, and those qualities of the physical world that the words *landscape* and *nature* once designated were altered by the fighting; nature appears in poems and in paintings in order to be disfigured, annihilated, and made irrelevant to the reality of the conflict (Hynes, 1990, p. 201).

Gardening is a recurrent theme in *Battle of the Somme* to underline the civilian nature of the men who volunteered to fight. In addition to panning shots of well-maintained Commonwealth Grave Commission cemeteries, programmes seek to re-establish the landscape and memory of the soldiers who fought in 1914–18. *Battle of the Somme* shows footage of the garden cemeteries to accompany a voice over reading a soldier's, Arthur Hubbard's, letter to his family: 'I can imagine how things must look at home and the garden, as you say, must be almost at its best.' Coming from a nation of gardeners, British soldiers were unlikely to miss the opportunities for irony in pretending that 'thickets' of barbed wire were something like the natural hedges of the English countryside. One soldier wrote home describing the wire snarled at the bottom of mine crater near Pozières, declaring 'the characteristic war-flora [...] represented here as usual by derelict snarls of *Barbedwira volubilis'* (Farrer, 1918, p. 82). Pastoral parodies can also be found in the popular trench newspaper, the *Wipers Times,* with a column entitled 'In My Garden', a satirical take on the weekly magazine *Country Life*: 'It must be remembered that the planting of toffee-apples on the border of your neighbour's allotment will seriously interfere with the ripening of his gooseberries'[1] (Fussell, 1975, p. 238).

Continuing the horticultural imagery, *Battle of the Somme* states that the Somme area of Picardy was where 'the flower of the war generation fell.' This imagery of the scything down of healthy men is widely used with reference to citizen volunteers. Television's concentration on this group has placed greater emphasis on volunteer soldiers at the expense of conscripted soldiers who made up just over half of the BEF in the second half of the war (Bet-El, 1999). Popularly known as 'Kitchener's men', they volunteered in the opening months of the war in response to the calls for recruits to free Belgium from German invasion. Often from the same towns, factories, villages and sports teams, many 'pals' battalions fought and died together along the Somme in 1916. The myth of the volunteers continued through to 1976 and beyond. During *Battle of the Somme,* an actor's voice is heard over archive footage of inexperienced troops marching towards the Somme at the end of June 1916, saying, 'You came of your own accord, you didn't have to be fetched: you bloody fools!' *Battle of the Somme* underlined that after many months of training and preparation, these volunteer battalions 'were two years in the making and ten minutes in the destroying'. *Battle of the Somme* did not feature any old soldiers because the idea of the programme was to show that the war was fought by young men. This was heavily emphasized in the programme's script, which underlined that

> At last the moment had arrived for which the young men of 1914 had volunteered. Men in their twenties, men in their thirties and boys in their teens. [...] Junior officers who might have been at school a year before, stood looking at their watches, whistles in their mouths as the last seconds ticked away. Now the war was no longer in the hands of the generals and the commanders, but in the hands of these young men.
>
> (BBC, 1976, p. 23)

Battle of the Somme underlines that the landscape of the Western Front is imprinted with the war memories of the men who fought there. Like many veterans, the writer Edmund Blunden experienced nightmares, especially about the Somme, and he felt compelled to revisit the sites of war because he felt as he had left some part of himself there. In 1919, Blunden described himself as a 'a harmless young shepherd in a soldier's coat', but out of today's most popular war writers he spent the most time in the firing line.

Blunden remained a pastoral poet in a war setting, not having developed a new wartime artistic style like Paul Nash, or found a new voice like better-known poets Siegfried Sassoon, Wilfred Owen or Isaac Rosenberg. Blunden's war poems 'concentrate on the courage of his comrades, the nature of the landscape or life away from the Front Line; the horrors and ironies are muted, the tone still often deliberately literary, as if he were striving to keep the role of observing poet separate from that of active soldier' (Webb, 1990, p. 57). This was a theme Blunden expanded in *Undertones of War* (1928). He was 'unable to say "Goodbye to all that" and memories and allusion to warfare were cruelly faithful companions. A row of trees, the quality of light on a landscape, the sound of the wind – any of these could transport him back to the trenches' (Webb, 1990, p. 57).

The music used in each programme has been carefully chosen to evoke a range of emotional responses. Television documentaries about the First World War have utilized music to heighten the emotional register of the events portrayed on the screen, providing signals that cue moments of drama to evoke the appropriate emotion in the mind of the viewer (Lacey, 1998, p. 54). For example, the sounding of the Last Post is the musical signification of remembrance and solemnity. Most significant, however, is the way in which some documentaries about 1914–18 use music as an atmospheric device by using music composed by men who were serving in the Army during the war itself. *Battle of the Somme* was the first British television documentary to use the trumpet motif from the slow movement of Ralph Vaughan Williams' *Symphony No. 3* ('Pastoral'). The composer had served on the Western Front, and he was deeply affected by the events he witnessed, in addition to the loss of his close friend, the composer George Butterworth. As a result of his wartime experiences Vaughan Williams' musical language changed to reflect his own experiences and emotions in a rapidly changing world (Mellers, 1989, pp. 260–1) The 'Pastoral' was written while the composer was serving on the Western Front, and it was first performed in London in 1923. The use of a natural trumpet in the second movement is used to stunning effect in *Battle of the Somme*. Out-of-tune partials prescribed in the score are echoes of some of Vaughan Williams' wartime memories:

> Lodged in the composer's mind was a recollection of camp life with the RAMC at Bordon in Hampshire where the bugler hit the 7th as a missed shot for the octave. The symphony was incubated during Vaughan Williams' military service, and in so far as any particular locality is depicted in the symphony it is northern France, where he went after being commissioned in the Royal Garrison Artillery in 1917. The scenery in the Pastoral symphony is not spectacular and northern France with its willows and streams is much like southern England.
>
> (Howes, 1954, pp. 22–23)

The trumpet motif is a mediated version of the traditional Last Post that has sounded in remembrance of the fallen since 1914, played every Armistice Day and at the Menin Gate in Ypres every evening. By using Vaughan Williams' 'Pastoral', *Battle of the Somme* is seeking to access the memory of the Somme via the composer's musical recollection. The *Mars* movement from Gustav Holst's *The Planets* also features in *Battle of the Somme*. In the programme's closing scene, as the present-day landscape fades into Paul Nash's 'We Are Making a New World', the music's gradual fade-in fosters the impression that after the start of the Somme fighting in midsummer 1916 a new period of warfare began. In addition, the reference to Mars as the Greek god of war, a planet thought to be barren and inhospitable, also draws parallels between descriptions of areas of the Western Front as being cratered and desolate, like the surface of the moon. In this way, composers like Vaughan Williams, and painters like Nash, are tangible 'voices' of the First World War.

Producer Malcolm Brown intended that McKern would tell the story of the battle with a long and patient build-up. It was intended that the shock that was to follow was made all the more powerful because the story of the battle 'was not widely known then [as it is today]' (Hanna, 2004). The BBC's Audience Research Department found that it did make a profound impression on reporting viewers 'inducing feelings of horror at the extent of the slaughter [...] and sadness at the futility of it all' (BBC, 1976, VR/76/345). The overall opinion of the series was that it had been most effective in conveying what it must have been like to be one of the 'poor bloody infantry' (BBC Written Archives Centre VR/76/345). Television reviews focused largely on the theme of remembrance, and the number of casualties suffered on the first day of the battle, 1 July 1916. One newspaper quoted Brown describing the Somme 'as though six Waterloos were fought side by side and five were lost' (Brown, 1976, p. 18).

Reviewers understood that the programme was underpinned by remembrance. One respondent wrote that listening to McKern's narration 'was like listening to a trumpet voluntary' (Clayton, 1976, p. 13) and that the 'vivid commentary, delivered with conviction by Leo McKern, was sternly equal to this terrible story' (Lennon, 1976, p. 36). The battlefield itself was described as 'still scarred by the memory of war, where military cemeteries stretch as far as the eye can see' (Jackson, 1976, p. 19), and the method of measuring miles gained by lives lost announced that '2 million casualties were inflicted for a 7$^{1}/_{2}$-mile advance' (Anonymous, 1976, p. 22). When *Battle of the Somme* was repeated on 26 June 1986, it had lost none of its emotive force. *The Times* spoke of 'So many thousands, and too young to sleep forever – except that euphemism really won't do: they didn't fall asleep; they died painfully, horribly, and alone – especially alone, buried in the mud in which they fell' (Watkins, 1986, p. 14). It was described as the 'harrowing and powerful' story of the 'Terrible Great War confrontation in which 1,200,000 men were killed or wounded in the devastated landscape of Picardy' (Smithies, 1986, p. 30). *Battle of the Somme* resonated with viewers' understanding of the Somme as a portal to futile and industrialized mass slaughter.

Battle of the Somme (1976) was the first documentary about 1914–18 to show how the men who fought on the Western Front felt about it at the time, not 50 years later when they were being filmed for a large-scale documentary. Lyn Macdonald's popular books, for example *They Called It Passchendaele* (1978), continued to give voice to the many thousands of men who had fought on the Western Front in the words that they used at the time. In parallel to these publications, surviving First World War veterans became a central component of television documentaries about 1914–18. Documentary makers thought it made good television to take veterans back to the battlefields on which they had fought, often thinking that they would be filming and witnessing the veterans' last visit to the landscape of the First World War. The influence of *Battle of the Somme* can be seen in later programmes such as *A Slow Walk Over No Man's Land* (Channel 4/Ulster TV, 1986), an evocation of the Ulster Division's experience on the Somme, in addition to *The Somme 1916* (Tyne Tees TV, 1994), *The Somme: 70 Years On Old Soldiers Remember* (Central TV, 1986) and *Voices of War* (Channel 4, 1988; Gliddon, 1996, p. 176). Television documentaries became increasingly focused on remembrance, landscape and memory. Memorial programmes such as *Gone for a Soldier* (Scottish TV, 1985), *Very Exceptional Soldiers* (BBC, 1986), *A Time for Remembrance* (Channel 4, 1989) and *A Game of Ghosts* (BBC,1991), along with Richard Holmes's *War Walks* (BBC, 1996) and *Western Front* (BBC, 1999) all filmed present-day scenes of the battlefields to demonstrate the physicality of the geographical area where fighting had occurred.

After the successful broadcast of *Battle of the Somme* and subsequent nominations for Emmy and BAFTA awards, Malcolm Brown went on to make *Peace in No Man's Land* (BBC, 1984), publish a number of books about twentieth-century history and act as historical adviser on several programmes about the First World War. In 2004, Brown was asked to act as historical adviser on *The Somme* (Channel 4, 2005). Brown guided the director Carl Hindmarch through the archive material he had used for *Battle of the Somme* in 1976, concentrating on the soldiers' letters and diaries that are stored at the Imperial War Museum. Hindmarch recalled that Brown insisted it was still important to hear the voices of men who died in the battle because the material is 'refreshing – it has none of the bitterness and cynicism of hindsight. It has irony, sarcasm, vulgarity, but not retrospective knowledge' (Sierz, 2005). The scenes involving a cast of actors and more than 100 extras were all filmed in Poland in July 2005 over a period of 3 weeks. *The Somme* was broadcast shortly after Remembrance Day. The two-and-a-half hour programme was watched by 2 million viewers – approximately 10 per cent of the available audience.

The most vociferous reviewer of *The Somme* was *The Times'* columnist A.A. Gill, who complained that the events of the summer of 1916 is 'a familiar and overworked story, mined and mulled over by hundreds of novelists, military historians and tooth-sucking, lachrymose commentators'. He did not like the fact that diaries and letters from soldiers were added to a voice over which paraphrased it, then 'an extra with a stuck-on moustache in a hole would mime it in case we didn't quite understand.' He thought that the 'mawkish music informed us of an appropriate emotional response' and that the result was 'both farcical and ghastly' (Gill, 2005, p.14), Gill would have found Brown's *Battle of the Somme* (1976) more palatable because the programme did not attempt to recreate any battle scenes. The re-enacted element was the principal complaint about the most controversial First World War documentary series *The Trench* (BBC, 2002), which Gill thought 'tragedy as vain farce' (Gill, 2002, p. 9).

Battle of the Somme shows us that images of landscape in British television documentaries about the First World War are instantly accessible to the audience because they refer back to pre-existing artistic representations of 1914–18. By presenting the emotional and physical ties of remembrance between the former Western Front and Britain's popular memory, programmes can engage with the disturbing nature of the conflict by rendering the war's colossal scale of destruction and loss within viewers' understanding.

A Note on Availability

Battle of the Somme (1916) is available on DVD at the Imperial War Museum, and the full DVD set of *The Great War* (BBC, 1964) is now widely available. Richard Holmes's *Western Front* (BBC, 1999) can also be purchased on VHS. The other programmes mentioned in this chapter are not currently available, but copies of some may be held at the British University's Film and Video Council or the British Film Institute.

Note

1. Gooseberries were thick balls of barbed wire five or six feet in diameter used to block trenches or fill gaps in wire entanglements. Toffee-apples were globular projectiles about a foot in diameter fired from the British trench mortar.

Filmography

Battle of the Somme (IWM Film, 1916).
The Battle of the Ancre and the Advance of the Tanks (IWM Film, 1917).
The Great War (BBC, 1964).
Battle of the Somme (BBC, 1976).
Peace in No Man's Land (BBC, 1984).

Gone for a Soldier (Scottish TV, 1985).
Very Exceptional Soldiers (BBC, 1986).
A Slow Walk Over No Man's Land (Channel 4/Ulster TV, 1986).
The Somme: 70 Years On Old Soldiers Remember (Central TV, 1986).
Voices of War (Channel 4, 1988).
A Time for Remembrance (Channel 4, 1989).
A Game of Ghosts (BBC, 1991).
The Somme 1916 (Tyne Tees TV, 1994).
War Walks (BBC, 1996).
Western Front (BBC, 1999).
The Trench (BBC, 2002).
The Somme(Channel 4, 2005).

Bibliography

Bet-El, I. (1999) *Conscripts: Lost Legions of the Great War* (Stroud: Sutton Publishing).
Connelly, M. (2002) 'The Great War, Part 13: The Devil Is Coming'. *Historical Journal of Film, Radio, and Television,* vol.22, no. 1, 21–8.
Cork, R. (1995) *A Bitter Truth: Avant-Garde Art and the Great War* (London: Newhaven).
Curtis, R. and Elton, B. (1999) *Blackadder: The Whole Damn Dynasty, 1485–1917* (London: Penguin).
Derez, M. (1997) 'A Belgian salient for reconstruction', in Peter Liddle (ed.), *Passchendaele in Perspective* (London: Leo Cooper).
Dyer, G. (1994) *The Missing of the Somme* (London: Penguin).
Farrer, R. (1918) *The Void of War: Letters from Three Fronts* (London: Constable & Co.).
Fussell, P. (1975) *The Great War and Modern Memory,* (Oxford: Oxford University Press).
Gliddon, G. (1996) *Legacy of the Somme 1916; The Battle in Fact, Film and Fiction* (Stroud: Sutton Publishing).
Howes, F. (1954) *The Music of Ralph Vaughan Williams* (Oxford: Oxford University Press).
Hynes, S. (1990) *A War Imagined* (London: Pimlico).
Jones, D. (1963) *In Parentheses* (London: Faber & Faber).
Lacey, N. (1998) *Image and Representation: Key Concepts in Media Studies* (London: Macmillan).
Lloyd, D. (1998) *Battlefield Tourism* (London: Berg).
Macdonald, L. (1978) *They Called It Passchendaele* (London: Penguin).
Masefield, J. (1918 [1972]) *The Old Front Line* (London: Spurbooks).
Mellers, W. (1989) *Vaughan Williams and the Vision of Albion* (London: Barrie & Jenkins).
Schama, S. (1995) *Landscape and Memory* (London: Fontana).
Sillars, S. (1987) *Art and Survival in First World War Britain* (London: Macmillan).
Webb, B. (1990) *Edmund Blunden: A Biography* (London: Newhaven).
Winter, J. and Prost, A. (2005) *The Great War in History: Debates and Controversies, 1914 to the Present* (Cambridge: Cambridge University Press).

Interviews

Malcolm Brown to author (by telephone), 9 August 2004.

Newspapers and Magazine Articles

Brown, M. *Daily Mail,* 29 June 1976, p. 18.
Brown, M. *BBC History Magazine,* March 2003, p. 42.
Gill, A.A. *The Sunday Times,* 17 March 2002, p. 9.
Gill, A.A. *The Sunday Times,* 'Culture', 20 November 2005, p. 14.
McKern, L. *The Radio Times,* 29 June 1976, p. 3.
Watkins, M. *The Times,* 27 June 1986, p. 14.

Reviews

Anonymous, *The Guardian,* 29 June 1976, p. 22.
Clayon, S. *Daily Telegraph,* 30 June 1976, p. 13.
Jackson, M. *Daily Mail,* 29 June 1976, p. 19.
Lennon, P. *The Sunday Times,* 4 July 1976, p. 36.
Smithies, S. *The Guardian,* 26 June 1986, p. 30.
Watkins, M. *The Times,* June 27 1986, p. 14.

Websites

Interview with Carl Hindmarch by Aleks Sierz as reproduced on Channel 4's 'Lost Generation' website: http://www.channel4.com/history/microsites/L/lostgeneration/somme/film1.html. (Accessed 28 February 2006.)

8
Mediated Collective Memory and the Political Process Towards Democracy in Spain

An Analysis of the Spanish TV Historical Documentary Series *La Transición*

Sira Hernández Corchete

Introduction

If we understand the concept of *collective memory* to be a social process for the construction and reconstruction of the past lived by a certain group, community or society in order to guarantee their cohesion and preserve their identity (Halbwachs, 1968), we must admit that today, reconstruction depends less than ever before on a specific collectivity, and more on the media that play an informative role in its use. Thus, not only do they mediate in the conveyance of the current reality, but they also have a decisive influence in forging a mythical past with which this collectivity may identify itself. This point has been made, for example, by Thompson (1995, p. 34), who admits that, even when 'oral tradition and face-to-face interaction continue to play important roles in shaping our sense of the past [...], they operate increasingly in conjunction with a process of understanding which draws its symbolic content from the products of the media industries'; or by Sampedro and Baer (2003, p. 94), who note that 'since media are display windows for the dissemination of information about the past and the typical socialization vehicles of current societies, they play an increasingly important role in the consolidation or destruction of collective memories, especially when generational memories decrease over time.' Hoskins (2001, p. 336) goes even further by talking about a 'new memory' to refer to this collective memory, which has been 'mediated' especially by television, and, in his opinion, has changed from being merely its electronic support to become also 'the medium of its *production*' [italics in original].

In spite of its restrictions, this mass-mediated reconstruction of memory has obtained, according to several studies (Zelizer, 1992; Schudson, 1993), a *de facto* popular legitimization. In the case of audiovisual media, it is due, according to Su Hi Choi (2005, p. 2), to the special privileges their professionals enjoy within society. This gives them access to visual archives dispersed worldwide, the technology needed for manipulating images and the control of the channels distributing interpretations of visual footage. As the same author concludes, 'mass media have legitimized the way in which they interpret the past with the aid of technological aesthetics and institutional power.'

In television, the narrative expression of collective memory has been reflected in diverse genres, formats and products. Among them, historical documentaries are among the main reference points for the general public, not only because of the credibility they still inspire, but also due to the responsibility assumed by documentary makers themselves. Simon Schama, the presenter of the series *A History of Britain* (BBC, 2000–2002) thus appealed to their responsibility in the opening session of the First World Congress of History Producers, held in Boston in 2001: like the persons who, after the fall of the Twin Towers, worked among the ruins in search of survivors, 'we [television documentary makers] too are duty bound to rescue from the smoking rubble of particular griefs and sorrows the shattered shape of our shared tradition.'

In current democratic and Europeanist Spain, the 'shared tradition' cited by Schama starts from a political process known as 'the Transition', which, after the death of General Francisco Franco in 1975, made it possible to move from dictatorship to democracy. Despite having been criticized during recent years, this process still remains, in the collective memory of the Spaniards, as an exemplary process. This positive, unforgettable event in collective memory has clearly been the result of two causes. First, a memory policy implemented by successive democratic governments to magnify the meaning and the historical relevance of the change of system, so as to make it a reason for national pride (Pérez Serrano, 2004, p. 111). Second, the socially aware role played by academic historiography in regard to the democratization process, above all, of 'media historiography' (Martínez Gallego, 2004, pp. 6–7), and, more specifically, of television historiography. If, as it has been publicly recognized, the Spanish press played a significant role in the advent of democracy during the Transition, then television strongly contributed, in subsequent years, to give it legitimacy, by means of the 'mythification' of the political process itself.[1]

The object of study of this chapter is one of the TV programmes that has most successfully contributed to this 'mythification': the historical documentary series *La Transición* [The Spanish Transition], directed by Elías Andrés and written and narrated by the journalist Victoria Prego. This series, opened on the Second Channel of Televisión Española (TVE2)[2] in 1995, the 20th anniversary of King Juan Carlos I's appointment as Chief of State, was the first audiovisual effort to rescue the most significant images of the attainment of democracy in Spain by giving them a unitary and global cohesion. It attracted, through its praise of the political reform process an average of 2 million viewers (*Anuario de la televisión* 1997, pp. 33, 148) – a record audience for this type of historical production in Spain.

The chapter begins by presenting the commonplaces which, according to two national surveys, comprise the current collective memory of the Spaniards in regard to the first stage of the above-mentioned political change process (1973–1977), and which systematically coincide with those that predominate in the historical reconstruction carried out by the series *La Transición*. The chapter also analyses two of the main strategies of documentary rhetoric – the voice over and the dramatization/customization of the history – through which Andrés and Prego bestowed interest and credibility upon the historical account and the corresponding argument. These strategies probably helped the series to 'remodel' viewers' memories with regard to the democratization process of Spain, and to its main actors.

Commonplaces of dominant collective memory about the Spanish transition at the beginning of the twenty-first century

In 1975, the death of General Franco – self-proclaimed Chief of the Spanish State after the Civil War (1936–1939) – put an end to 40 years of dictatorship and opened the door to one of the most significant periods of Spain's contemporary history: the political transition towards democracy. In just 2 years, through pacific means and without interfering with the legal system in force, the dictatorship's institutions were replaced by democratic ones, endorsed by all the political actors involved and subsequently legitimized by the Spaniards in the elections held in June 1977. The success of the reformist strategy to emerge from the dictatorship, reflected in numerous historical and journalistic accounts and fostered by the commemorations promoted by the political authorities and endorsed by the mass media, immediately settled in the collective memory of the Spaniards. Thus, the Spanish transition was raised to the category of 'myth' and became a reference point for other countries – both Latin American and Eastern European – also immersed in processes of political change.

However, by the end of the twentieth century, in some intellectual circles, voices of protest arose against the – until then – undisputed view of the Spanish transition to democracy. Specifically, those 'revisionist' authors denounced the Transition's roots in an 'oblivion deal', tacitly subscribed to by the most open politicians of Franco's regime, and by representatives of the democratic opposition in order to overcome a traumatic past and favour future coexistence. In their opinion, this pact imposed 'from above', without the participation of the Spaniards, had produced a kind of collective amnesia with regard to the national conflict and the subsequent repression by Franco's forces, which ultimately had produced a 'mediocre, low-quality democracy' in Spain (Colomer, 1998, p. 10), unworthy of a model transition (Navarro, 2002).

However, these views were neither welcomed by the public nor able to reconfigure the hegemonic collective memory of the Spaniards with regard to the exemplary character of 'their' transition. As will be seen below, the indisputable international reputation that said political process currently holds is equal to the one it has within Spain. In order to prove the truth of this assertion, and at the same time gather the main common places that characterize the prevailing memory – the dissemination of which in the series *La Transición* will be analysed in the following paragraphs – we appealed to the results of two national surveys performed in the years 2000 and 2006 about the collective memory of twenty-first-century Spaniards with regard to Franco's political regime and the political transition. The first survey was carried out by the Centro de Investigaciones Sociológicas (CIS) (Center of Sociological Research) with 2500 adults, in 2000, the year of the 25th anniversary of Franco's death, and of the succession of King Juan Carlos I de Borbón as Chief of the State.[3] The second survey coincided with the commemoration of the 70th anniversary of the start of the Spanish Civil War. Thirty years after the end of Franco's dictatorship, Spaniards were asked to give their views about the most significant aspects of Franco's regime. The survey was conducted by the company *Sigma Dos* for the newspaper *El Mundo del Siglo XXI* among 1000 citizens aged over 18.[4]

The first element in the collective memory of the Spaniards with regard to the political reform (which can be inferred from both surveys) is its exemplary character. According to the first survey, citizens almost unanimously approve the way in which democracy was attained in Spain. 'Up to 86 per cent of the citizens surveyed think that *the way in which the transition towards democracy was achieved is a source of pride for the Spaniards,* against 8 per cent who disagreed and 6 per cent who abstained from answering this question' (Moral, 2001, p. 20). These data confirm that the passing years have not undermined in any way the positive view that the Spaniards have in regard to the Transition. Since 1985, when the CIS started to 'measure' collective memory about the political reform process, the percentage of citizens who feel proud about it has never been less than 75 per cent, and the results for the year 2000 were the highest (Moral, 2001, pp. 20–1).

More specifically, and considering the results of the second survey in the year 2006, 68 per cent of the Spaniards surveyed approved of the fact that the replacement of Franco's regime by a liberal democracy had been made by means of a reform of Franco's regulations. Forty-one per cent of them thought that the reformist option had guaranteed a nonviolent transition, instead of the rupture, an option sponsored mainly by the Partido Comunista de España (PCE) (Communist Party of Spain) and the Partido Socialista Obrero Español (PSOE) (Spanish Socialist Workers Party), endorsed by 24.5 per cent of the citizens surveyed (*El Mundo del Siglo XXI*, 7 August 2006, p. 14). Moreover, in this same survey, 60.6 per cent of the Spaniards supported the decision that had been made in favour of the restoration of monarchy in the person of Prince Juan Carlos, at present King of Spain, as a solution to replace Franco's regime, instead of proclaiming the Third Republic, an option supported by a 24.4 per cent in 2006 (*El Mundo del Siglo XXI*, 8 August 2006, p. 10).

The second element of Spanish collective memory with regard to the Transition is the role assigned to Juan Carlos I and to Adolfo Suárez during the process of change. Leaving aside the political context, the Spaniards think that the role played by the King of Spain was the main factor for the success of the political transition. As a matter of fact, according to the first of the surveys, a large majority *agrees that without the presence of the King, the transition towards democracy would not have been possible*: almost three-quarters of the persons surveyed (72 per cent) agree on this, while a minority of 18 per cent disagrees' (Moral, 2001, p. 78). This majority opinion about the significant role played by Juan Carlos during the Spanish transition is also in agreement with the general trust of the Spaniards in the democratic feeling of the King. This was manifest in the Sigma Dos survey, according to which 72.6 per cent of those surveyed in 2006 thought that the King 'disagreed with pro-Franco values […] and that his consent to the succession proceedings established by Franco was a means to reform the political regime itself, and thus attain a democratic system' (*El Mundo del Siglo XXI*, 9 August 2006, p. 14).

Among the Spanish political leaders and parties that contributed in a greater or lesser degree to the restoration of democracy, the Spaniards surveyed in 2000 agreed that the most remarkable role was played by the executor of the change, President of Government Adolfo Suárez. He was granted 7.9 points (two decimal places lower than Juan Carlos I, on a scale of 1 to 10) for his contribution to the democratic transition. The leaders of the main democratic opposition parties were left far behind: Felipe González (PSOE) and Santiago Carrillo (PCE) obtained marks of 6.6 and 5.7, respectively, below the Spanish society (7.8), the workers' movement (7.3), the press (7.2), the students' movement and the intellectuals (6.9) (Moral, 2001, pp. 22–3).

Features and production and broadcasting context of the series *La Transición*

The production of *La Transición* had an initial budget of half a million euros, and was the result of the work of 6 years (1987–1993) by a small team, composed, apart from the above-mentioned Elías Andrés, its director, and Victoria Prego, scriptwriter and narrator, of the following seven professionals: the producer Itziar Aldasoro, editors José Luis San Martín and Carlos Bragado, and researchers Lola Santa Cruz, Susana Olmo, Pilar Moreno and Concha de Unamuno.

The series has all the features typical of a television historical documentary. Its 13 episodes of around 1 hour chronologically and panegyrically narrate, in a reliable, trustworthy way, by means of the traditional narrative resources of this genre – a voice over, archive footage and talking-head testimonies – the main events that occurred during the first stage of the transition from dictatorship to democracy in Spain. They cover the period from 20 December 1973, the date of the assassination of Admiral Carrero Blanco, and 22 July 1977, the day of the celebration of the first joint session of the Spanish Courts, born from the democratic elections held on 15 June of that same year.

The series was put on air under conditions very unfavourable to reaching the general public: in summer, from 23 July to 15 October 1995, on Sundays at 10:00 PM, on the minority Second Channel of Televisión Española. However, against all predictions, the average audience who watched *La Transición* during that first broadcast exceeded 2 million viewers, a number that, after the liberalization of the television market in Spain at the beginning of the 1980s, had only been reached by one other history documentary, *Los años vividos* [The Years Lived] (1992). However, the latter aired at primetime through the First Channel of TVE.[5]

The excellent reception that the Spaniards gave to the series – also supported by favourable reviews it received both from Spanish historians and journalists and by the sales of this series to the main foreign television channels and many European and Latin-American universities – implied an actual popular legitimization of the historical reconstruction made by *La Transición* about the way to recover democracy in Spain. This legitimization can be explained on the following grounds. The series met for the first time – in front of Spanish society – the need which, according to certain studies (Pennebaker and Basanick, 1998, pp. 31–47), all groups and societies have of looking backwards – also from a filmic point of view – across 20- or 30-year cycles. But, above all, at a time when Spanish society was puzzled, discouraged and disoriented due to the corruption cases accrued by the socialist government under which democracy had become established (1982–1996), it offered a mythical, commemorative narration, which viewers could ponder, find themselves within and then share with others. As Josetxo Cerdán (2002, p. 2) said:

In view of the success of the product, we can infer that when this series arrives on the screens, almost at the end of the last socialist mandate, already it can be said that a desire exists to celebrate the Transition. It is possible to conclude, therefore, that Spaniards have a desire to see themselves on TV in this historical moment which they have carried out and already given up as closed. The idea of having lived and having carried out a unique event has consolidated society: it is time to begin to address that moment with suitable images and for that nothing is better than television.

This corroborates the assertion that '*TV producers and audiences are similarly preoccupied with creating a "useable past," a longstanding tenet of popular history, where stories involving historical figures and events are used to clarify the present and discover the future*' (Edgerton, 2001, p. 4).

Analysis of the series *La Transición*

Since *La Transición* belongs to the documentary genre, together with a historical account on the events that made it possible to move from an autocratic to a democratic system in Spain, an argument was provided about the historical world represented. As Nichols (1991, p. 29) points out, 'we process the documentary not only as a series of highly authentic sounds and images that bear the palpable trace of how people act in the historical world, but also as the serial steps in the formation of a distinct, textually specific way of seeing or thinking.'

This argument, the basic elements of which coincide with the main elements typical of the current collective memory of the Spaniards about the Transition – praise of the exemplary, peaceful mode in which democratization was carried out in Spain and of those who made it possible – effectively reached the viewers of Elías Andrés and Victoria Prego's series, and contributed to feed this memory through a set of rhetorical strategies inherent to the documentary genre itself.

In the following discussion, two of the most important elements are analysed: (i) the presence of a predominant, authoritative voice over, whose comments are supported and legitimatized by the testimonies of eyewitnesses to the events included in the programme, and (ii) the dramatic structure that the story adopts so as to keep the attention and interest of the audience, the consequence of which is the customization of history.

Voice-over narration: the voice of history

One of the main elements that form documentary rhetoric is, undoubtedly, the voice over, that is, 'oral statements [...] spoken by an unseen speaker situated in a space and time other than that simultaneously being presented by the images on the screen' (Kozloff, 1988, p. 5). This is not only because, as Nichols (1991, p. 21) points out, the underlying arguments of documentaries 'require a logic that words are able to bear far more easily than images', but also, and above all, due to the trust inspired in the audience by this voice that, due to its invisibility, omniscience, and the generalized use of a self-confident, cold, neutral or distant tone, has been called the 'voice of God', or rather, in this case, the 'voice of history'.

On the one hand, the mere perceptible presence of a narrator generates in the audience of classic documentaries an expectation of reality, since it moves the genre away from the speech codes prevailing in fiction movies. Because these are more 'mimetic' than 'diegetic', the characters usually interpret the story in front of the viewers, thus avoiding the explicit mediation of a narrator. On the other side, in these documentaries, the public sees the voice over as trustworthy, because their words can be verified by the images and the testimonies – if any – of the talking heads, that is, of the protagonists and witnesses of the events told, or of the experts in the subject matter considered. These other voices, which are also strategically used with the rhetorical purpose of lessening the authoritative, powerful image of said omniscient voice, do not deprive it, however, from authority at all, since they often get subordinated to it and are only used to support or justify the argument. 'The voices of others […] retain little responsibility for making the argument, but are used to support it or provide evidence or substantiation for what the commentary [voice over] addresses' (Nichols, 1991, p. 37).

If we look at *La Transición*, we can see that the arguments about the exemplary, model character of the political change process in Spain, which, as we have stressed, preside over the series, are transmitted to the viewers mainly by means of a voice over. The narrator's omniscient knowledge inspires confidence, while historical records and the testimonies of the talking heads add credibility to his statements. His omniscience is revealed to the audience through his mastery of time and space – which enables him to narrate actions that take place simultaneously in different scenarios and anticipate events that will happen later on – and through his access to the inner world of the historical characters. However, despite featuring this omniscient character, the narrator leaves in the hands of the characters the personal narration of the events they witnessed or took a direct part in. He thus enhances his own credibility and the credibility of the series itself. As Sergio Alegre (2000, p. 170) points out, the testimonies 'reinforce the idea that what is being told is what really happened. "How couldn't it be true if the person speaking was actually there and lived that moment?" we cannot avoid wondering.'

Featuring such qualities as omniscience, truthfulness and credibility, the voice over of *La Transición* appears before the audience as 'the voice of history', thus playing the role of a trustworthy spokesman for the argument about the exemplary character of the democratization process in Spain. This argument includes, in the first place, praise of the choice of a reformist strategy, instead of the option of a democratic rupture, since the former was able to bestow a peaceful character to the Transition. As we have noted, the social view that it was a model process is based precisely on this idea. This is what can be inferred from a comment made by the voice over in the seventh episode, which hints at the starring role of King Juan Carlos I as the engine of political change:

> Two options for the future of Spain lie before the King: a total rupture with the laws and institutions of the regime, in order to build a new political system starting from scratch, and a legal though deep reform of Franco's

regime until a democratic system still not well defined is reached. There are still no really dependable opinion polls, but the King's political intuition tells him that Spanish society is expectant and ready for a change, but that it does not want to be exposed to frights or adventures, that it wants to achieve democracy without compromising stability. And thus the King started the reform operation.

Later, the narrator of the series omits other likely alternatives or projects raised during the Spanish political transition, and, invoking reasons of stability, insists on the convenience of the reformist option, through statements such as the following:

Suárez needs to convince the opposition about the sincere democratic willingness of his project for change, and persuade Franco's followers that change is unavoidable, and that his project is the only one able to ensure moderation and peace (tenth episode), and

Since the Government's reformist project is not just a fantasy, but a realizable project, and above all, the only feasible one, the managers of the Communist Party have heard in Guadalajara, from the lips of his Secretary General [Santiago Carrillo], that the party's intention is to get on the train of reform, not to overthrow the system (eleventh episode).

Both statements show that the control – and therefore, the success – of the democratization process can be credited to the government of Adolfo Suárez, and that the members of the democratic opposition (in this case, Santiago Carrillo and its party, the Communist Party of Spain) were secondary actors in the so-called 'agreed upon reform'. This idea is present in the collective memory of Spaniards, as seen in the results of the above-mentioned surveys.

The second important idea on which the voice over of *La Transición* rests to support the exemplary character of the political process is the careful planning and absolute accuracy with which the promoters of the change carried it out. Thus, it shows that some key decisions of this historical period were made after careful consideration. Such was the case of the appointments of Torcuato Fernández-Miranda as President of the Courts and the Council of the Kingdom and of Adolfo Suárez as Head of the Government, on whom the King would rest 'to perform a delicate operation: intending to move from an authoritative regime to a democracy without violent confrontations or legal ruptures' (seventh episode) or the preparation of Franco's procurators to approve the Law of Political Reform that would enable the country to reach democracy without breaking the legal system in force. In regard to the planning for this poll, the voice-over sounds categorical:

> The reform operation has been carefully planned by the Government, by the President of the Courts and by the King, and then accurately executed [...]. The Government, under the direction of the King, has crossed the Rubicon. The way to democracy is now open. Franco's courts have authorized the political reform, and Franco's regime has begun to be a thing of the past (eleventh episode).

The fact that, as in the last example given, the decisions carefully considered by the partisans of the reform finally materialized in actions helped to conceal the mistakes they surely made, and gave them an image of historical responsibility and exemplary character, which spread to the transition process itself.

Dramatic structure and customization of the history

The second strategy of the documentary rhetoric in which *La Transición* took part to disseminate its laudatory message of the political change process to the audience is the dramatic structuring of the account, that is, the arrangement of the story in the opening, development and closing stages of the conflict. This structuring intends, firstly, to awaken and keep the attention of viewers, because the spectators of historical documentaries shown on television are not 'a captive audience' (Kuehl, 1976, p. 180), and 'historical events rarely occur with the kind of shape, order and intensity that will keep an audience in its seats' (Rosenstone, 1995, p. 125). However, dramatization of the history implies the use of certain narrative skills that, as well as keeping viewers in front of the screen, promote a discussion on the past, which is the object of the producer. The following lines make reference to the use that Elías Andrés and Victoria Prego made of one of these skills: the customization of history. This allows us to categorize this series within the documentaries that Rosenstone himself rated as 'history as homage', in which the end is 'not analysis or theory [...], but the evocation of emotion, the etching of individual character, the magic ability of verbal and visual memory to bring an earlier world and earlier selves into the present, where they can be experienced, shared and even admired' (1995, p. 117).

In the case of the series *La Transición*, the voice over organizes his account around a fundamental conflict: the political battle for 'the conquest of democracy' (first episode) in which, within Franco's regime, partisans of openness and change fight against the conservative, who are in favour of continuity and want to avoid democracy at all costs. Out of the system, the players are the same men who – coming from the regime – promote openness, and the main members of the democratic opposition. In the latter case, both bands pursue the same objective: attaining democracy, though they disagree in the methods they proclaim to achieve this goal. While the former want a political reform, respecting the legal system in force, the latter would like democracy to be implemented in the country on the basis of a full rupture with Franco's laws.

The term 'conquest' used by the voice over to refer to the persecution and the achievement of democracy during the Spanish political transition implies that the democratic system is good in itself and a future asset – as opposed to Franco's regime, identified with the past. The voice tacitly associates other values with the achievement of democracy, such as monarchy – which is featured, not only as the best political solution after the dictatorship, better than the Republic, but as the only way – and the reconciliation of the two Spains that fought in the Civil War. Therefore, the narrator assigns to those who fought for implementing this democratic system in Spain the role of protagonists in the historical account, by commenting on their character and actions, whereas those who threatened and hindered the political change are featured as opponents.

These opposing roles are played – so as to enable a better identification of viewers with the values and countervalues proposed in the series – by several individual and collective characters. Some of the opponents are: the contradictory Carlos Arias Navarro, the last president of the Government appointed by Franco, who, after Franco's death, is in favour of the continuity of the Franco system without Franco; the so-called 'bunker', composed of the most intransigent Franco partisans, and the terrorism implemented by ETA and ultra-rightist movements, about which the voice over says in the second episode: 'this will be the largest and most tragic threat for the Spanish democracy, which is still just a silent purpose of the majority'. Among the protagonists it is worth mentioning Torcuato Fernández-Miranda, the creator of the legal texts that made possible a transition with no ruptures; the main leaders of the opposition, Felipe González (PSOE) and Santiago Carrillo (PCE) who, according to the voice over, impelled from their positions a consensual reform; the democratic press, which instructed public opinion in favour of political liberties; Spanish society, an expectant witness and extraordinary player in some events where its active participation was vital; and, above all, those who, according to the last national surveys, are considered by the collective memory of the Spaniards to be the real heroes of the political transition: King Juan Carlos I de Borbón, and the President of the Government appointed by him to undertake the political reform process, Adolfo Suárez.

The narrator builds a positive image of Juan Carlos I even before he is proclaimed King, by alluding to his attitudes including his disagreement with Franco's regime while he was a Prince. This, in addition to making him likeable for the viewers, showed that Juan Carlos I had certain qualities that would be very useful to lead Spain to democracy: cultural background, initiative, prudence, discretion, gentlemanliness, spirit of service to his country, courage and political intuition. Later, on the basis of this profile of the Prince, the narrator starts to outline the role assigned to him after his coronation: an engine of political change. This role becomes evident not only through the narration of several of his initiatives, but also by means of explicit statements, such as in the ninth episode, as a result of the official journey to Washington of the Spanish monarchs in 1976, which, according to the voice over 'is fully successful, and consolidates the image of Juan Carlos both inside and outside Spain as the indisputable leader of the process towards democracy'.

In regard to Adolfo Suárez, described as the political executor of the transition process in Spain, the omniscient, reliable narrator underlines his boldness and capacity to undertake risks, his open spirit, and his negotiation and strategy skills. Some of these qualities are shown, for example, in the account of successive encounters with members of the democratic opposition, among which the voice over refers to the meeting of Suárez with Santiago Carrillo to consider the legalization of the Communist Party of Spain before the elections scheduled for 15 June 1977:

> 27 February is a Sunday. Early in the afternoon, Adolfo Suárez is to attend a secret, risky meeting. The President of the Government has agreed to meet face to face, and for the first time, with the Secretary General of the Communist Party. Suárez is aware that the time is coming when he must make a historical decision, with unforeseeable consequences. A bold step that, if taken, could by itself doom to failure the process of reform initiated, or, to the contrary, seal a final victory in the effort to achieve democracy (thirteenth episode).

Conclusion

The creation and maintenance of collective memory within a society is a dynamic process, in which the mass media play an increasingly significant role. Historical documentaries produced for television have special importance for the reconfiguration of the past starting from the present. Their popular retrospective accounts, vested with credibility and persuasive efficacy, conveyed by means of a set of rhetorical strategies inherent to the documentary genre itself, become the 'voice of history' and are welcome and legitimized by most viewers.

In Spain, collective memory of the political process which, after the death of Franco in 1975, enabled the country to move from an authoritative regime to a democratic system still holds to the idea that the process, in which the current, democratic, Europeanist Spain is rooted, developed in an exemplary way, and that it was possible thanks to the courage, intuition and good deeds of two men in particular: Juan Carlos I, the present King of Spain, and Adolfo Suárez, first president of the recent Spanish democracy. This memory has remained alive not only due to the memory policy implemented by the successive governments as a reminder of the foundational milestone of the current Spain – the political transition – and as an attempt to build the future of the nation on this basis, but also, and above all, to the role played by the media. With commemorative products such as the historical documentaries series *La Transición,* debuted by Televisión Española on the 20th anniversary of the appointment of King Juan Carlos I as Chief of the State (1995), and broadcast for the last time on the 30th anniversary of the first democratic elections after the Spanish Civil War (2007), they have fed the collective memory and reinforced a positive vision of the political reform process in Spain and of those who made it possible, which is still predominant in the minds of Spanish citizens.

A note on availability

La Transición is available on DVD (remastered version), released by Radio Televisión Española (Spanish Radio and Television Corporation).

Notes

1. In the years immediately following the political transition process in Spain (1980s), Televisión Española produced and broadcasted a large number of historical documentaries that considered the main events of Spanish contemporary history, among which the Civil War was assigned great importance. Through these series, this public TV channel wanted to teach a history lesson to the Spaniards, by disclosing the fact that historical conflicts had been overcome during the political change process and thus legitimized the recently recovered democracy (Hernández Corchete, 2007, pp. 569–79).
2. Television Española (TVE) is the national state-owned public-service television broadcaster in Spain. The First Channel (TVE1, also known as 'La 1') started broadcasting on 28 October 1956, and a second channel (TVE2, or 'La 2') followed on 15 November 1966. Until the 1980s, they were the only two networks in the country. The monopoly of Televisión Española was partially broken with the appearance of the first regional public channels at the beginning of the 1980s, and totally broken by the introduction of the first three private networks: Antena 3 and Telecinco (free channels) and Canal+ (pay channel), at the end of the 1980s. Since then and, above all, after the introduction of DTT (digital terrestrial television) in Spain (completed in April 2010), the number of channels has not stopped increasing. However, this audiovisual map may change in the future due to the existence of several merger agreements (or negotiations) between competitors that have arisen as a result of the passing of the Law 7/2009, July 3rd 2009, on urgent measures in telecommunications.

   In 2009, the most important national Spanish networks, publishing group and main shareholder (in parentheses) were as follows: TVE1, La2, Teledeporte, 24 Horas and Clan TV (Spanish Radio and Television Corporation); Antena 3, Neox 8 and Nova 9 (Antena 3 Group/Planeta); Telecinco, La 7, FDF and Cincoshop (Gestevisión Telecinco /Mediaset); Cuatro, CNN+, 40 Latino and Promo (Sogecable/Prisa); La Sexta and Gol TV (GIA La Sexta/Mediapro); Intereconomía TV and Disney Channel (Net TV/Vocento) and Veo TV 7, Sony Entertainment TV/AXN and Tienda en Veo (Veo TV/Unidad Editorial).

3. The results of this survey were published in Moral (2001).
4. From 18 July to 26 August 2006, the newspaper *El Mundo del Siglo XXI* published the results of this survey in a segment of the section *Spain* called 'El franquismo a debate 30 años después'.
5. This number of viewers has only been surpassed by that obtained by *Memoria de España* [Spanish Memory], a series broadcast in 2004 and 2005, also prime time on TVE1, which achieved an average of 3 million viewers (Hernández Corchete, 2008, pp. 159–61).

Bibliography

Alegre, S. (2000) '*La Transición española*, un documental histórico', *Film-Historia*, 10.3, 169–94.

Anuario de la televisión 1997 (Madrid: GECA).

Cerdán, J. (2002) 'Dos o tres conclusiones, desde el presente, sobre el binomio Televisión/Transición', *Área Abierta*, 3 July. http://revistas.ucm.es/inf/15788393/articulos/ARAB0202230007A.PDF. Accessed 9 September 2002.

Choi, S.H. (2005) 'History, Collective Memory, and TV Documentary: Analysis of *Battle for Korea* (PBS, 2001)', paper presented at the annual meeting of the International Communication Association, Sheraton, New York, NY.

Colomer, J.M. (1998) *La transición a la democracia: el modelo español* (Barcelona: Anagrama).

Edgerton, G.R. (2001) 'Television as historian: a different kind of history altogether', in G.R. Edgerton and P.C. Rollins (eds), *Television Histories: Shaping Collective Memory in the Media Age* (Lexington: University Press of Kentucky).

'El franquismo a debate 30 años después' (2006), *El Mundo del Siglo XXI*, 18 July–26 August.

Halbwachs, M. (1968) *La mémoire collective* (Paris: Presses Universitaires de France).

Hernández Corchete, S. (2007) 'La voluntad democratizadora de las series documentales históricas producidas por TVE en los ochenta', in E. Moreno et al. (eds), *Los desafíos de la televisión pública en Europa* (Pamplona: Eunsa).

Hernández Corchete, S. (2008) *La historia contada en televisión: El documental televisivo de divulgación histórica en España* (Barcelona: Gedisa).

Hoskins, A. (2001) 'New memory: mediating history', *Historical Journal of Film, Radio and Television*, 21.4, 333–46.

Kozloff, S. (1988) *Invisible Storytellers: Voice-Over Narration in American Fiction Film* (Berkeley: University of California Press).

Kuehl, J. (1976), 'History on the public screen II', in P. Smith (ed.). *The Historian and Film* (Cambridge: Cambridge University Press).

Martínez- Gallego, F.A. (2004), 'Memoria social e "historiografía mediática" de la Transición', Actas del VII Congreso de la Asociación de Historiadores de la Comunicación '25 años de libertad de expresión', Universidad Pompeu Fabra, Barcelona, 18–19 November.

Moral, F. (2001) *Veinticinco años después: La memoria del franquismo y de la transición a la democracia en los españoles del 2000* (Madrid: Centro de Investigaciones Sociológicas).

Navarro, V. (2002) *Bienestar insuficiente, democracia incompleta* (Barcelona: Anagrama).

Nichols, B. (1991) *Representing Reality. Issues and Concepts in Documentary* (Bloomington: Indiana University Press).

Pennebaker, J.W. and B. Basanick (1998) 'Creación y mantenimiento de las memorias colectivas', in D. Páez et al. (eds), *Memorias colectivas de procesos culturales y políticos* (Bilbao: Servicio Editorial de la Universidad del País Vasco).

Pérez Serrano, J. (2004) 'Experiencia histórica y construcción social de las memorias: La transición española a la democracia', *Pasado y Memoria: Revista de Historia Contemporánea*, 3, 93–122.

Rosenstone, R.A. (1995) *Visions of the Past: The Challenge of Film to Our Idea of History* (Cambridge, MA: Harvard University Press).

Sampedro, V. and A. Baer (2003), 'El recuerdo como olvido y el pasado extranjero: Padres e hijos ante la memoria histórica mediatizada', *Revista de Estudios de Juventud*, special edition, 93–108.

Schudson, M. (1993) *Watergate in American Memory: How to Remember, Forget and Reconstruct the Past* (New York: Basic Books).

Thompson, J.B. (1995), *The Media and Modernity: A Social Theory of the Media* (Palo Alto, CA: Stanford University Press).

Zelizer, B. (1992) *Covering the Body: The Kennedy Assassination, the Media, and the Shaping of Collective Memory* (Chicago: University of Chicago Press).

Part III

Televised History, Memory and Identity

9
Television Fiction: A Domain of Memory
Retelling the Past on Dutch Television

Sonja de Leeuw

Introduction

The most remarkable Dutch television event in 2001 was the top-listed production *Wilhelmina*, on the present queen's grandmother. A conventional historical drama series in four parts, it traces the story of the queen's life until her abdication in 1948. The series focuses especially on her role during the Second World War, reflecting the ongoing public debate on the question whether her decision to leave the country (for England) was well chosen. Its number-one ranking can be explained by the way this series brings together the two main points of reference in Dutch national history: the relationship between the state and the monarchy, and the Second World War. This series demonstrated how Wilhelmina wanted to stay to help her people, but could not due to the circumstances. Moreover, the series showed how tough her struggle was against the male politicians around her and how she demanded the utmost of her self to really become the motherly symbol of her country in the times of occupation. The popularity of the series can also be found in the way it celebrates the nation's unity in post-modern times. It stresses the importance of historical drama in telling and retelling the stories of the recent past, from different points of view, including its controversies and its changes.

Although the present generation does not have any personal experience with the Second World War, it does have memories of it. These are continuously constructed through the transmission of stories in multiple forms. This chapter discusses how Dutch historical television fiction mediates in this ongoing process by using memory both as a dramatic device and as an act of history making. We will not address the relationship between historiography and audiovisual representations of history as debated by Rosenstone (1995), Sobchack (1996) and many others; rather we are interested in the construction of collective (popular) memory through narratives of the past in the context of globalization.

We will focus on drama about the Second World War, a topic that by definition has a strong national connotation, at the same time containing dominant myths about how the nation sees itself and wants to be conceived. Nonetheless, especially fiction about the Second World War can take a different strategy. It is generally assumed that popular media need to draw on the stories and images of shared memories to connect to the knowledge and interests of the audience. According to Morris-Suzuki (2005, p. 18) media forms and memories do shape each other in the context of an evolving popular media culture. That is not to say that this is only to confirm existing practices of remembering the past. By recreating history, television fiction can potentially open up the past and extend the archive of collective memory, revealing a plurality of stories. With the help of examples from Dutch television fiction in the 1990s, we will show how historical television fiction is able to act against the dominant myths, so as to offer a diversified notion of history, as well as becoming a growing domain of contemporary memories.

Multiple memories

Historical film and television productions may be considered the liveliest artefacts witnessing the existence of a past. It is therefore relevant to discuss the stories that are being told about the past as these reveal what we are expected to remember, collectively. We are indebted to Maurice Halbwachs' theory about the construction of memories. He points to the fact that people do indeed remember things they did not experience themselves. Halbwachs (1877–1945) calls this 'borrowed memory', which builds up by reading about historical events, listening to witnesses. Although Halbwachs wrote his theory on collective memory long before the emergence of film and, notably, television as dominant forms of popular culture, his writings on the construction of memory highly apply in the media age. According to Halbwachs (1991, p. 7) memory is always collective. This is true for both personal and historical memory. Personal memory is autobiographical and consists of memories of events we have experienced ourselves. Historical memory consists of stories, performances, data, formulae, pictures, books and descriptions we have heard or read (Halbwachs, 1991, p. 17) and – as we should add – seen by watching movies and television productions. Personal and historical memories are connected in that historical memory provides a schema, which is open to take in personal memories. Memory to a great extent can therefore be considered a reconstruction of the past based upon information derived from the present; the perception of information in turn is informed by earlier reconstructions and memories (Halbwachs, 1991, p. 24).

What is important here is the understanding of memory as a dynamic process, which moves between, and incorporates, both personal and historical remembrance. No matter how much personal memory and historical memory are connected, Halbwachs made a distinction between memories as a collective experience and history *pur sang*. Collective memory is continuous, a flow, while history as a succession of periods tends to also emphasize ruptures and discontinuity (Halbwachs, 1991, pp. 31–2).

In the media age collective memories are increasingly stored in media, which provide endless databases and sources from which we manufacture both history and memory (Hoskins, 2001). Remembering has become a process that is now increasingly 'media-afflicted', as Hoskins puts it, and in this affliction television is the primary medium of memory (Hoskins, 2004, p. 110). Television is capable of making history in real time, as it has the possibility of transforming 'original' images, recorded images into a visual commemorative sign (Hoskins, 2001, p. 338). Hoskins mentions examples such as the attack on the Twin Towers (Hoskins, 2004), but we would suggest also including 'fiction', as fiction enables viewers to experience, for example, the history of the Second World War over and over again, identifying with different characters that offer different perspectives on the events. The medium manufactures 'new memory', which is at the same time the instantaneous moment of historical occurrence and the way it is represented (Hoskins, 2001, pp. 343–4). To put it differently, media, and television in particular, have literally become a mediator of memory.

Memory and the notion of the national and the global

What then are we supposed to remember and how are we supposed to make that memory useful in our own lives? Historical film and television productions may not have replaced historical memory completely, yet they do contribute to the construction of memory in that they have taken over the function of preservation and remembrance. This is even more true in the digital age, where film and broadcasting archives are providing access to their collections to a larger audience, and new channels such as You Tube on the Internet also present historical images. Halbwachs' notion of history has become obsolete as film and television enable a creative use of history, transforming it into a popular cultural memory, which is collective in the sense that it is shared by 'viewers' as much as it is dynamic in that it challenges historical discourse (Anderson, 1991, pp. 19–20).

The most popular 'memory banks' are indeed televised and filmed histories, and eventually they create *lieux de mémoire* – physical places and spaces that can be visited and revisited (Nora, 1989). In representing the past, they conceptualize notions of the nation and construct collective memories and identities (Morley and Robins, 1995, p. 91). Like other sites of memory, television fiction productions are bridges between past and present; they help to construct the collective identity of a nation. To put it differently, they help to constitute myths that serve the construction of the identity of communities in the present (Strath, 2000, p. 19). These are 'imagined communities', a term coined by Benedict Anderson (1983) to underscore the fact that national identities exist in representations. Communities are held together by stories, and by images and symbols that represent shared meanings about the past.

Within the post-colonial and plural society the concept of national identity has become problematic and has also generated new demands for representations across national cultures. The problems that nations face are best expressed in terms of the time–space separation discussed by Giddens (1991, pp. 16–17). Giddens sees the separation of time and place as typical of modern societies that are characterized by migration and communication flows, in which place no longer mediates between 'when' and 'where'. Rather, place becomes something that is not exclusively geographical, but something to be created, a cultural space where identities are being formed and (re)defined. One of the dynamics he observes is the global creation of a standardized past. Kaes (1989) has argued how much the past has become a collection of recycled images and stories that replace not only historical experience but also historical imagination. That is not to say that the distinction between professional and popular history is a valid one. Popular media such as film and television contribute to our experience of the past in their own right. Thus they are engaging people in using the past to find their identities in the present global post-modern world.

Processes of globalization and Europeanization at the same time have reinforced the rethinking of the national in cultural terms. These processes necessarily seem to require a discussion and repositioning of the nation by focusing on its roots, its continuities and the inevitable changes in its history. This is where popular media culture finds its content. According to Morley and Robins (1995, p. 87), there is a desire to be 'at home' in the new and disorienting global space. European discussions on the relationship between European and national cultural identity as well agreements on co-operation between European media production companies cannot conceal a tendency in many European countries to return to the confines of single national cultural traditions. Facing European unification, national identity became a relevant issue in many European countries, reflecting feelings of fear for the unknown 'other', meaning both the new countries entering the European Union and the EU as an entity in itself.

No matter how much the notion of nation is contested and no matter how much national identities are – at least theoretically – being replaced by multiple identities within the new European and global media culture, what we see are attempts to construct narratives of the nation that represent shared meanings about nationhood. These narratives emphasize the traditions and continuity of a nation, which is challenged by the circulation of global cultural discourse (Barker, 1997, pp. 190–2). The retelling of a nation's past remained an especially important cultural strategy in constructing (new) collective identities, new *lieux de mémoire* offering stories that are able to make or remake history and to construct notions of 'home' in particular (Morley and Robins, 1995, p. 91).

This ties in well with the fact that, despite globalization, most television production is produced for a national audience, created by the national culture in the national language. From a European perspective it is acknowledged that viewers in European countries demand programmes that enable them to connect with their own cultural experiences and social reality (McQuail, 1996). At an economic level, however, European audiovisual policy is very much oriented towards the creation of a European communication space, to strengthen European audiovisual markets. That is to say that the European media culture at the same time is global (in terms of an international market) and local (in terms of the deeper content). In the context of this chapter, the latter is most interesting because content reflects the attempt to construct and reconstruct a national identity within a changing European and global media culture.

Identity is firmly rooted in history (either that of an individual, a community or group) and poses the question of how history relates to what we want to be and become. Morley and Robins (1995, pp. 85–8) argue how much history and geography have been connected in Europe and how much this connection has informed notions of identity. Because identity contains contradictory values it discusses the relationship between our collective needs as human beings and our individual needs as members of a specific community. In answering this question, stories – narratives – play an important role.

Televised storytelling in the Netherlands

Historical television drama is considered an ideological liaison between past and present, roughly allowing for two representational strategies: (i) the reproduction of an empirical notion of history and (ii) the challenging of historical reconstruction (Tulloch, 1990, pp. 96–8). Anderson (2001, p. 30) discusses how particular television series that proliferate 'counter-narratives' deal with historical representation in an experimental way, thus demonstrating that 'history is open to interpretation and modification.'

The function of television fiction in retelling our own history is then to reflect not only the actual social debates on how to conceive and remember national history, but also to help us to give meaning to an increasingly complex society. It is accordingly important to discuss to what extent historical television fiction about the Second World War (by definition a national topic) has reproduced or undermined dominant myths about national history. Has television drama in the Netherlands been working to reconstruct dominant nationalistic myths or did it produce 'counter-narratives' and if so, what were the ideological biases?

Our analysis involves televised historical representations, which by definition mean public broadcasting service exclusively, as in many other European countries. Because historical fiction is the most expensive programme category, broadcasters are forced to invest, which they do either for cultural or for commercial reasons. Revenues from advertising do not, however, compensate the high costs of historical fiction; nor does income from license fees and state money. For commercial channels this is the end of the road, while public channels can apply for money at the Dutch Cultural Broadcasting Promotion Fund, founded in 1988 and financed out of advertising revenue interest with the objective of encouraging quality production in public broadcasting cultural programming. Before 1988, historical drama was also present on Dutch television, which at that time had not yet seen the arrival of commercial channels; these appeared in 1989.

In the 1970s, public broadcasting companies started developing classical series, set in the past, in the city and countryside alike, projecting present-day values and standards onto an historical mirror. These series did not as yet dramatize war experiences. They were very popular among audiences, not only from a nostalgic point of view, but also because these epic series stressed aspects of Dutch history and culture as collective experience, focussing on individual struggles against the rules of a time. These prestigious series also appealed to supposed experiences, values and standards of the traditional target group of the broadcasting company involved. I am referring here to the history of public broadcasting in the Netherlands, which goes back to the 1920s (with radio) when important religious and social currents in the Netherlands (neutral, Catholic, socialist, Protestant) took the initiative of founding broadcasting companies. Dutch society in those days was marked by the concept of *pillarization*, a way of realizing pluriformity. Pillarization is an invented phrase, referring to a segmentation of society into different social and religious currents that were called 'pillars'. The segmentation of public spheres along the lines of social and religious beliefs that pillarization allowed for, was dominant in the Netherlands since the end of the nineteenth century. Schools, political parties, sport clubs, newspapers and universities, were all 'pillarized' institutions, and pillarization was eventually extended to broadcasting. All of the early founded broadcasting companies still exist; they are no longer exclusively bound up with specific pillars in society, though. Yet they are still obliged to represent certain religious, cultural, spiritual and social currents in their programmes. Here the legacy of pillarization is still visible, albeit somewhat blurred. Broadcasting companies adapted their beliefs to social and cultural changes that took place over the course of years. In the Netherlands several broadcasting companies are sharing a channel now, and since 1995 companies operating on one channel are forced to cooperate. As a consequence, more then in the past, the audience will be challenged to identify with a whole channel instead of with each of the companies itself. Still, the original identity of broadcasting companies is informing programming content, and this has proven valid for historical fiction in particular.

Considering the experiences of the Dutch people during the Second World War, the Netherlands being an occupied country, with the largest percentage of Jews of all Western European nations killed in German camps, it is not surprising to see the Second World War dramatized on Dutch television. Until the end of the 1980s, historical drama dealing with the Second World War was closely connected to the contemporary public moral debate about how the Dutch behaved during the war in terms of right and wrong.

Nearly all historical fiction on the Second World War was single memorial drama, a form of what Ebbrecht and others have called 'historical event television' (Ebbrecht, 2007, p. 36), broadcast in the first week of May, the high season of commemorative ceremonies that take place everywhere in the country. These ceremonies are broadcast live on television, and the memorial drama productions that were screened in the same season did frame these transmissions in their own right. Moreover, most of these were broadcast by the nonpillarized broadcasting foundation responsible for such programming as the daily news, sports and cultural topics that are not addressed by the pillarized broadcasting companies. Evidently, the dramatized commemoration was used as a means of confirming the concept of nationality, of the nation as one cohesive unit. As such, historical drama on the Second World War positioned itself among other memorial events, thus becoming part of 'contemporary memory culture' (Ebbrecht, 2007, p. 37). Basically it supported an institutional view of the Second World War and the creation of an historical memory about it.

In the last decade of the past century, however, some changes started to be observed: drama on the Second World War came in the form of series produced by the pillarized broadcasting companies and revealed changes in how they presented wartime behaviour as well as discussed incidents and aspects that had been hidden from the public to that point. Also striking is that the series addressed the Second World War not as the central event, rather as a part of a chain of events, thus reflecting a view of history as a continuum, which became noticeable in innovative storytelling. To underline this development we will discuss three drama series, each of which stands out for the way it deals with memory and history as well as for its representational strategy.

Historicizing the Second World War: *In Retrospect*

The production of epic series in the 1990s emphasized the quality-seeking activities of public broadcasting companies, looking for and developing new standards in fiction production that could be highly competitive. Directed by filmmaker Frans Weisz, who offered a filmic approach, *Bij Nader Inzien* [In Retrospect] (1991) set a new standard for television drama production in the Netherlands. The years of restoration after the war are reflected in the present, 40 years later. This six-part series was broadcast by VPRO, a broadcasting company traditionally rooted in liberal Protestantism, which had taken a progressive stance since the end of the 1960s. As a result of its deeply rooted interest in avant-garde and advanced representational strategies, this broadcasting company aims at exploring in television drama the relationship between fiction and reality, experimenting with new dramatic forms.

The series *In Retrospect* concentrates on the experiences of six classmates who form a group after the war in Amsterdam and swear to be friends forever. In 1949 they lose sight of one another, but are brought together by the suicide of one of them (committed after his wife died), 40 years later. The parts set in the past are based on a Dutch novel; the present-day parts are originally developed. Every episode is dedicated to one of the friends, bringing them all together in the last episode where they attend the funeral of their friend. Every episode starts in the present time, introducing one of the friends' personal lives until the moment he or she receives the farewell letter of their friend. In the personal letter friendship is assessed. *In Retrospect* is about lost ideals, and about friendship that turns out to be based on false expectations, unmasked as an illusion. But the series is also about the relationship between personal and historical memories.

The series is unconventional in the way it flies backwards and forwards between past and present. The roots of present life are made visible to be present already in the past, although at that time they are not recognized. In lighting, camerawork, acting and style the two worlds are completely different, though related. Flying backwards and forwards the series makes visible and palpable how 'time' affects people and how their present-day acting is rooted in the past, the post-war years. On top of that it is the memory of each individual of their gatherings in the post-war years that is set in motion by reading the farewell letter and that forms the start of the construction of a common history that turns out to be very individual at the same time. This is underscored by the screening in each of the individual story lines of one identical scene from the past, which was witnessed and attended by all characters, yet is remembered in very different ways. Thus, the series expresses a view on history as construction.

By way of its narrative concept the series illustrates how post-war values and standards determined the late twentieth-century Dutch mentality of a group that was looked upon as the hope of the nation, and how much historical memory is informed by personal memory. It reveals the incompetence of the former students to live up to the past promises regarding the building of the nation. The most striking in this respect is the indifference shown towards the Jewish character, David, more specifically towards his war experience, hiding from the Germans. Only in one scene from the past, where he plays the piano as he does a lot, is there a slight reference to his background. In a way this reflects the lack of attention to the experiences of returned Jews in the years after the war, even up to now. But in the series it is not explicitly revealed as an omission. Still, the others do look away, not even in shame, leaving David locked in his own personal past. Apparently his personal memories cannot be shared; neither will these then become part of historical collective memory. This is also articulated in that David is shown to have failed building up personal relationships, hiding in a night life filled with drugs and booze, somehow according to his life as art trader. The memories are drowned and the Second World War has become part of the continuing life.

History as a nondramatic process of adaptation: *Time to Live*

Lack of attention to the experiences of returned Dutch Jews, even more the incapability and impossibility of speaking about these experiences, is dramatized in a very subtle way in one of the episodes of a ten-part series, *Time to Live*, broadcast by the Catholic broadcasting company in 1996. It reflects the speaking position of the Netherlands, the nation acknowledging that it has neglected an essential part of collective history that still has to be turned into collective memory.

For the first time in the history of Dutch television drama, post-war history is represented as a chronicle, situated in a little Catholic community in the eastern part of Holland between 1945 and 1985. Living in the small village is framed, not by big historical events, but by small, everyday happenings. Along the stories of three generations the series demonstrates how the village community is slowly opened up to the outside world. Big historical events only reflected in village community life after some time, or rather are summarized within the margins of the story. As the proprietor of the local café puts it, 'It looks like the five years of war have not touched upon the village.' The son of the Jewish smith returns home, smarting from the loss of the rest of his family. He finds his father's business already taken over by the locals and encounters but insensibility and a sense of shame that keeps his former neighbours from communicating with him. He leaves for Israel.

These dramatic actions take place in relatively silent scenes. The series not only tries to stay away from big historical events; it also avoids strong dramatic moments and in doing so it follows a nondramatic narrative strategy with climaxes taking place between the episodes instead of within them. It focuses on family history, framed by the history of the region, and in doing so the series investigates the relationship between individual and community in a period that can be characterized by economic and social cultural changes. We see how these changes touch upon the characters, and how they become insecure as a result of that, as well as the efforts they make to find their way in modern times. *Time to Live* writes the cultural history of a time and is mainly confined to values of family life. Modern times are embraced;

the past is cherished. Communal sense is a central issue in this series, albeit at the expense of individual happiness, as with the Jewish character. Communal sense and its possible manifestations when the community is put under pressure always have been a central issue in television drama produced by the Catholic broadcasting company. And in this sense, *Time to Live* is just another way of demonstrating the centrality of the community in Catholic thinking, where people are supposed to share the same attitude towards life, and learn to accommodate themselves to changing social conditions, albeit at the cost of individual members, keepers of unpleasant memories. The community is presented as a place that provides memory and thus identities in the sense of the 'home'. History is shown here as something that is constructed so as to serve the collectiveness of a community. Collective memories seem to be able to exclude individuals indeed. In this series memory thus is not so much a narrative device as it is shown to be an act of history making, even if this might also involve 'looking away' from the shameful parts of it.

The source of inspiration for *Time to Live* was *Heimat* – at least the first 11 parts – the epic series that German filmmaker Edgar Reitz released in 1984. Covering the period between 1919 and 1982 and representing the histories of ordinary people in a small community in a culturally defined region, Reitz presented 'a history from below'. Like *Heimat,* the series *Time to Live* presents history as a chain, be it in a different way because of the different histories of Germany and the Netherlands in terms of the Second World War. Reitz looked for continuities in German history, cruelly ruptured by Fascism. He intended to give back the Germans their history and by doing so he intended the constructing of identity positions, which were able to construct notions of 'home' ('Heimat'; see Morley and Robins, 1995, pp. 88–9). *Heimat* and *Time to Live* pose and explore the question of how time has affected us, even slipped from us, and how we have lost hold of it.

Unlike *Heimat* both *Time to Live* and *In Retrospect* do not include the Second World War in their narratives. This could either point to seeing 1945 as a new beginning or to notions of 'home' that were not destroyed by the Second World War, if only this would exclude again the Jewish survivors. Considering the storylines as outlined above, the latter seems more plausible. The concept of an undestroyed post-war nation does not, however, seem to help to bring about a change in reworking a collective traumatic event; neither does it support the national process of remembrance. It is here that we observe a new direction in representing the past, opening up to personal memories that challenge the notion of a collective memory at large. On top of that, the students setting in one series provides the notion of an untouched past, which is revealed as less innocent than remembered. The regional setting in the other series defines communal identities, looking for cultural roots, and thus point at cultural differences (the use of dialect underscores this). Also, both series articulate how much the Second World War experiences are historicized, and are given a place in history, not as exceptional events to be nationally commemorated at special times and places. The Second World War experiences rather seem to have become marginalized, subordinated to the notion of history as continuous passage of time, merging into history as a continuum.

The process of remembrance: *The Partisans*

Both the idea of history as construction and the function of memory in keeping up with one's own history are dramatized in the three-part serial *De partizanen* [The Partisans] (Catholic Broadcasting Company, KRO, 1995). It deals with a rather unknown incident that took place in Fall 1944 in the resistance movement in one of the southern Catholic provinces of the Netherlands. A little group of inexperienced partisans by accident gets hold of a group of more than 30 German soldiers, disarms them and holds them captive, waiting for the Allies at the verge of liberating the south of Holland. But the Allies are not yet coming, being defeated in the Battle of Arnhem, and as a consequence the Dutch partisans and the Germans are forced to live together more than 2 months. The harsh circumstances of their wanderings have blurred the distinction between captives and captors, between right and wrong. Moral dilemmas are strongly felt and articulated in discussions about carrying out an execution or not, which in the end was performed indeed.

This story of failure in its narrative construction does not pose a narrative closure; it rather questions a final narrativization of history by linking past to present (flying backwards and forwards), connecting what must have happened to how people recollect it. In order to realize this concept of history as construction and as the result of a process of remembrance, the scriptwriter presents two fictional worlds – one situated in the past, telling the story of the hostage in 1944, and the other set in present, a half-century later. In the present we follow a local radio reporter, who sets out on a quest for the local history in question by interviewing five survivors of the partisan action. It soon becomes apparent that the memories of the five survivors are inconsistent. The experiences of the radio reporter, being a professional searcher for truth, run parallel to the experiences of one of the main characters, a man from the North of Holland who joined the resistance movement in the South and later became a judge, which represents another way of searching for truth. The questions that occupy his mind – for example, about the execution, about the line between terrorism and anti-terrorism – also become the questions of the viewer. His recollections of the incident in the end, when he finally consents to meet the reporter and to tell his story, help to bring about a change in reworking the past, admitting that in fact it was a senseless undertaking; and above all this holds true for the execution of two Germans captives and the death of one of the resistance fighters.

After 50 years, myth has become unmasked; history is presented as only existing in the minds of people. This is a very universal message, though at the same time the regional setting, foregrounded by the use of dialect as the main language in the serial, provides a specific context for a specific Catholic part of history. The serial refers implicitly to the myth of absence of Catholics in the resistance movement, the dominant view in Dutch history – and maybe even worldwide – for a long time. *The Partisans*, recounting a bizarre story, reveals the myth of Catholics as only bystanders in the Second World War, and at the same time it does not replace one myth for another. The diverse personal memories of the survivors blur the historical memory of the action.

More than anything else this drama production discusses the construction of memory and of history. The myth of resistance and the myth of memory as a reliable source of information are deconstructed. In its narrative construction the past is commented upon as a domain of various truths and thus of various memories. It is here that we see the formation of collective memory at work. Memories are touched up and accommodated to present ways of thinking. It is not important what has happened, rather how that is remembered so as to serve the reworking of the past in the present.

Conclusion

The three series show how the past should not be seen as a closed territory; rather it is open to a plurality of memories, continuously produced in the present. No matter how much the plurality of memories is supported by the plurality of opinions and beliefs represented by (pillarized) broadcasting companies, it certainly is a result of a post-modern view of history. Historical television drama in the Netherlands in the 1990s does not reproduce an empiricist notion of history; rather it discusses the process of history making.

The 1990s series produce a noninstitutionalized view of the Second World War, opening up historical memory to new constructs, which are in turn the results of processes of remembering. Remembering is shown to be constitutive of collective memory, constantly changing. As such it is a dramatic device, as in *In Retrospect* and *The Partisans*, and an act of history making alike, as shown in all three series. All series also produce counter-narratives, challenging the content of the official culture of memory. They reveal strategies of community building by revealing silence about the unusable past in *Time to Live*, and also deconstruct existing myths that informed collective memory, such as on the braveness of the Dutch. In all cases, these strategies confirm memory as a representation.

The notion of national identity (in terms of pluriformity) is either denied, or expressed in the regional as a new *lieu de mémoire,* and in the chronicle as a domain of memories in Dutch television drama from the 1990s. It is in this sense that historical fiction in the last decade of the past century provides a cultural space where (new) memories can be constructed and shared.

A note on availability

Wilhelmina, Bij Nader Inzien [In Retrospect] and *De partizanen* [The Partisans] are available on DVD (in Dutch), released by the respective broadcasting companies. *Time to Live* is not available.

Bibliography

Anderson, B. (1983) *Imagined Communities: Reflections on the Origin and Spread of Nationalism* (London: Verso).

Anderson, S. (2001) 'History TV and popular memory', in G.R. Edgerton and P. Rollins (eds), *Television Histories: Shaping Collective Memory in the Media Age* (Lexington: University Press of Kentucky).

Barker, C. (1997) *Global Television: An Introduction* (Oxford: Blackwell Publishers).

Ebbrecht, T. (2007) 'Docudramatizing history on TV: German and British docudrama and historical event television in the memorial year 2005', *European Journal of Cultural Studies*, 10.1, 35–53.

Giddens, A. (1991) *Modernity and Self-Identity: Self and Society in the Late Modern Age* (Cambridge: Polity Press).

Halbwachs, M. (1991 [1950]) *Het collectief geheugen* (Amersfoort: Acco).

Hoskins, A. (2001) 'New memory: mediating history', *The Historical Journal of Film, Radio and Television*, 21.4, 191–211.

Hoskins, A. (2004) 'Television and the collapse of memory', *Time Society*, 13, 109–27.

Kaes, A. (1989) *From Hitler to Heimat: The Return of History as Film* (Cambridge, MA: Harvard University Press).

McQuail, D. (1996) 'Transatlantic TV flow: another look at cultural cost-accounting', in A. Van Hemel, H. Mommaas and C. Smithuijsen (eds), *Trading Culture: GATT, European Cultural Policies and the Transatlantic Market* (Amsterdam: Boekman Foundation).

Morley, D. and K. Robins (eds) (1995) *Spaces of Identity: Global Media, Electronic Landscapes and Cultural Boundaries* (London: Routledge).

Morris-Suzuki, T. (2005) *The Past within Us: Media, Memory, History* (London: Verso).

Nora, P. (1989) 'Between memory and history: les lieux de mémoire', *Representations*, 26, 7–24.

Rosenstone, R. (1995) *Visions of the Past: The Challenge of Film to Our Idea of History* (Cambridge, MA: Harvard University Press).

Sobchack, V. (ed.) (1996) *The Persistence of History: Cinema, Television and the Modern Event* (New York: Routledge).

Strath, B. (ed.) (2000) *Myth and Memory in the Construction of Community: Historical Patterns in Europe and Beyond* (Brussels: P.I.E. Peter Lang).

Tulloch, J. (1990) *Television Drama: Agency, Audience, Myth* (London: Routledge).

10
Facing the Truth, Pain and Reconciliation

Aileen Blaney

Since the signing of the Good Friday Agreement in 1998, the normalization of broadcasting practices in the UK has all but consigned to history the governmental policing of airwaves formerly in operation there. By contrast, during the protracted period of political conflict known as 'the troubles', programme-makers' freedom of expression was enormously limited. In a great many respects, a broadcaster–government consensus which existed in the Republic of Ireland during this same time mirrored the situation in the UK: here, too, factual and even entertainment programming that deviated from an establishment consensus on the North invariably generated political controversy and/or attracted state interference.[1] For many journalists, the likelihood of their investigative endeavours being misconstrued as support for paramilitary campaigns of violence made them reluctant to contextualize the conflict outside of the state's terms of reference. Betty Purcell's aptly phrased expression 'the silence in Irish broadcasting' (Purcell, 1996, p. 253) was regularly invoked to refer to this media phenomenon, one whereby although ' "facts" were in abundance' (Rolston, 2007, p. 347), analysis and explanation of the conflict were conspicuously absent.

The British 'Broadcasting Ban' – which came into being via legislation introduced by the British Home Secretary Douglas Hurd in 1988 – banned from the airwaves members belonging to Sinn Fein or one or other of a further ten proscribed organizations, but did not legislate against broadcasters from showing any of the above from appearing in silhouette accompanied by voice overs by actors reading from transcripts of their exact words (one actor was even dismissed for being too adept at mimicking Sinn Fein leader Gerry Adams' voice). Notwithstanding this degree of leeway available to broadcasting organizations, faced with the prospect of professional ruin few television producers or executives during the 'troubles', in either the UK or Ireland, were willing to run the risk of putting their support behind projects with the potential to challenge state strategies of information management. However, that is not to say that all programming uniformly adhered to the broadcasting status quo. For example, when 'At the Edge of the Union' (BBC, 1985) – an episode from the *Real Lives* documentary series, which, crucially, included a sequence recorded at home with Sinn Fein representative and member of the Northern Ireland Assembly, suspected IRA member and now deputy First Minister of the current Northern Irish Assembly Martin McGuinness – was planned for broadcast, BBC governor Daphne Park had cause, as she saw it, to object to its depiction of 'terrorists' as 'lovable people with babies' (*Guardian*, 2005a). The British Home Secretary's attempt to intercept the programme's broadcast; the fallout between BBC management and the board of governors, who voted unanimously – with the exception of one of its members – in favour of its banning; the subsequent protest strike called by BBC staff; along with the affair's negative impact on public perceptions of the independence of the national broadcasting organization, together illustrate the many obstacles in the way of making television on the theme of 'the troubles', as well as the extent of governmental involvement in broadcasting during this period.[2]

For the benefit of readers unfamiliar with Irish history, notably since the partition of the island into two distinct jurisdictions in 1921, it is worth pointing out that the irreconcilable constitutional aspirations of Northern Ireland's Catholic and Protestant communities are widely regarded as root causes responsible for the outbreak of 'the troubles' – the term most commonly used to refer to the most recent period of civil unrest and violent political conflict in Northern Ireland. While a sizeable proportion of Northern Ireland's Catholic population identify themselves as being Irish and vote for nationalist and republican political parties that are pro-reunification of Ireland, the Protestant population by and large identify themselves as being of British extraction, and support Unionist political parties steadfast in their commitment to retaining the union with Great Britain. The bipartisan demographic composition of Northern Ireland's population has been traced back to the 'plantation of Ulster' in 1609 when the native Irish were dispossessed of confiscated lands so that they could be acceded to English and Scottish settlers (Darby, 2005, p. 3). As John Darby points out: 'By 1703, less than 5 per cent of the land of Ulster was still in the hands of the Catholic Irish' (Darby, 2005, p. 3).

In historical accounts of 'the troubles', its start invariably circulates around three key dates: (1) a Civil Rights march in Derry on 5 October 1968, which went ahead despite being banned by the Stormont government; the subsequent television footage of police brutality against marchers sparked rioting throughout Derry; (2) the 'Battle of the Bogside' on 12 August 1969, when residents of the Bogside area of Derry engaged in open combat with riot police and erected barricades cordoning the neighbourhood off from the rest of the city in their attempt to claim jurisdiction over it; and (3) the event known as 'Bloody Sunday', when soldiers from the British Army Parachute Regiment opened fire on a Civil Rights march in Derry on 30

January 1972 shooting dead 13 civilians, more than half of them teenagers (O'Dochartaigh, 1997). Ireland subsequently experienced a period of sustained bloody conflict involving Irish republican paramilitaries, who were fighting for a united Ireland; loyalist paramilitaries, who wished to defend the union with Great Britain and retain loyalty to the British Crown; the RUC (the Royal Ulster Constabulary), who were in charge of policing in Northern Ireland; and the British Army deployed under Operation Banner in 1969 (which concluded in 2007, making it the longest continuous deployment of British troops in history), to assist the RUC in preventing Protestant Loyalist attacks on Catholic communities in Derry. During this period of violent atrocities committed on the part of all of the above parties, 3600 people were killed, and over 30,000 injured. On Good Friday, 10 April 1998, after at least 2 years of political talks involving members of the British and Irish governments and Northern Ireland's major political parties, and many more years of behind-the-scenes activities, the signing of the Belfast Agreement took place. The following 22 May, this agreement was endorsed in separate referenda by the people of Northern Ireland and the Republic of Ireland. The Belfast Agreement – by providing a framework for peace and reconciliation between the opposing political factions and communities in Northern Ireland – inaugurated a new phase in the history of Northern Ireland, one which by all accounts is still in progress.

Annette Hill (invoking Seaton, 2005) points out that 'the historical tradition of news, and in particular news about violence, has always drawn upon emotions and the body in order to communicate to the public' (Hill, 2007, p. 14). Hill's observation, however, could hardly be applied to the dispassionate reporting of the conflict in Northern Ireland prior to the peace process there. Owing to a state-led propaganda war, which denied actors, and, as often, nonactors in the conflict, as former British Prime Minister Margaret Thatcher would have put it, the 'oxygen of publicity', television could not fulfil the role it often plays in other democratic societies as a 'central public site for confessing one's innermost feelings' (Aslama and Pantti, 2006, p. 167). Subsequent to the first IRA ceasefire in 1994, however, dramatic changes were afoot in both the UK and Ireland's broadcasting worlds – the ending of the 1988 British 'broadcasting ban' being not least among them, while a broadcasting ban that operated in Ireland's case under the conditions set out in Section 31 of its Broadcasting Act was lifted in 1993 by Minister for Arts, Culture and the Gaeltacht Michael D. Higgins. The BBC series *Facing The Truth* (BBC, 2006) – in which victims and perpetrators of Northern Ireland's 'troubles' come face-to-face in the presence of Nobel Peace Prize winner and convenor of South Africa's Truth and Reconciliation Commission, Archbishop Desmond Tutu – is exemplary of the type of 'permissive' (McLaughlin, 2008) programming being produced in the post-conflict context. Notwithstanding that *Facing the Truth* appeared more than 10 years after the rescinding of the ban, its staging of confessional encounters between victims and perpetrators was nonetheless unprecedented in the context of UK broadcasting.

Beginning with the notorious inquiry in 1972 into 'Bloody Sunday' – widely referred to as the 'Widgery Whitewash' – the deficit of truth that has been associated with state-led inquires into events linked to Northern Ireland's 'troubles' has considerably curtailed the public's faith, both in the UK and Ireland, in their respective government's commitment to the principles of truth and justice. Rolston expresses a considerable amount of pessimism in this regard: 'As Hegarty (2003, p. 1189) concludes, the tension has been between "state interests" and "truth telling," with the cards stacked in favour of the former' (Rolston, 2005, p. 559). When, early in 2004, the Secretary of State for Northern Ireland, Paul Murphy, and the Chief Constable of the Police Service of Northern Ireland (PSNI), Hugh Orde, jointly called for a truth and reconciliation commission along the lines of the South African model, victims' groups in Northern Ireland – despite having previously voiced their support for such an initiative – expressed objections (Rolston, 2005). According to Rolston, their opposition stemmed from a shared perception of Orde's perspective of a truth commission 'as a means to rescuing the PSNI from multiple inquiries into what he classifies "historic crimes" and of "drawing a line" under the past (cited in Brown 2003)' (Rolston, 2005, p. 562). Rolston applies similar reservations with regard to *Facing the Truth* in a provocative and insightful narrative analysis of the series; he points out that the reconciliatory objectives that the panel members (Leslie Belinda, a former aid worker who lost her husband in the Rwanda genocide in 1994; Donna Hicks, an Associate at the Weatherhead Center for International Affairs at Harvard University; and Archbishop Desmond Tutu) conspired to achieve might have precipitated hasty responses from participants. He adds that an expectancy that victims conform to the notion of an 'ideal victim' (Rolston, 2007, p. 357) exerted inordinate pressure on them to become reconciled with and forgive the perpetrators of violence. While I would agree that the eliciting of responses from participants does indeed function in this way, as a counterweight to Rolston's argument, I would like to turn to Minna Aslama and Mervi Pantti's invocation of Nick Couldry's insight that 'it is not even the authority of the host of the show or the audience that sanctions the confession; rather, "the authority who requires the confession" is the authority of *television itself*' (Aslama and Pantti, 2006, p. 179). Although Couldry's own claim that TV is constitutive of social reality might call for revision, especially considering the inordinate communicative role currently being played by information technologies in this respect, participants in *Facing the Truth* who, far from performing regardless of whether or not they would be on TV, perform emphatically *for* the TV cameras and respond to this very authority of television.

In an analysis of the performance dynamics characterizing the address made by the subject in documentary to a future audience, Stella Bruzzi writes:

> We are invited not to observe but to scrutinize them, their mannerisms, their words; the effect of this scrutiny functioning as an indication that each time these people speak they are doing so with their audience very much in mind. . . . These subjects are not caught unawares or merely talking about themselves in an unpremeditated fashion, rather they are conscious of their involvement in a performative event, one that is simultaneously a description and an enactment of their lives and lifestyles.'
>
> (Bruzzi, 2000, p. 160)

In line with Couldry's theorization of the authority of television, here the camera does not record a pro-filmic scene which takes place independently of it, since it in itself calls forth the 'performative event'. Documentary film scholar Michael Renov makes a similar point in reference to video confessions by contending that the presence of the camera is sufficient in itself to 'spur self-revelation' (Renov, 2004, p. 204). He goes on to argue that 'in the case of video confessions, the virtual presence of a partner – the imagined other effectuated by the technology – turns out to be a more powerful facilitator of emotion than flesh-and-blood interlocutors' (Renov, 2004, p. 204). Similarly, in *Facing the Truth*, the camera, as a surrogate for both the authority of television and a mass television audience, to at least some extent precipitates the modes of confessional dialogue and acts of performative display enacted by confessants.

Turning to Couldry once more, and taking into account his observation that 'television's role in our social and individual lives is above all as the frame through which we gain access to what is marked off *as* social, from the merely individual' (Couldry, 2002, p. 284), it can be appreciated how *Facing the Truth's* affording of victims *and* perpetrators a platform to recount their personal histories provide viewers with points of identificatory engagement hitherto unavailable to them. With respect to perpetrators who participate in the series, it is worth giving consideration to Renov's description of how, in criminological contexts, the confession operates as 'a threshold moment, marking the possibility of the criminal's first step on his way back to society: 'By confessing, he finds the first possibility of a return to the community after he had put himself, through his deed, outside its limits [Reik, 1945, p. 205]' (Renov, 2004, p. 212). Broadcasting the series under the auspices and fanfare of 'event television' and placing it 'in the heart of the BBC TWO schedule for three consecutive nights to create maximum impact with as wide an audience as possible' (BBC, 2006a), the BBC attempts to enact a comparable 'threshold moment' and to readmit, or even reintegrate, perpetrators into Northern Irish society.

Anticipating objections to its broadcast of a programme that made claims of healing 'historic wounds' during a tentative period of the peace settlement's infancy, the BBC made every effort to ensure that their pre-publicity activities would win public support for the series. As part of its promotional strategy, it mobilized the rhetoric of reconciliation already in circulation, which, prematurely according to widespread accounts, assigns divisive bipartisan political and ethnic affiliations to history and accentuates supposed commonalities that are perceived as uniting the people of Northern Ireland. More specifically, in a press release for the programme, BBC 2 Controller Roly Keating's championing of *Facing the Truth* as 'groundbreaking current affairs which explores a tough issue from a human, rather than political, perspective' (BBC, 2006a) endorses its supplanting of the political concerns, typically present in current affairs, with human interest ones. Furthermore, by describing the shooting period as 'a positive experience for all those involved' (BBC, 2006a), Keating relates *Facing the Truth* to claims made both by its makers – that it constituted an important step in the rehabilitation of both of the concerned parties – and to factual TV trends more internationally where, as media scholar Dominique Mehl points out, there has been a 'new focus on the discourse of the uninitiated and the account of personal experiences' (Mehl, 2005). The framing of the testimonies of victims and perpetrators – they are described as being 'in their own words' – presents participants' accounts as authentic acts of self-disclosure and at the same time downplays the role of the series producers and panel in the programme's proceedings.

Although the BBC's assurance that the series allows participants to tell their stories in their own words equates confessional dialogue in *Facing the Truth* with self-disclosure, the interview framework within which the confessions take place ensures that the panel's role in the proceedings is a substantial one. By contrast, in the case of video testimonies made not for broadcast but for archival purposes, the role of the interviewer is kept to a minimum. Take, for example, the case of the Fortunoff Archive for Holocaust Testimonies at Yale University's department of Manuscripts and Archives, where '[the] interviewing methodology stresses the leadership role of the witness in structuring and telling his or her own story. Questions are primarily used to ascertain time and place, or elicit additional information about topics already mentioned, with an emphasis on open-ended questions that give the initiative to the witness. The witnesses are the experts in their own life story, and the interviewers are there to listen, to learn, and to clarify' (Fortunoff, 2005a). Given the leadership role played by the witness, the video testimonies recorded at Yale emerge as 'purer' forms of testimony if compared to those found in *Facing the Truth*, where the nature of the co-performance between panel members, the host and participants limits the degree of autonomy that can be exercised by confessants over their statements. Renov's observation with regard to 'documentaries of the interactive mode in which the interview format prevails', that confessants are 'more spoken than speaking' (Renov, 2004, p. 200), is echoed in Rolston's criticism of the BBC that it acted more in the capacity of progenitor than midwife with respect to the statements made by victims and survivors: 'the victims and survivors may speak or be spoken to, but the framing is still in the hands of the programme makers. It is hard to imagine such a powerful institution handing over control to victims and survivors' (Rolston, 2007, p. 3). Many of the reservations expressed by Rolston, including the above, are instructive with respect to items of crucial concerns in this chapter, namely with respect to how victims and perpetrators' experiences of coming to terms with historical suffering are presented to a viewing public via the series.

The opening sequence of *Facing the Truth*'s first instalment, in which a British soldier meets the sister of a suspected IRA member whom he killed while on active service in Northern Ireland, offers a good point of entry into this line of inquiry. Although the family of the deceased – Michael McLarnon – have tirelessly protested his lack of any paramilitary involvement, ex-soldier Clifford Burrage's testimony in court contributed to a verdict that attributed IRA membership to Michael. Following Mary McLarnon's emotionally distressing account of the last night in her brother's life, and her family's attendance at his death, Mr. Burrage is asked by Archbishop Tutu to give his account of the night so that he might 'enhance their sense of God's presence' in the room. Throughout his account, Burrage gestures approximate a reliving of the lead-up to and eventual shooting of Michael: when he describes how he silenced a woman at the scene, he smacks his hand across his mouth, and recalling the orders he gave the woman's husband to sit down, he points to where a couch would have been located.

Similarly, he accompanies the statement, 'I looked through the nightscope like this,' with gestures that mimic the action being described, and, in what must have been a painful moment for McLarnon, he raises his arms as he shouts hooray in a demonstration of the jubilation he and his colleagues expressed subsequent to receiving confirmation of the death of a gunman, being Michael in this case. The confluence of words that speak of, and gestures embodying, the night he says erected a wall in his life from which point he could never cross back are highly convincing, so much so that they approach a re-enactment of the night in question. It is all the more remarkable then how quickly his narrative collapses under the pressure to recant, firstly by Archbishop Tutu who says 'you might have shot an unarmed civilian because of that anger,' and then by Hicks who says, 'Why was that burden so great when you thought it was a gunman?' What had begun as an element of doubt in Mr. Burrage's memory of events: 'I don't think he was the man I shot at,' is swiftly supplanted by the almost complete certainty that 'he [Michael] was definitely not…he wasn't the man you described to me as your brother.' Once more, there is a transition from doubt – in the statement: 'there is that definite shadow of doubt about it [the identity of the gunman]' – to certainty: 'I'm willing to say for certain now that the man I shot at was a gunman, but I hit Michael instead.' Notwithstanding that his embodied memories of the night of the shooting, the shedding of tears, and desperate pleas to McLarnon for forgiveness inspire faith in Archbishop Tutu's assurances that, 'This is not something we could have contrived,' the changes made to his confession suggests that the more fully the panel inhabits the role of interviewer, the more McLarnon's authorial control over his testimony diminishes.

To augment his argument regarding the dispossessing of victims and perpetrators of authorial control over their own histories, Rolston criticizes how the religious rhetoric pervading the series encourages participants to commune in the here and now at the expense of dealing with the past. For Rolston, a foreclosing of the past via an almost exclusive focus on the participants' interactions in the present, and which are presented in terms of Christian concepts of forgiveness entails that 'participants were in effect presented as having a *reason* for participating but without a *history* which brought them to the point where they might be willing to participate' (Rolston, 2007, p. 353). Not forgetting either Rolston's critique of *Facing the Truth's* evacuation of history or that participants willingly comply with the religious framing of the programme – two of them are even born-again Christians – it is worth investigating further the nature of the 'safe haven', to borrow a term used repeatedly by Archbishop Tutu throughout, installed by the TV series, and the extent to which it does, if at all – again in Tutu's words – 'facilitate [their] story [or history] being told'.

Although Archbishop Tutu's argument that historic wounds be opened to allow for 'a healing that will redulge to the blessing of all of the people of this land' indicates a level of engagement with the past, the stress on Christian concepts of forgiveness and repentance situates the encounters in distinctly ahistorical terms. Compare how in the first programme he explains to participants how 'God enlists your participation in the process of making Northern Ireland a place where people can live together' to his reminder to Sylvia Hackett of 'God's presence' in the room before he requests that she shake hands with Michael Stone – a named suspect in her husband's murder, who in addition served a prison term for opening fire on the crowd at an IRA funeral, killing three mourners. Despite the inordinate pressure brought to bear on Sylvia to forgive, and her apparent compliance with Archbishop Tutu's religious injunctions to do so – she even offers Stone her personal assurance that he is forgiven – the groundswell of emotion that immediately precedes her dramatic exit undermines Tutu's insistence that participants have been touched by 'God's grace [and] healing'. For instance, although Sylvia does acquiesce with Archbishop's Tutu's request to shake hands with Stone, a loyalist and former member of a paramilitary association, the Ulster Defence Association, immediately after doing so, her visible disorientation and distress as she dashes from the scene undercuts the notional 'healing' on offer. Sylvia's disclosure of raw emotion here – the shedding of tears and tremors in her voice as she cries out in anguish, 'Oh my God! Let me go!' – are indicative of how 'through emotions, the past persists on the surface of bodies. Emotions show us how histories stay alive' (Ahmed, 2004, p. 202). While these unscripted emotions make compelling if uncomfortable viewing, and are scarcely effective as a model of closure or Christian forgiveness, perhaps more pertinently they betray the persistence of a past that is not easily forgotten.

The procedures that elicit Sylvia's emotional responses here and the question put to Stone by Archbishop Tutu, when he asks him, 'When you look across the table, what do you think and *feel* [my emphasis]' strongly resonates with Annette Hill's observation that 'the focus on emotions has become a trademark for many factual programmes, where the premise is to observe or put people in emotionally difficult situations' (Hill, 2007, p. 15). Archbishop Tutu says as much when he thanks participants of this particular episode for 'allowing us the privilege of looking and seeing your anguish and your pain'. Moreover, in an interview with the Archbishop published on the BBC News website, referring to *Facing the Truth*, he states: 'Even though we might think we're hardened to reality television, real-life, raw emotion is still quietly shocking, catching you unawares' (BBC, 2006b). Here, Archbishop Tutu, by underlining the centrality of 'emotion-based authenticity' (Aslama and Pantti, 2006, p. 177) of the series, aligns it with one of the central purposes of reality television, which, according to Aslama and Pantti, is 'to disclose what truly occurred and how it was experienced' (Aslama and Pantti, 2006, p. 177). Jerome de Groot meanwhile points out that such is the exhibition and display of authentic experiences in 'reality history' programmes such as *The 1940s House* and *The Edwardian Country House* that 'the only difference between us as viewers and those we see is "social and material".' The experience of the audience is significantly and importantly different due to the involvement of people 'like us' in 'reality history' (de Groot, 2006, p. 398). de Groot notices a striking dissimilarity between this mode of addressing viewers, who are asked to 'put [themselves] in their place' (de Groot, 2006, p. 401) and Reithian BBC models where the 'power of television as a transmitter of information' (de Groot, 2006, pp. 399–400) condescends to educate audiences about the past. While reality history TV programming is easily susceptible to denigration on the basis of a variety of shortcomings with respect to issues of historicity, as de Groot notes, by bringing forth the 'gap' separating past and present, it offers invaluable insights into the historical differences between '*now* and *then* [my emphasis]' (de Groot, 2006, p. 402). In a variation on this theme, emotive speech-acts in *Facing the Truth* present the impact of *then* on *now*, since they are as informative of experiences of reliving the traumatic past in the *present* as they are of events as they actually happened in history. Accordingly, the continuity announcer who asks viewers, at the beginning of episode 2, to 'watch, listen and wonder how you'd react – now on BBC 2 – moments of great courage and raw emotion in a remarkable new series…,' stresses the centrality to the series of contemporary *feelings* about the past as opposed to historical 'facts'.

Facing the Truth then, for being exemplary of a type of 'living history', where the emphasis lies with the 'living' elements of history, reflects wider shifts in the dynamics between 'living' memory, or private testimony, on the one hand, and archival resources, on the other. Erin Bell says as much by calling to attention how numerous scholars 'are recognising the way in which, as German film historian Matthias Steinle puts it, since the 1990s there has been an increasing shift so that archive images are contextualized through memory, rather than the other way around: memory and eyewitness testimony has become central to understanding of images, he suggests' (Bell, 2008, and in this volume). Steinle and Bell's insights are borne out in the dynamic interplay between performativity and textuality in *Facing the Truth*: the testimonies of bereaved family members and survivors that recount experiences of suffering along with perpetrator confessions retrospectively contextualize archival images of the dead, and also of perpetrators, that appear at the beginning of each face-to-face meeting. Consequently, the still images increase in affective force long after they have disappeared from the screen.

Like the victims, survivors and even perpetrators who took part in *Facing the Truth*, participants in the West Belfast-based Victims and Survivors Trust (VAST)[7] archive (Cathal McLaughlin describes VAST as 'a politically nonaligned organisation which campaigns on issues of justice, and runs workshops for personal and socially therapeutic purposes' (McLaughlin, 2004, p. 100)) who wish to 'tell their stories to the public, to be listened to, and to be acknowledged' (McLaughlin, 2004, p. 102) are equally invested in reanimating history by bringing it *up-to-date*. An evaluation by representatives for the Fortunoff Video Archive of the suitability of the television medium to the transmission of personal histories, which might equally be applied to the BBC's initiative, suggests some further points of overlap in this regard: 'It was felt that the "living portraiture" of television would add a compassionate and sensitive dimension to the historical record' (Fortunoff, 2008b). The privileging of living history here, as in *Facing the Truth*, reflects growing levels of acceptance for performance as a site of history, and also for its suitability as a supplement – as opposed to a replacement – to archival artefacts and historical argument.

To encourage viewers to emotionally engage with the confessional statements, at the end of the first two programmes, the presenter's announcement of 'Tomorrow on *Facing the Truth*…' accompanies highlights from the upcoming episode; in the case of the first programme, these highlights include a father who sets the scene for his son's murder, an admission of a desire to kill, followed by one of homicide: 'My son was lying in this dirty ground, and someone had killed him./I wanted them dead/I set myself up as judge, jury and executioner, and I took that young man's life.' The editing strategy here of splicing together a number of encounters from different points in the series sensationalizes each one in turn. Although these speech acts retain their factual authenticity, in so much as they are in participants' 'own words', editing techniques that refashion the order and context of their occurrence are indicative of the challenges in this type of popular factual programming of both transmitting the experiences of perpetrators and victims, and appealing to a viewing public accustomed to the entertainment dimensions of reality television.

Traditionally, media scholars, on conservative and ethical grounds, saw the necessity of maintaining divisions separating entertaining and factual modes of addressing viewers, and the very ones that are typically disregarded in contemporary examples of popular factual television. Paddy Scannell's allusion to the cross-fertilization of televisual modes betrays a level of anxiety in this regard. He asks, 'But how, for instance can we (as viewers) distinguish between being informed and being entertained – the answer, in large part, is that they both depend on very different kinds of performance, different ways of staging the program-event, different styles of talk etc etc' (Scannell, 2006, p. 8). *Facing the Truth,* on the other hand, aims to both make 'good television', via the sensationalizing of testimony, and at the same time inform viewers about a range of experiences of suffering – ones belonging to perpetrators as well as to victims. Notwithstanding the problematical aspects of the dual function of the 'popular factual' approach adopted in this series – because it offers viewers a complexity of engagement with experiences of historical suffering – its relevance to discourses of conflict transformation should not be underestimated.

Even though Rolston is highly critical of the slowness of programme makers to take advantage of the new broadcasting dispensation available to them subsequent to developments in UK/Ireland media environments, he does commend the BBC for finally – more than 10 years after the first IRA ceasefire in 1994 – producing a programme which he argues constitutes 'the most significant and imaginative example to date of the broadcasters not merely vigorously reporting on conflict transformation but also attempting to contribute towards such transformation' (Rolston, 2007, p. 348). In common with sites of public history, such as museums and memorials, which have flourished subsequent to the political resolution of the conflict, *Facing the Truth* attempts to deal with the legacies of the past in contemporary Northern Ireland and its neighbouring jurisdictions. Ironically enough, though, the series appears to succeed most at engaging viewers where its apparent failures lie, notably those acts of performative display – or scenes of emotional breakdown – that are at cross purposes with the discourse of healing and closure that frame its narrative. Sarah Ahmed puts forth a convincing case with respect to dealing with historical suffering by saying that ideally 'healing does not cover over, but exposes the wound to others: *the recovery is a form of exposure* (Ahmed, 2004, p. 200). In *Facing the Truth's* unscripted sequences, far from achieving closure vis-à-vis the past, participants' wounded feelings of pain, guilt and regret present to viewers the persistence of historical suffering. Via these 'living portraitures' then, *Facing the Truth* gives *exposure* to a past that has not passed, bringing viewers into affective relationships with first-hand experiences of individuals belonging to a post-conflict society in transition. Notwithstanding that the practicalities of television programme-making only permit a select few the opportunity of telling their stories, the series, at least in some small manner, gives voice to and puts flesh on historical suffering associated with contemporary Northern Irish history.

A note on availability

Unfortunately *Facing the Truth* is not available on DVD. However, extracts from the series can be accessed via the BBC website: http://search.bbc.co.uk/search?uri=%2Fprogrammes%2Fb007m4j1&go=toolbar&tab=av&q=facing%20the%20truth&scope=all.

Notes

1. Bill Rolston sums up the media's adherence, during the 'troubles', to a state-led consensus vis-à-vis the conflict in Northern Ireland as follows: 'News coverage therefore served less to enlighten or encourage dialogue which might lead to political resolution than to enable the public to close ranks around a number of agreed responses to "mindless violence". A number of familiar tropes quickly emerged: the Northern Ireland problem was about "terrorism"; the army was there to keep the peace; and there was a "hierarchy of death" (Greenslade, 1998) which ensured that some victims were more newsworthy than others' (Rolston, 2007, p. 347).
2. According to a report in *The Guardian*, compiled from what were at the time newly released files made available to them from the BBC under the Freedom of Information Act, the impact of the Real Lives controversy caused irreparable damage to the inner workings of the BBC. In this article, Lisa O'Carroll writes: 'Within a month the board did a U-turn, deciding the programme could be shown with minor changes. It was transmitted in October. But the mistrust between management and governors was never repaired; within two years Milne was gone. "It was an unpleasant time, but it was an honourably made programme and the governors' minutes bear that out," said Hamann after seeing the documents for the first time last week' *Guardian* (2005a).

Bibliography

Ahmed, S. (2004) *The Cultural Politics of Emotion* (New York: Routledge).
Aslama, M. and M. Pantti (2006) 'Talking alone: Reality TV, emotions and authenticity', *European Journal of Cultural Studies*, 9.2, 167–84.

BBC (2006a) Press releases: *Facing the Truth*: www.bbc.co.uk/pressoffice/pressreleases/stories/2006/02_february/14/truth.shtml. Accessed 7 March 2009.

BBC (2006b) BBC News: The go between: http://news.bbc.co.uk/2/hi/uk_news/magazine/4723320.stm. Accessed 8 March 2009.

Bell, E. (2008) History on television, Lincoln: Advisory board meeting, 28 February 2008; Discussion: 'Dramadoc, reenactment and memory': http://tvhistory.lincoln.ac.uk/Bell%20introduction.htm. Accessed 12 December 2008.

Bruzzi, S. (2000) *New Documentary: A Critical Introduction* (London: Routledge).

Couldry, N. (2002) 'Playing for celebrity: big brother as ritual event', *Television & New Media*, 3.3, 283–93.

De Groot, J. (2006) 'Empathy and enfranchisement: popular histories' *Rethinking History*, 10.3, 391–413.

Fortunoff Video Archive for Holocaust Testimonies (2005a) About the archive: Introduction: www.library.yale.edu/testimonies/about/index.html. Accessed 7 March 2009.

Fortunoff Video Archive for Holocaust Testimonies (2005b), About the archive: History: www.library.yale.edu/testimonies/about/index.html. Accessed 7 March 2009.

Hill, A. (2007) *Restyling Factual TV: Audiences, News, Documentary and Reality Genres* (New York: Routledge).

McLaughlin, C. (2004) 'Telling our story: recording audiovisual testimonies from political conflict', in R. Barton and H. O'Brien (eds), *Keeping It Real: Irish Film and Television* (London: Wallflower Press).

McLaughlin, G. (2008) 'Changing Hearts and Minds? The Media and Conflict Transformation in the North', Seminar at the Centre for Irish Studies, NUI Galway. 18 February.

Mehl, D. (2005) 'The public on the television screen: towards a public sphere of exhibition', *Journal of Media Practice*, VI.1, 19–28.

O'Carroll, L. (2005) 'The truth behind real lives', *The Guardian*: www.guardian.co.uk/media/2005/dec/12/mondaymediasection.northernireland. Accessed 7 March 2009.

Purcell, B. (1996) 'The silence in Irish broadcasting', in B. Rolston and D. Miller (eds), *War and Words: The Northern Irish Media Reader* (Belfast: Beyond the Pale Publications).

Renov, M. (2004) *The Subject of Documentary* (Minneapolis: University of Minnesota Press).

Rolston, B. (2005) 'In the full glare of English politics: Ireland, inquiries, and the British state', *The British Journal of Criminology*, 45.4, 547–64.

Rolston, B. (2007) 'Facing reality: The media, the past and conflict transformation in Northern Ireland', *Crime, Media, Society*, III.2, 344–64.

Scannell, P. (2006) An interview with Professor Paddy Scannell, http://www.wmin.ac.uk/mad/PDF/WPCC-Vol4-No2-Tarik_Sabry_Paddy_Scannell.pdf. Accessed 6 November 2008.

11
Women and War

Margit Rohringer

Traditional war films, be they feature or documentary, usually show soldiers fighting against their enemies. The main discussion then refers to the loss or gain of territory, to border movements, to the official status of a region and the like. In recent times, however, the unofficial realities of war have also gradually become issues of public discourse and media representation. New questions that have arisen so far include what wars mean to civil society and how civilians experience them. A mainly unasked question that has recently received at least peripheral attention addresses the role and the fate of women both as active players and as victims in war.

To study the fate of women one has to study their relational position in a patriarchal society, and I will do so in the course of this case study. In this chapter, I will concentrate on a documentary film chosen for its representation of the victimization of women in the war in Bosnia, and which had one of the largest TV audiences of all documentaries made in the Balkan region after 1989: *Calling the Ghosts*, made by Mandy Jacobson and Karmen Jelinčić (USA/Croatia, 1996).[1] The film covers a very sensitive topic that usually falls into the category of the 'unspeakable' and is therefore often taboo. Despite the exponential increase of TV programmes within the last two decades dealing with history, including recent wars, the topic of rape as a war crime was more or less ignored on the 'small screen' until the end of 1993.[2]

Though the focus of this book is on the 'representation' of history on television and the use of film languages, other chapters use a sociological approach, because the issues demand an interdisciplinary discussion and contextual knowledge. The main questions of this chapter are the following: What does war mean for the individual woman in the everyday war context, and what are the patterns of representation of women's fates during the war in the films? Furthermore, the discussion will lead to the question of how – apart from the focus on individual fates – the construction of 'collective victims' is supported and shaped by the filmmakers, the channels distributing the documentary (e.g., TV) and also by institutions outside the film/media world as well.

One basic conclusion of the research work of the Belgrade-based non-governmental organization Women in Black[3] is that during the war, violence against women increased significantly, and not only in the 'public war sphere' but also in 'private spaces'.[4] Women in Black, whose main political goal in the 1990s was resistance to the war in Bosnia, push the borders of taboos when they publicly mention violence against women and children by their own husbands, fathers and sons, returning from the front. The abuse of women was silently accepted in the Second World War and long after its end.[5] The conclusion of Women in Black is that militarism and violence in the family are connected.[6] Staša Zajović, the founder of the group, further criticizes the West for the fact that, as she sees it, as soon as the West speaks about the protection of human rights in relation to the Third World and to the Balkans, they mean *collective* human rights – the rights of discriminated minorities. But nowadays she thinks it is more important to speak first about individual civilian rights in the region.

Individual suffering versus the collective victim

Though I agree with Zajović that the trend of collectivization is a preferred approach of the West when it considers Balkan societies, this tendency could be observed and was even maintained inside the former Yugoslavia, and is even representative of the Balkan region as such. The main collective group that experienced a revival in the masses and that was used as a 'mediating force' shortly before and during the war years when the collective Communist legacy had officially been put aside was the traditional patriarchal family. This kind of re-traditionalism, as the group Women in Black agrees, indirectly supported a national re-awakening. Communism had no longer any power to impede the values of patriarchal thinking and behaviour that manifested itself in the traditional patriarchal family. Still, what can be observed in many other films produced in the Balkan area constitutes a kind of paradox because this longing to be seen as an individual seems to derive not only from externally produced stereotypes and stigmatization, but also from a desire to free oneself from the collective forces inside the (former) Yugoslav/Balkan culture. The problem of 'collectivist' thinking is discussed further in the next section, which deals with *Calling the Ghosts*, the film that focuses on the victimization of (raped) women in war. Though this film reveals the experiences of women in war by showing their individual fates, it usually also places the female victims and male perpetrators in collective ethnic groups, thus making us once again aware that we need to explore the interdependence of regional, gender and national/ethnic identifications.

Calling the Ghosts: Let's play a game in order to survive

Some decades ago, authors such as Brownmiller (1975) and Bergman (1974) (see Olujić, 1995) started to discuss rape as a tactic of terror in warfare, in relation to the First World War, the Second World War and the war in Vietnam. The difference, in the context of the war in the former Yugoslavia, is the widespread publicity that rape received, even though this was only true in regard to a very short period of time, particularly the years 1992–1993, when the (print) media considered this topic. *Calling the Ghosts*, which predominantly addresses (mass) rapes committed during the war in Bosnia,[7] has been aired on more than 30 TV channels since its first release on Danish television in 1996, and its basic appearance comes very close to traditional TV aesthetics. It was only aired on the Bosnian national television network in 1997, shortly after its Bosnian premiere at the Sarajevo International Film Festival in September 1997.[8] The title *Calling the Ghosts* is a reference to a game that the women imprisoned in a camp partly believed in, and which they played during their captivity in order to keep themselves occupied and, by doing so, survive the conditions for 2 months.

Mandy Jacobson is a multiple award-winning director who has been working out of New York and South Africa for more than 10 years. She also completed four documentaries on Nelson Mandela as part of SABC's flagship series to celebrate the former Presidents' global contribution to human rights. Jacobson's fieldwork has taken her across the globe including the US, Brazil, Bosnia, Rwanda, Bangladesh, Cuba, Mozambique and South Africa. With her work she wants to make heard stories not typically covered by the mass media.[9]

In *Calling the Ghosts*, especially when the protagonists of the film remember certain situations, the images are often shown in slow motion and the musical score is frequently melancholic or we hear threatening piano tunes; sometimes we listen to a slowed-down violin that sounds particularly sad. The narrative is not developed in a chronological pattern but rather on the basis of flashbacks. The slow-motion images are often blurred and thus seem to hide part of the 'stories' told, which are presented as if hidden in a fog. In contrast, images that show the streets of Mostar before the war – the town near the homes of the main protagonists (both were in Prijedor when the war broke out)[10] – are very bright and colourful, and the sound is cheerful. Images that refer to the 'more recent past' frequently show destruction: burning buildings, refugees and corpses. It is clear that we are not confronted with the authentic places and bodies we are told about, but with re-enacted images that corroborate what is said. In some scenes, a contrast is made by telling gruesome stories and combining them with less cruel images; showing, for example, male prisoners in the canteen collecting their modest meal and eating it.

The lack of voices and images

Being aware of the general lack of 'female voices' in the public sphere, one realizes how hard it must be to show the fate of women who were raped in the war, including the experiences and consequences of mass rapes. Apart from the generally unfavourable reception in wider society of reports on the sensitive topic of (mass) rape, footage of such rapes does not usually exist, and because no images exist that would prove these violent acts, their status as a war crime is often disputed. Potential audiences' expectation of pictorial proof, despite the absence of images, fosters a need to create visual material that will represent this 'invisible crime'. But real evidence is usually only given by testimonies, thus, as Jadranka asserts, the pressure to speak about it is enormous because the victim is aware of the fact that if she does not tell her story, it will simply not exist. Secondly, as rape is a taboo subject, it is not only difficult for women to speak about it, but there are also no clear rules regarding *how* to speak about it. There is not only a lack of images but also a lack of language. Nusreta and Jadranka usually use neutral words such as, for example, 'experience', and omit the word 'rape', We are not allowed to forget that it is still taboo to speak openly about sexuality as such, apart from clichés that maintain traditional gendered behaviour. Nevertheless, most of the films that deal with violence and rape are predominantly dependent on verbal statements made in interviews, and here the level of the background images is usually created either very neutrally or exaggerated, offering artistically highly constructed images. The latter, in combination with sound, are usually highly manipulative.

A basic question here is: can film be an alternative platform for these 'nonexistent' voices, and if so, what kind of discourse can be established in order to not only break a taboo but also include a wide range of approaches without resorting to the strategy usually applied by the mass media, which offers highly manipulative images but does not dare to 'really' provide a voice for those affected. Film and media analysis is confronted, then, with the following problem: If scholars focus on media products and concentrate on recorded verbal statements, as 'real' images of rapes simply do not exist, they fail to focus on the film's immanent character, which *is* the inclusion of images. Apart from this specific problem, it is generally difficult to focus on the discourse of violence against women for the reasons already mentioned. In my view, we need to analyse not only the documentaries that follow mainly mass-media aesthetics, as we find them most often on television, but also those that are more innovative and show a new potential for dealing with images in the war context which help to reflect on the issues rather than manipulating the audience. These films do exist but are present at film festivals rather than broadcast on TV. In the case of *Calling the Ghosts*, it is the rather manipulative visual means that can be related to the mass-media style, and which we will consider shortly. But before we go on to focus on the ambivalent construction of images of *Calling the Ghosts* in more detail, let us concentrate on another ambivalent issue: the definition of mass rape.

Ambivalence in the definition of mass rape

It is difficult to speak about the representation of 'real' fates of rape victims and not to provide the 'real contexts'; fates of individual victims usually depend on, for example, the period of time after the violence. I will therefore provide a short overview of the legal framework of rape as a crime. One legal definition of 'mass rape', commonly used as a term in the mass media during the 1990s but also in scholarly works, was more or less equated with the term 'genocide'. It explained mass rape as an attempt to 'destroy in whole or in part a national, ethnic, racial or religious group' (Mladjenović and Hughes, 1999, p. 6). Another similar but more detailed definition specifies mass rape in the Bosnian war as genocidal when speaking of 'forced pregnancy, repeated rape, and the prohibition of the woman to abort so that she is forced to carry the "Serbanized" baby to term' (Copelon in Dombrowski, 1999, pp. 22–3). Significantly, Copelon implies here that Serbian women were not victims of mass rapes.

The judge at The Hague Court shown in the film *Calling the Ghosts*, Elizabeth Odio Benito, confirms the earlier view when she asserts that the 'systematic use of rape has been an essential instrument of any cleansing policy.'[11] Niarchos, among others, criticizes this perspective, as 'from a feminist perspective, international human rights law has mischaracterised the crime and has ignored its gender aspects. Rape is regarded not as a violent attack on women but as a challenge to honour (whose honour is not entirely clear), but it has yet to be recognised as an assault motivated by gender, not simply by membership in the enemy camp.' She sees international human rights law as gender-biased (Niarchos, 1995, p. 674). In the Statute of The Hague Tribunal, rape is explicitly treated as a crime against humanity (Article 5) only when it is systematic and widespread, in other words, when it is seen as a part of ethnic cleansing (Smiljanić in Nikolić-Ristanović, 2000, p. 79). Like Niarchos and Smiljanić, Copelon states that rape and genocide are separate atrocities (Copelon, 1999, p. 334) and attention should be given to both the particular ((mass) rape in war) and the general (sexual violence in daily life) as well as to the tension between them. She argues that one also needs to capture the multilayered relationship between gender and ethnicity (Copelon, 1999, p. 335). And finally, she criticizes that 'the distinction commonly drawn between genocidal rape and "normal" rape in war or in peace time is proffered not as a typology, but rather as a hierarchy,' which 'obscures the atrocity of common rape' (Copelon, 1999, p. 342). A third camp of scholars thinks that rape is violence against an 'individual' woman in the first place and not a collective – be it an ethnic or gender group – and so cannot be prosecuted collectively.

Certainly, by concentrating on ethnic collectives, violence against women was manipulated for political goals. Regretfully, the historical and political macro-perspectives of scholars were also in the fore in many countries, and predominantly legitimized the 'collectivist' view, thus promoting collective responsibility and guilt (Blagojević in Nikolić-Ristanović, 2000, preface, pp. x–xi). The approach that I personally favour is the third, which focuses on the individual victim and does not neglect those who do not fit into dominant groups; for example, Serbian women or male rape victims.

The film's construction of victims

Returning to *Calling the Ghosts*, the main protagonists, Nusreta, a Muslim, and Jadranka, a Croatian, both intellectuals, use the term 'genocide' and through that construct primary ethnic affiliations of victims and perpetrators. By following this approach, the directors of *Calling the Ghosts* mainly adhere to the theory of 'collective guilt'. Such extreme positions are arguably caused by moral pressure and the fear of hurting somebody by having a different opinion to official discourse. Furthermore, in my view (mass) rape is rather a psychological 'problem' than a straightforward political action as it is often qualified by war parties. At the same time, to allow us to understand what this crime means to the afflicted women, we need to leave the supposedly 'safe' area of definitions that many official bodies have tried to use, and rather look at the grey areas between these categories, at the women's 'real' life-stories and fates.

As discussed already, *Calling the Ghosts* primarily shows the intimate story of two women; both were tortured and raped in the Omarska camp during the war in Bosnia. Altogether, 36 women were in the camp for 2 months. The only reason the women were set free after 2 months of torture was because journalists, among them Ed Vulliamy, foreign correspondent of *The Guardian* newspaper, were about to break into the camp.[12] It may be that placing the camp's victims in ethnic collectives was an unconscious strategy by the directors of the film to find an approach appropriate to existing national and international discourse, in order to fight for justice.[13] In addition, *Calling the Ghosts* was funded by the Soros Documentary Fund (now known as the Sundance Documentary Fund), The Open Society Institute and many other international funds and trusts, and distributed by Women Make Movies, which may have made the directors even more dependent on the ongoing international point of view at that time. As a result, the film was shown at many festivals and on many TV stations (all in all it was aired in 35 countries), and it was one of the films that later – as intended by the directors – helped spur legal action at the Court in The Hague. In other words, the 'collective guilt' approach of the film helped the women to be heard there at all.[14] Let us, then, see in more detail how the victimized women's fate is constructed in *Calling the Ghosts*.

The construction of female fates in war

We need to be aware that most of the images of the film illustrate life before and after Omarska and are, for a large part, invented as there was no camera present at the time to tell the 'story'. But then we must admit that for most periods of film history it has been common to re-enact scenes in order to represent 'truth' in documentaries. Still, the question remains how sincerely this was done. Further scenes in the film recording the present are also highly manipulative. We usually see the faces of Jadranka and Nusreta in close-up, including those of other women, who do not speak, and keep silent about their 'experiences'. Sometimes even extreme close-ups are used if the subject is very traumatic or of high importance. Part of the close-ups are shown in black and white to foster appreciation of the historical significance of the images and to stress the 'evidence of truth' of them.

When Jadranka speaks about her first rape experience, we see her face in close-up, then there is a cut and we see hands in the dark, the camera moves upwards and we get to know the perpetrator, the camp commander's face, but still the image is very dark and at the same time in black and white. Then we see Jadranka in colour and again in close-up and she informs us that she was summoned by Mejakić, the commander. Another six or seven men were in the room. We again see the room in Omarska where the rapes took place in black and white, and we listen to her words that tell us that she was raped by Mejakić in front of the other men. When she gives this testimony, we repeatedly see her in close-up, then black-and-white images follow, fading in and out. They first show Jadranka, then another woman, and then fade out again to a close-up of Nusreta. The worst sadism, says Jadranka, was when Mejakić, the man who most often initiated this torture of women, asked the following morning if anyone had raped them, and if they had, to tell him. This shows clearly the psychological terror; another level of violence representing the commander's absolute power over them. Mejakić is usually shown through very dark images; when we see him the first time in close-up, there is a dark shadow on his face. The camera zooms first in and then out again. This makes the images appear even more dangerous and give the impression that the audience is confronted with 'evil'. Most often we see Mejakić from behind in slow motion, when he walks through the dark corridors of the Omarska building, underscored with dull violin tunes – sometimes he cannot even be identified. Only at the very end of the film, we see him in an outdoor shot and recognize his face clearly. Here a contrast is created by means of these very dark images that are usually related to Mejakić and the very bright images of the innocent victims. Jadranka is usually dressed in white and placed in a white environment, such as the room she is interviewed in; Nusreta is usually presented in front of a bright pink background. The scenes that refer to the time after the victims' release are shot with a yellow filter so the colour yellow, with the sun shining, seems to be the colour of freedom after the dark days.

Productions such as *Calling the Ghosts* basically follow news reportage style. Hrvoje Turković, a film scholar from Zagreb, sees a general 'predominance of the television format' in this sort of documentary that has led to the stereotype of the 'Big Mac'-dramaturgy: 'a slice of verbal testimony, a slice of environmental (nontestimonial, contextual, observational) vistas with musical underscore, and a reiteration of this bi-segmental structure to the end of the film' (Turković, 2008). The specifics of *Calling the Ghosts* are the *per se* missing images of what the women experienced and, as a consequence, the understandably higher 'need' for their invention. In addition, the more a subject is taboo, the more there is the danger of constructedness and polarization. When trying to somehow understand a rapist, it would be too risky to rely on just one case, where a rapist admits his deed, for example, in the documentary film *Confessions of a Monster* (Ademir Kenović and Ismet Arnautalić, Bosnia and Herzegovina, 1992). But every single voice may be able to contribute a new aspect to this under-researched and therefore also polarized topic.

Returning to taboo topics, we need to be aware that there is also a barrier to watching such films, especially if one feels indirectly involved. So the reception of films such as *Calling the Ghosts* is a topic on its own, worthy of scholarly analysis. It remains a fact, though, that there are conditions in any society that limit discourse on such sensitive issues. It is a mental and psychological limitation and reflects the 'inability of language'. Further, there is a total lack of power on the part of the victims, and the construction of images highlights this fact but also shows a high degree of manipulation. Arguably, 'collective guilt' is the dominant message in the film, but in my view this is an unhealthy approach. In order to enable in-depth understanding and show the danger of the collectivist view, and at the same time its roots, the topic needs to be discussed in the framework of regional patriarchy.

The patriarchal framework and the question of guilt

The following scene exemplifies the need to include the patriarchal framework in the discussion of guilt. Nusreta, who met her husband in Zagreb after 6 months of separation, repeats what her husband said to her: 'My God, if anything did happen to you, you were not to blame.' At first, this statement infers that he does not know what happened to his wife but also something even more important, which I consider shortly. Then Nusreta tells us the story of another woman who told her that her husband divorced her as he could not cope with what had happened. She adds: 'If he can't forgive her for something that was out of her control....' Both statements, that of Nusreta's husband and Nusreta's own, let the audience realize that both think it is a matter of forgiveness and prove how guilt is still associated with women in the context of rape, although it is obvious beyond any doubt that they are the victims. The attitudes of patriarchal society indirectly justify the male's violent behaviour while at the same time finding fault with the wife (Nikolić-Ristanović, 1994, p. 411). Such fundamental attitudes confirm my earlier argument that the role of women and the construction of their fate – in real life and in film – must always be considered in relation to the specific patriarchy of the region in which they live.

Maria B. Olujić elaborates that this abject humiliation is especially prevalent in the Balkans where the *honour/shame complex* is still strong and 'female chastity' is central to family and community honour (Schneider, 1971; Davis, 1977, in Olujić, 1995). In the Balkan region patrilinear thinking, a specific form of patriarchal identity, constitutes a framework in which the specific value of honour remains stronger than in the rest of Europe (Rohringer, 2008). In comparable societies, war rape and other forms of sexual assault have long been categorized as 'an attack against "honor" in national and international regulations because they violate the honour of the man and his exclusive right to sexual possession of his woman as property' (Copelon, 1999, p. 336). There remains also legal ambiguity, as the indictments represent the rape of women as a 'wilful infliction of great suffering', but not as 'torture' (Copelon, 1999, p. 339). The latter is the case only if sexual mutilation of a male prisoner happens (Copelon, 1999, p. 339), which surely confirms the objectivization of women once again, as there is no logic in this given (and also hierarchical) difference.

When Jadranka speaks about her first experience of rape, she lets us know that she did not tell anyone what had happened to her, and that the women did not ask: 'It was an unspoken rule that we not talk to each other about what happened during those absences.' This again can be explained by the taboo of speaking about rape, by the feeling of shame and also by the lack of language to express what happened. Finally, though, it is also the fear that they could be left by their husbands if it became known. As Nikolić-Ristanović asserts, we are not allowed to forget that raped women who do not speak about their fates protect themselves against stigmatization (Nikolić-Ristanović, 2000, p. 24). Thus, even in the cases finally made public, certain taboos (at least on a language level) seem to live on.

The majority of authors agree that the problem of violence between men and women starts in a patriarchal system that legitimizes violent behaviour. It started long before modern warfare and is a consequence of the unequal access to power of women and men in patriarchal societies. We can speak of a kind of 'shifting' of the violence perpetrated by males from the private sphere to a public or semi-public one. How otherwise could we explain the rape of men's own wives and lovers in the first place? This does not mean that the victim is always a woman, but our societies are structurally built on hierarchical and unequal chances for men and women when it comes to the rise to power, especially in the context of forming one's identity and protecting one's integrity as well as one's interests and needs/desires.

Giving voices back to the individuals

According to Olujić, and connected to the unequal power to define one's position and identity, war propaganda manipulated the individual body into a body of politics and used 'political rapes' to 'tempt' military action by the West (Olujić, 1998). Olujić states that we are responsible for transforming and reformatting the social body back into the individual body and, as I have argued here, for predominantly showing individual fates (Olujić, 1998). Mass rape in Bosnia captured world attention largely because of its association with 'ethnic cleansing' or 'genocide' and not as a crime of gender. Indeed, 'for many, rape remains an inevitable by-product of war except when it is a vehicle of genocide' (Copelon, 1999, p. 333). This development needs to be changed, and films may manage to do so when they show the 'faces' of the individuals behind the anonymously constructed ethnic groups of victims, who encountered violence in many different ways. Films can be better equipped for giving insight into these individual fates than any written texts as they (even though they may be highly manipulative, as *Calling the Ghosts* shows) depend on, but at the same time allow for, more diverse levels of expression than a written text. One example, a rather innovative project in terms of its film language that in my view manages to break taboos by showing the individuals' 'real' experiences and feelings exactly because of its alternative filmic approach, is Vesna Ljubić's film *Ecce Homo* (Bosnia and Herzegovina, 1994).

Speaking images

The (semi-)absence of words characterizes not only films about rapes in war, but is also characteristic of other films on war violence in the former Yugoslavia. In this context, *Ecce Homo* is one of the most interesting examples. Its director, Vesna Ljubić, a Jewish Croat from Sarajevo, did not aim to construct a film without words, but realized during the process of filming that she 'could make it without any words'.[15] What she wanted to express could be done by a certain arrangement of images, sounds and quotations. Regretfully – apart from countless and many successful festival and conference releases, in Europe and the US (e.g., the film received awards in Berlin 1994, Amsterdam 1994 and Cretey/Paris 1995, opened the World Peace Conference in 1994 in Washington D.C. and met as well with good reception at the Second International Conference on Documentary Films in Los Angeles in 1995, held by the Academy of Motion Picture Arts) – *Ecce Homo* was only shown on Bosnian state TV and TV Amsterdam in 1994, where it reached its biggest audience.

Ljubić studied philosophy at Sarajevo University and simultaneously film directing at the Experimental Center and RAI in Rome, where she temporarily also worked as an assistant to Federico Fellini. With her film *Ecce Homo* she created a graphic record of people living and dying together in her native town Sarajevo, where she lived throughout the war. After the end of the war Ljubić continued to work as an editor of drama and documentary programmes for the radio/television network of Bosnia and Herzegovina.[16]

The film *Ecce Homo* expresses thoughts and feelings through a combination of visual metaphors, which are constructed in a totally different way to *Calling the Ghosts* and which, unlike *Calling the Ghosts,* are aiming for a conscious reception by the potential viewer. Lubjić uses a poetic language on the level of images in order to convey the 'state of being' in the city of Sarajevo during the siege. The 'state of being' includes the life of animals in the city, especially dogs. By applying a minimalist film language she succeeds in gradual insight into what is happening in this war, in this city. We realize that war makes life the same for everyone in the city: living means surviving, no matter if you are Jewish, Catholic, Serbian or Muslim, a dog or a human being. As the seasons change, the city's nature changes too; the only difference to the previous season is that more people have been buried: the available space in the graveyard has decreased. We are brought back to the essence of life and feel the absurdity of killing living beings, of extinguishing life. At the end of the film the city is again covered in the snow. A song projects a better life in the future.

The unconventional narrative construction that we experience in Ljubić's film is symptomatic of these new modes in documentary film, as are her decisions to use collage as a narrative device and the personal and at the same time poetic and emotional approach. The films share the need to construct taboo themes and unspoken realities, and chose different ways of dealing with them. In comparison to *Calling the Ghosts, Ecce Homo* invites people to reflect on essential issues rather than drawing them in, though *Calling the Ghosts* was also created with only good intentions.

Conclusion

Today, television is still the first place that can provide a platform to reach huge audiences, and we still depend on it when we are aiming to break the taboos dealt with in the films discussed in this text. We should not judge these films based only on their potential viewing figures. On the other hand, TV formats, which usually aim to communicate with the masses, need not necessarily be manipulative or reliant on 'Big-Mac'-dramaturgy to reach their audiences. As Rada Šešić, another documentary film author, film curator and lecturer who grew up in Bosnia and Herzegovina as well, confirms, this sort of filmic approach usually finds its way into TV slots, most often in productions of the national TV-channels themselves or ordered by a production company outside television and later on also aired on TV.[17] But there can and should be developed also new patterns of telling a 'story' and of reading which invite the audience to reflect, for example, by confronting them with the experiences of individuals on the (small) screen, which show fates with which the potential viewer can identify him/herself. Such alternative TV programmes are made step-by-step, but regretfully are not yet common. In these changing times we need to change the conventions of how to communicate history and to reconsider the criteria that legitimatize a topic as historical. In this process the traditional TV format, with inherited modes of production functioning as a restrictive medium with conventions that require sensationalism, only one of many potential and possible forms, may need to be set aside: for example, to offer a space for more innovative film concepts. We will always have to deal with conventions relating to how one communicates history on the basis of letters, sounds and images, but these could more often meet our current ways of identifying ourselves with certain issues and states of being. Films such as *Ecce Homo* can be understood by everyday people, and yet it is a very complex and artistically ambitious film project. By giving space to these newer formats, the probability may increase that female voices and/or female concerns and fates will be more often included when talking about history, since history before such films were made was more or less a hugely 'male narrative' of the past.

A note on availability

Calling the Ghosts is available on film, VHS, and DVD and can be ordered at Women Make Movies, http://www.wmm.com/. The distributor offers different conditions for sale or rental for universities and institutions on the one hand and for K–12, public libraries and select groups on the other. The film *Ecce Homo* can be ordered from its director, Vesna Ljubić.

Notes

1. Jacobson is a sociologist from South Africa; Jeliničić was born in Croatia and was brought up in the US.
2. Jacobson, personal communication, 18 February 2008.
3. A film dedicated to this group, made by Zoran Solomun and Helga Reidemeister (Germany, 1997) was, apart from many festival screenings, also aired on German television (in May 1997 and March 2002 on 3-sat, and in July 1997 on WDR). Some members of the group were also represented in the film *Unsatisfied* (Casey Cooper Johnson, UNMI Kosovo, 2005), which is part of the film project 'Under Construction' – a serial of different documentary films on the post-war and/or post-Communist period showing a cross-cultural approach to the Balkan region, which was also aired on RTK (Radio Television of Kosovo).
4. A study entitled 'Violence Against Women' conducted by SOS Hotline (Belgrade) in the period 1991–1993 shows that the rise of nationalism, militarism, war and the economic crisis intensified violence against women in Belgrade (Mršević and Hughes, 1997, p. 2). Almost 12 per cent (11.7 per cent, $N = 90$ out of 770) of the women reported that they had been raped (Mršević and Hughes, 1997, p. 3).
5. After the Second World War, it was still taboo to address openly how women coped with the changed personality of their husbands who returned from the war. In the 1990s, Atina Grossman's article about German women in the Second World War (Grossman, 1999, pp. 176–7) and Copelon's work refer to rape as a war crime as well as to ethnic cleansing (Copelon, 1999, p. 346). Mladjenović concludes that in the Yugoslav wars of the 1990s many women refugees were

raped while they were escaping or staying at a friend's home, by their male hosts and even relatives (in Mršević and Hughes, 1997, p. 10).

6. One of the sharpest increases in violence since the beginning of the wars on the territory of the former Yugoslavia has been young men's violence against their mothers. The percentage of calls from women who were battered by their sons almost doubled from 1991 to 1993 (6.4 per cent to 11.1 per cent) (Mršević and Hughes, 1997, p. 8). A scene in the documentary *Road of Fraternity and Unity* (Maja Weiss, Slovenia, 1999) impressively demonstrates this (new) type of violence when a son attacks his mother in a sort of video clip that the director incorporates in her film.

7. As agreed upon by international organizations (e.g., the European Community), the number of women raped during 5 years of war was set at 20,000. The Sarajevo State Commission for Investigation of war crimes states 50,000 (Jones, 2000, p. 3).

8. Furthermore, the film had a week-long theatrical release at the Cinema Village in New York City in October 1996, but finally was disqualified for the Academy Awards because it was already aired then on Danish television. Excellent reviews brought the film also to the attention of HBO and CBS's '60 Minutes'. Among other awards it received the Emmy Award for Outstanding Individual Achievement in a Craft in News and Documentary Programming: Directing, the Emmy Award for Outstanding Investigative Journalism Program, the 1998 Robert F. Kennedy Journalism Award, the 1997 Cable ACE Award for the Best International Informational Special and the 1996 Nestor Almendros Award (personal communication, Mandy Jacobson, June 2008). While Women Make Movies acquired theatrical and educational rights, Jane Balfour Films handled international television sales. A nonprofit UK company, namely The Television Trust for the Environment, acquired distribution rights for developing countries on a flat fee basis (personal communication, Mandy Jacobson, June 2008).

9. See https://www.msu.edu/unit/phl/devconference/Jacobson.htm date. Accessed 27 September 2009.

10. Prijedor is a city in the Northwest of Bosnia and Herzegovina, part of the Serb Republic.

11. In 1992 the UN Security Council and in 1993 the European Community (EC Report, 1993), following the statement of Kajosevic, also joined this position: www.women.it/cyberarchive/files/Kajosevic.htm. Accessed 26 June 2009.

12. This happened after Radovan Karadžić's statement announcing that all prisons were open to inspection by international organizations: Interview with Karadžić, United Press International, Belgrade, 23 December 1992: http://www.women.it/cyberarchive/files/kajosevic.htm. Accessed 26 June 2009.

13. The two main protagonists of the film, Jadranka and Nusreta, also met with Kofi Annan, then Secretary of the United Nations (personal communication, Mandy Jacobson, June 2008).

14. Even some American feminists, who confirmed the view of collective guilt, became supporters of particular nationalist causes at the expense of general 'feminist' ones (see Korac, 1996).

15. Author's interview with Ljubić, 15 October 2002.

16. Author's interview with Ljubić, 15 October 2002.

17. Interview with Rada Šešić, curator of various film festivals in the region and also in other parts of the world, held in September 2009.

Filmography

Calling the Ghosts (Mandy Jacobson and Karmen Jelinčić, US and Croatia, 1996).
Confessions of a Monster (Ademir Kenović and Ismet Arnautalić, Bosnia and Herzegovina, 1992).
Ecce Homo (Vesna Ljubić, Bosnia and Herzegovina, 1994).
Road of Fraternity and Unity (Maja Weiss, Slovenia, 1999).
Unsatisfied (Casey Cooper Johnson, UNMI Kosovo, 2005).
Women in Black (Zoran Solomun and Helga Reidemeister, Germany, 1997).

Bibliography

Brownmiller, S. (1975) *Against Our Will: Men, Women and Rape* (New York: Simon & Schuster).

Copelon, R. (1999) 'Surfacing gender: reengraving crimes against women in humanitarian law', in N.A. Dombrowksi (ed.), *Women and War in the Twentieth Century* (London: Routledge).

Dombrowski, N.A. (1999) (ed.) *Women and War in the Twentieth Century* (London: Routledge).

Grossman, A. (1999) 'A Question of silence: the rape of German women by Soviet occupation soldiers', in N.A. Dombrowksi (ed.), *Women and War in the Twentieth Century* (London: Routledge).

Jones, A. (ed.) (2000) *Gendercide and Genocide*: http://jonestream.blogspot.com. Accessed 13 January 2007.

Kajosevic, I. (2000) *Understanding War Rape: Bosnia 1992*: www.women.it/cyberarchive/files/Kajosevic.htm. Accessed 18 February 2008.

Korac, M. (1996) 'Ethnic conflict, rape, and feminism: The case of Yugoslavia', *Research on Russia and Eastern Europe*, 2, 247–66.

Mladjenović, L. and D.M. Hughes (1999) *Feminist Resistance to War and Violence in Serbia*, http://uri.edu/aetsci/wms/hughes/warvio1.htm. Accessed 17 February 2008.

Mršević, Z. and D.M. Hughes (1997) 'Violence against women in Belgrade, Serbia: SOS Hotline 1991–1993', *Violence Against Women: An International Interdisciplinary Journal*, 3.2, 101–28.

Niarchos, C. (1995) 'Women, war, and rape: challenges facing the international tribunal for the former Yugoslavia', *Human Rights Quarterly*, 17.4, 649–90.

Nikolić-Ristanović, V. (ed.) (2000) *Women, Violence and War: Wartime Victimization of Refugees in the Balkans* (Budapest: Central European University Press).

Nikolić-Ristanović, V. (1994) 'Nasilje nad ženama u uslovima rata i ekonomske krize', *Sociološki pregled*, 28.3, 409–17.

Olujić, M.B. (1995) 'Women, rape, and war: the continued trauma of refugees and displaced persons in Croatia', *Anthropology of East Europe Review*, 13.1. http://condor.depaul.edu/~rrotenbe/aeer/aeer13_1/Olujic.html. Accessed 18 February 2008.

Olujić, M.B. (1998) 'Embodiment of terror: gendered violence in peacetime and wartime in Croatia and Bosnia-Herzegovina', *Medical Anthropology Quarterly*, New Series, 12.1, 31–50.

Rohringer, M. (2008) *Der jugoslawische Film nach Tito. Konstruktionen kollektiver Identitäten* (Münster: LIT).

Turković, H. (2008) 'Preface', *Catalogue of the GoEast-Festival Wiesbaden, Germany* (Frankfurt am Main: Deutsches Filminstitut).

12
History in Popular Television Drama
The Flemish Past in *Wij, Heren van Zichem*

Alexander Dhoest

Can history be reconciled with the laws of mainstream television? If so, how do popular programmes relate to and influence historical consciousness? To explore these issues, this chapter reflects on the position and importance of history on television in Flanders, the Dutch-language community in Belgium. It focuses on the monopoly period of public broadcasting, from 1953 until 1989, when history was a crucial domain for television. Despite evolutions within this period, it presents remarkable continuity and coherence as to the broadcasting philosophy and policies leading to the production of innumerable historical programmes. After providing an overview of historical programming, this chapter takes a closer look at the most successful period serial, exploring the impact of contextual factors and historical actors (producers, audiences, critics) on the representation of the past. To conclude, this chapter reflects on the potential impact of such period drama on the formation of a national historical consciousness.

History on Flemish TV

In the monopoly period, Flemish television operates in a typical Western–European public service context, prioritizing information and education while also providing an extensive but discursively marginalized offer of entertainment programmes (Dhoest, 2007a). As a region, Flanders gradually gains economic, political and cultural confidence, which inspires a great dynamism and ambition among broadcasting personnel. Working within a Reithian ethos, the BRT (Belgische Radio- en Televisieomroep) officials strive towards enlightenment of viewers, conceiving television along the lines of what they think is important and worthwhile. With a typical background in education, press journalism, philology, history, literature and theatre, they represent and broadcast the views of the intellectual and artistic middle class. Their views are reflected in innumerable informative and educational programmes dealing with current affairs, history, literature and the arts. Interviewing great men, revisiting great scenes, showcasing great monuments, performing musical masterpieces and staging great plays: most television is conceived along the lines of the tradition of culture as 'the best that has been said and done'. In this endeavour, culture and history are strongly intertwined, the past being presented as the most important repository of cultural accomplishments.

In this period, history is omnipresent, in various genres and in different sections of the broadcasting institution. Historical references also appear in many nonhistorical genres such as quiz shows. The historical approach is so self-evident that programme descriptions often fail to mention it (Theuwissen, 2002). Most obviously, there are proper historical programmes, often documentaries or historical reconstructions. Within the section of Artistic and Educational Broadcasts, many documentaries focus on the past, with an early appetite for arts history because images of paintings and buildings are easy to make (de Maesschalck, 2007, p. 282). As a period of Flemish prosperity and artistic productivity, the Middle Ages is a privileged object of historical arts programmes, with a focus on painting (Flemish primitive painting) and architecture (such as cathedrals). School television and adult education are other fields where many historical programmes are made, with an obvious educational objective. The section of Sciences also has a high historical output, often commemorating anniversaries of important events. Both archive footage and interviews with eyewitnesses are popular techniques to reconstruct the more recent past. While often international in scope, many programmes return to a relatively recent (twentieth-century) and close (Belgian) past, with a predilection for national political events and the Second World War (de Maesschalck, 2007). These choices are inspired not only by a view of what is important in the past, but also by pragmatism (there is more material available for more recent periods) and by audience preferences, as viewers (are assumed to) identify most with what happened in the last three generations (de Maesschalck, 1989, p. 113).

Drama is another central category, with a host of historical reconstructions and single dramas based on historical figures. Some of it is historically sound docudrama, inventively remedying the lack of visual material for older history. Some of it is more fictionalized, often using literary material as a source for artistic renditions of the past. Within the Drama section, for a long time single drama is the privileged form for serious and literary material. However, it is gradually supplanted by serial drama providing a higher (audience) return on investment, as historical reconstructions are a particularly expensive enterprise for a relatively small broadcaster working on shoestring budgets. Many of the series and serials made between 1953 and 1989 are set in the past (20 out of 32). Only four of them are clearly historical, explicitly dealing with historical figures (such as the painter Rubens) and reconstructing actual historical events (such as the Belgian battle for independence). Beside a courtroom drama reconstructing actual cases and a comedy situated in the recent past, the other 14 shows are 'period serials' set in the past and occasionally referring to actual events or persons but predominantly giving fictional accounts of life in the past.

Taken together, these period serials form the strongest and most consistent trend in drama until 1989. All return to the rural Flanders of the late nineteenth and early twentieth centuries, showing the village or small city life of 'common people'. Often based on literary work, they show everyday dramas situated in the context of historical changes: world wars, industrialization, urbanization, modernization and so on. They also deal with the strong but waning power of the Catholic Church and the rise of liberalism and socialism. However, these changes remain in the background, the foreground being occupied by the relatively simple and stable world of ordinary people. If addressed at all, these social tensions are incorporated by characters in their everyday occupations and personal relations. While varying in tone and seriousness, most dramas contain comic elements counterbalancing social critique and sympathetic types incorporating heavy themes. Although they are set in the past, these dramas mostly evoke a period atmosphere without serious discussion of historical events. They are extremely popular, thus justifying their high cost, but they are at odds with the overall informative and educational take on drama. Their content is often far from elevated and refined, the coarse manners of folksy types constituting the object of good-natured joy. This is essentially entertainment rather than enlightenment, with only the mostly literary sources offering some cultural justification and credibility. In this period, broadcasting officials show a marked resistance to such 'popular' drama (see Dhoest, 2004a), but it is undoubtedly the most successful variant of historical programming. This begs questions as to the importance and impact of its view on the past, a point I will investigate by taking a closer look at the prototypical example.

Wij, Heren van Zichem

The most famous period drama is *Wij, Heren van Zichem* [We, Lords of Zichem] (1969), a 26-episode serial based on the work of novelist Ernest Claes. Director and screenwriter Maurits Balfoort combined characters and storylines of different novels into an overarching narrative about the life of the proud people ('lords') in the actual village of Zichem. The tone is mixed, showing good-natured types and humorous situations, but also poverty and hardship, as indicated in the introduction of the serial to Dutch viewers: 'It is also a truthful chronicle of the poor, backwards circumstances in which a large part of the Flemish rural population lived at the previous turn of the century' (KRO, press release, n.d.). Ernest Claes was the most-read Flemish novelist of the time, although he got into trouble after the Second World War for sympathizing with the German occupier. All the same, his work was unquestionably part of the literary canon, as a middlebrow (literary but accessible) author with a knack for storytelling and evoking the atmosphere of rural Flanders. His most famous work *De Witte* [Whitey] (1920) recounts the adventures of little rascal Lewie, getting into all sorts of trouble but ultimately a naïve, good-natured lad. *De Witte* inspired a character in *Wij, Heren van Zichem,* which thus capitalizes on the fame of author Claes and his literary creations, also known through a successful film adaptation (*De Witte,* J. Vanderheyden, 1934; see Biltereyst and Van Bauwel, 2004). Claes became the single most adapted author on Flemish television, as his 'Heimat'-works were set in a familiar recent past and his vividly typed characters had 'flesh and blood'.[1] Director Balfoort describes his characters as follows: 'For their unadorned realness they have become the prototypes of the average person in his everyday existence, with his joy and sorrow, ups and downs, peace and turmoil' (Balfoort, n.d., p. 5).[2]

The breadth of 26 episodes allows Balfoort to create a whole world of related and interlinked characters representing different aspects of village life, as well as characteristics of and tensions within early twentieth-century life in Flanders. Thus, the young Lewie (de Witte) symbolizes the idealized free life in the countryside, also incorporating the 'typically Flemish' resistance to authority. He and his family represent the hard life of poor rural workers, while farmer Coene has worked his way up to become a rich farmer. As a Flemish prototype he is dramatically opposed to the francophone village baron Alex, rich and powerful by descent, thus addressing class tensions. Of Coene's sons, Herman in particular gets a central role in the later episodes, as the student who becomes involved in the Flemish language movement. Village priest Munte is another key protagonist, his church literally and figuratively standing central in village life. He is a good-natured but self-willed and old-fashioned little old man, coming to the defence of the outcasts. His legs are worn-out but his tongue is still sharp, which becomes apparent in his discussions with Mother Superior Cent, a physically and mentally strong woman with socialist inclinations. Munte is also opposed to Jef the blacksmith, a liberal, and to his maid Rozelien, who loves him dearly but who is terribly domineering and gossipy. These dramatic oppositions are not used to create big drama or explosive tensions, but they fuel good-natured teasing and bickering in intertwined storylines about everyday life.

The appeal of the serial is mostly to be situated in its evocation of village life in all its aspects, taking the time to show scenes from daily life such as family dinners or communal prayer. It's like a folkloric museum come to life, with characters in period costume (caps, clogs, aprons) living in period farmhouses and kitchens, working the fields with authentic tools and reviving old trades. Scenes take place in the farm kitchen, the blacksmith's workplace and the village cafe. The opening shot of the first episode is emblematic: a slowly panning camera follows a horse and cart riding through the typical flat Flemish landscape, through the green fields with the village and church tower in the background. Love for the village, the countryside and its people is an important undercurrent in all storylines. In the fourth episode, on a walk with Lewie, the priest Munte admires his village ('our beautiful Zichem') from a distance, praising the landscape ('God's face is imprinted in it') and the people ('peasant-like silent pious people'). The camera pans to show us the wood and fields, the church tower and the abbey in the neighbouring village, both actual cultural landmarks of the Zichem region. Catholic religion is a strong force in village life, with the priest and the nun as central protagonists, and crosses and Maria statues in every room. The villagers devotedly pray and go to church, but they also superstitiously whisper folk tales about ghosts. Most characters speak a juicy dialect, evoking the true speech of the rural working class. The soundtrack is full of folk tunes and instruments, with the accordion as a beloved instrument. While accurate period settings and details are important, the style is not visually overwhelming but quite intimate and sober. This is partly related to the content, the simple and relatively poor life of common people, but there is also a pragmatic reason, as grandiose period reconstructions are simply too expensive. The same is true for the long takes and the slow editing pace, which simultaneously symbolize the quiet life in the country and reflect the poverty of the producers who cannot afford multiple shots and takes. As director Balfoort comments, in the late 1960s, there is not even much money for the post-synchronization of dialogue, so the sound quality is very uneven (De Bie, 1981, p. 47).

If we want to assess the importance of this serial, its success is a first factor to take into account. Systematic audience research started in 1969 and found that *Wij, Heren van Zichem* was incredibly popular, with 3,120,000 viewers on average (of a population of about 6 million) and ratings up to 81.70 per cent (BRT, 1969, p. 3). The streets were allegedly empty at the time when *Wij, Heren van Zichem* was broadcast (BRT, 1978, p. 48). The actors quickly became celebrities, notably actor Luc Philips playing village priest Pastoor Munte, who capitalized on his fame to make public appearances in costume and who got actual offers to become a village priest (De Bie, 1981, p. 41). The serial had frequent reruns, the last one on the occasion of 50 years of television in 2003, when it was consecrated again as one of the great moments of Flemish television. In research on television memories, I found that *Wij, Heren van Zichem* was one of the best-remembered fiction programmes (Dhoest, 2007b). Viewer memories of this programme were predominantly positive, most viewers addressing the good acting and remembering quite a few characters and actors. The interviewees also commented on the recognition prompted by the portrayal of a world they knew or were familiar with through stories of their parents and grandparents. Nostalgia was definitely an ingredient of these fond memories, a longing for the simpler, communal life of the past.

The press response was mixed. As with most Flemish fiction, the tone was critical, commenting on the poor quality of acting (comparing it to amateur theatre), on the use of strong (and therefore sometimes hardly intelligible) dialect, on the fragmented and anecdotic nature of the script, on the slow pace and the overall old-fashioned nature of this serial (e.g., *Humo,* 30 January 1969; see also Dhoest, 2004b).[3] Quite a few commentators wondered why the BRT did not turn to more contemporary drama talking about contemporary people (e.g., *Het Volk*, 27 January 1969; *Het Laatste Nieuws,* 28 January 1969). However, there were also positive comments on some actors who played quite naturally, partly thanks to the authentic use of dialect. Also, many reviewers comment on the enormous success of the serial and attribute it to the need of viewers for such 'typically Flemish' serials (*Vlaams Weekblad*, 25 January 1969). Looking back, director Balfoort remembers the negative reviews but also the enormous success of the serial, which he attributes to recognition:

> …what kind of criticism didn't I get. It was *folklore*, it was *anti-culture*, it made the people *retarded* and what have you not. They blamed me for all kinds of things, while it was my purpose to show something about Flemish people with a human face. […] It was the start of something our own people did and I must have hit the mark: people recognized themselves and their parents in the figures, I think.
>
> (De Bie, 1981, pp. 33–9)

Again, recognition of a familiar world comes up as one of the strengths of *Wij, Heren van Zichem*. This sentiment is often linked to its Flemish nature, which was indeed a clear objective of public broadcasters at the time. They specifically wanted to educate the viewers into 'good Flemings', who knew their history and culture. This explains the choice for the adaptation of literary heritage with a historical setting. It also explains the choice for Claes, not only a good narrator but also a typically 'Flemish' author writing regionally specific novels. Elaborating a Flemish 'dramaturgy' was a clear intention of the broadcasters: 'The Flemish broadcaster has the cultural and legitimate task and moral duty to give the Flemish identity an adult emanation in Flemish television-dramaturgy' (BRT Annual Report, 1975). If possible, they opted for Flemish work, so that each annual report proudly proclaims what percentage of the fiction output was based on 'own' Flemish (or Dutch-language) sources. This conviction remains intact until the 1980s, when cable allows viewers to turn to (more popular) Dutch channels. In 1981, then head of drama Frans Puttemans proclaims: 'In the middle of the increased cable distribution, we think it is our duty to show the Flemish viewer the mirror of a recognizable Flemish world of civilization and life' (BRT Annual Report, 1981, p. 142; see also Dhoest, 2004a).

Heritage, history?

Although recognizable, the portrayal of Flanders in this and other serials is very selective: a particular period is focused upon, with particular experiences and characters. Similar images and discourses consistently return in television serials and films based on the same *Heimat* literature – a popular trend but only one among many in Flemish literature. Selectivity is unavoidable in reconstructions of history, but the specific selections that are made tell us something about the view on the past at a particular time in a specific cultural and institutional context. As indicated above, clear Flemish-minded broadcasting policies guided the choice of literature to be adapted. Not coincidentally, the Flemish-minded broadcasters chose the work of Claes, himself actively involved in the Flemish (nationalist) movement (de Goeyse and Keersmaekers, 1998, pp. 728–9). There are also more pragmatic factors at play, to do with financial and artistic restrictions: as there wasn't a tradition of Flemish screenwriting at the time, often existing work was adapted; 'folk'-narrators with colourful characters like Claes were most easy to adapt to the screen; the 'simple past' invoked by Claes and others was also the cheapest period to realistically reconstruct (Dhoest, 2004a). The audience success of two previous period serials, all by the same director, also played an important role in the start-up of *Wij, Heren van Zichem*, which clearly tapped into the *Zeitgeist*. At its core, however, the adaptation of Flemish *Heimat*-literature bespeaks an ideologically charged broadcasting policy.

This persistent return to a specific (version of the) past, based on a corpus of literary work, reminds of similar preferences for historical drama throughout European film and television. The British 'heritage' tradition forms a particularly interesting point for comparison, as it was also criticized for showing a limited and ideologically suspect image of the past. Higson (1993) denounces heritage cinema for turning away from the chaotic present and nostalgically looking back at an imperialist, upper-class, pastoral England, presented in a visually lavish and prettified way. Although typically addressing social tensions, heritage film and television generally presents a rosy picture of the past: 'the past is displayed as visually spectacular pastiche, inviting a nostalgic gaze that resists the ironies and social critiques so often suggested narratively by these films' (Higson, 1993, p. 109). Nostalgia is identified as the overarching structure of feeling, reflecting contemporary malaise and providing a redefinition of the national (Chase and Shaw, 1989; Wollen, 1991). Later accounts have criticized this one-sided ideological criticism of heritage drama and have pointed at its ambiguities and diversity (e.g., Monk, 2002). While discussion is possible on the ideological outcomes of heritage film and TV, its focus on certain periods, experiences and literary sources is undeniable.

I would argue that Flemish period drama has a similar function, although it represents the past very differently (see Dhoest, 2004c). As indicated in the above account on *Wij, Heren van Zichem*, it portrays a rural world of 'simple people', not the higher classes. It focuses on poverty rather than opulence, on 'real' problems rather than problems of the heart. Nevertheless, the mixed critical-nostalgic tone is equally present, criticism perhaps taking a more prominent position but nostalgia ultimately defining the structure of feeling. Although poor, the past is comforting, for it is presented as a time of simplicity, authenticity and communality. The world of *Wij, Heren van Zichem* is not exactly a rural idyll, but it is touching and endearing. It does not commemorate an empire, but a time when poor, honest and hardworking people were laying the roots for the current, prosperous Flanders. There is a degree of national auto-stereotyping going on, not aimed at an external market (unlike British drama, Flemish drama is hardly ever exported) but at self-definition. The Flemish myth of the 'underdog', both hardworking and resistant, is strongly present in all period drama. There is an interesting parallel with other more 'peripheral' or smaller nations, such as Ireland where the Gaelic myth of an isolated, rural Catholic population is kept alive and whose people are often represented as happy, innocent and welcoming (White, 1997; Barton, 2000). Ultimately, such period drama is an instrument for revisiting and reconstructing national history, returning to the past in order to create images for the present. It is no coincidence that period drama was thriving at a time when the Flemish movement for cultural and political emancipation was leading to the gradual reform of the Belgian state structure. As with all (sub-)nations, Flanders needed to define and reconfirm the national identity that its new political structures were deemed to reflect. The sense of a shared past and culture were strong sources of identification, so it is no surprise that period drama, with its connotations of historical and cultural legitimacy, became so prominent between the 1960s and the 1980s.

Presented in this way, period drama takes on many aspects of mythology, seeking the roots of the nation in a fictionalized past and naturalizing its portrayals by constant repetition. What, then, has this drama to offer from a historical point of view? Clearly, it is not intent on creating accurate pictures of 'the past', although 'surface realism' through the use of accurate period details is important. Costumes, settings, buildings, objects: every detail is selected to effectively and accurately evoke a particular episode from the past. As to the storylines and characters, the aim is predominantly to entertain rather than to instruct about history, although the historical context does justify a popularity of tone that was unacceptable in contemporary fiction of the time. The coarse humour and strong types became acceptable because of the historical distance, allowing both viewers and broadcasters some excuse for essentially entertaining viewing. So, on the whole, *Wij Heren of Zichem* does not offer much in terms of 'proper' history, but to dismiss it as completely historically irrelevant would underestimate its impact. Rather than 'official' history, such period drama is to be situated on the field of popular history and popular memory. According to Wollen, this is where the photographic image can have a tremendous impact: 'Photographic images [...] have a unique capacity to give the past an active existence in the present, and those which are seen by vast numbers of people construct popular memories shared on a significant scale' (Wollen, 1991, p. 186).

As pointed out by Anderson (2001), history is also to be found in programmes that are not 'about' history nor claim to be historically authentic. Film and television can effectively evoke the past, thus becoming part of popular memory. Research into popular memory deals with all the ways in which the past is constructed in society and social memories are formed, including mass media and especially historical dramas that 'select, amplify and transform constructions of the past produced elsewhere' (Popular Memory Group, 1982). As indicated above, research about television memories confirms that *Wij, Heren van Zichem* is well-remembered and has become part of collective Flemish memory (Dhoest, 2007b). Popular history typically simplifies the past and speaks to present concerns and needs (Spigel, 1995).

In many ways, popular memory is the antithesis of written history:

> It measures change genealogically, in terms of generations rather than centuries, epochs or decades. It has no developmental sense of time, but assigns events to the mythicized 'good old days' (or 'bad old days') of workplace lore, or the 'once upon a time' of the storyteller.
>
> (Samuel, 1994, p. 5)

Television, in its constant revisiting of the past, contributes to the formation of such popular memory: 'On the one hand television exalts the role of the individual in history [...]. On the other – anti-heroically – it insists on the primacy of ordinary, everyday life and resilience of the family in face of outside pressures' (Samuel, 1994, p. 15). Both tendencies are present in *Wij, Heren van Zichem*, where each character represents particular social positions and themes, while the overall narrative deals more with everyday life in the (undifferentiated, simplified) past than any concrete historical event.

Reflecting on the role of historical cinema in historical consciousness, Rosenstone (1995) claims that it is important not to compare historical cinema to written history, but to embrace its strengths while being aware of its conventions. Rather than focussing on factual inaccuracies and the compression of history into a single, linear and closed story, it is important to focus on the strengths of historical cinema: its ability to show the complexity and multidimensionality of actual history, its ability to recall the actual 'look' and 'feel' of the past and to evoke empathy among viewers. Hesling (2001) agrees that we have to be aware of the selectivity and narrative conventions in historical cinema but that we also have to acknowledge its impact on historical consciousness:

> In an age where audiovisual media have come to dominate practically every layer of communication, historical films, with their semi-fictional, dramatized portrayal of the past, have been able to exercise an

increasingly significant influence on our historical consciousness, that is, on what we assume to know or happen to believe about the past.

(Hesling, 2001, p. 190)

Historical drama, let alone period drama, may not tell or explain us (exactly) how it was, but it can show us what it was like. Thus, Helen Taylor (1989) found that *Gone with the Wind*, for all its historical distortions and propaganda, has some historical value to its female fans. They do not mistake it for history proper, but it tells them something about the past: 'So the "truths" which the work has successfully documented are not necessarily those of detail, or indeed of historical objectivity (whatever that may be), but more of a mythic, epic and indeed tragic nature' (Taylor, 1989, p. 208).

One of the major drawbacks of historical cinema comes from the narrative and temporal constraints of the feature-length movie, which typically tells a single, linear story. Even in films breaching the conventions of the classical narrative, there is little time to explore multiple characters or storylines, so the past is always necessarily overly simplified. This is where serial television drama has a definite advantage, as it has in adapting books for the screen: there is time for digressions and elaborations. Both in the production logic and in critical reception, serial drama has long been considered as an inferior form to the (essentially theatrical or novelistic) single drama. More recently, however, in the wake of an ever-growing output of high-quality drama, the serial is increasingly lauded as a form with much greater potential. In his defence of serial drama, Creeber (2004) enumerates its many advantages: thanks to its length, it allows more breadth of vision and a broader narrative scope; it makes room for narrative complexity, the weaving together of multiple interrelated storylines; character psychology can be more deeply elaborated and there is more room for character 'growth'. Thus, in historical serials (the so-called 'miniseries'), there is time to explore the complexity of the past while also evoking its emotional, 'lived' aspects.

The German serial *Heimat* (1984) is often referred to in this context. Creeber acknowledges its shortcomings in addressing actual German history (in particular the concentration camps), but he defends its subjective telling of everyday history of ordinary people going about their day-to-day lives; 'the camera often lingering lovingly and leisurely over frequently trivial and daily routines' (Creeber, 2004, p. 37). Sorlin praises *Heimat* as a specifically televisual (rather than cinematic) approach of the past: 'The intricacies of plots and subplots, the variety of characters and extras, the difficulty viewers meet when they decide who is doing what, are typical of serials that do not tell a story but set up an atmosphere and an unsteady network of personal relationships' (Sorlin, 1998, p. 217). While it is less obviously amnesiac, the same descriptions perfectly fit *Wij, Heren van Zichem*, as a many-voiced account of lived, everyday life in the past.

To conclude, it is safe to assume that *Wij, Heren van Zichem* was of historical importance. Although not made with straightforward historical intentions and at odds with the high-cultural bias of the broadcasters, it was tremendously popular. By taking a closer look at its context of production and reception, we can see how the intersection of multiple factors (ideology, pragmatism, nationalism, recognition, social changes, audience preferences, etc.) led to a specific programme that greatly resonated with contemporary preoccupations. Not despite, but on the contrary, thanks to its popular approach, it managed to capture the hearts and historical imagination of a whole generation of Flemish viewers. Its particular representation of the past (rural, nostalgic, social-realist but humorous) touched a sensitive chord in the rapidly modernizing Flemish community, which turned to the past in its search for national identity. In this way, *Wij, Heren van Zichem* has become part of popular memory, the kind of history 'for everyday use' on which mainstream television can have a fundamental impact.

A note on availability

Wij, Heren van Zichem is integrally available on DVD in three boxes released by VRT and Vintage Films as part of the series 'VRT Klassiekers'.

Notes

1. Although hardly comparable stylistically, Claes thus takes the central position taken by Dickens on British television, a similarly legible 'middlebrow' classic with colourful types (see Kerr, 1982).
2. All quotes are literal translations by the author.
3. Quotes from the press are based on newspaper clippings in the BRT archive, which only contain the newspaper title and date.

Bibliography

Anderson, S. (2001) 'History TV and popular memory', in G. Edgerton and P. Rollins (eds), *Television Histories: Shaping Collective Memory in the Media Age* (Lexington: University Press of Kentucky).

Balfoort M. (n.d.) *'Wij, Heren van Zichem', naar de vertellingen van Ernest Claes* (Antwerpen: Standaard Uitgeverij).

Barton, R. (2000) 'The Ballykissangelization of Ireland'. *Historical Journal of Film, Radio and Television*, 20.3, 413–27.

Biltereyst, D. and Van Bauwel, S. (2004) 'De Witte/Whitey' in E. Mathijs (ed.), *The Cinema of the Low Countries* (London: Wallflower Press).

BRT (1969) *Enkele algemene vaststellingen en ontwikkelingen van het kijk- en luisteronderzoek*, unpublished report of the Research Department (Brussels: BRT).

BRT (1978) *25 jaar televisie* (Brussels: BRT).

Caughie, J. (2000) *Television Drama: Realism, Modernism and British Culture* (Oxford: Oxford University Press).

Chase, M. and Shaw, C. (1989) 'The dimensions of nostalgia', in M. Chase and C. Shaw (eds), *The Imagined Past: History and Nostalgia* (Manchester: Manchester University Press).

Creeber, G. (2004) *Serial Television: Big Drama on the Little Screen* (London: BFI).

De Bie, I. (1981) 'Zichem dat is boven, maar waar is Balfoort?' *Humo*, 2134, 32–50.

de Goeyse, M. and Keersmaekers, A. (1998) 'Ernest Claes', in R. De Schryver (ed.), *Nieuwe encyclopedie van de Vlaamse Beweging* (Tielt: Lannoo).

de Maesschalck, E. (1998) 'Telehistorie: Hoe geeft de televisie ons verleden weer?' in R. Bauer et al. (eds), *Tussen herinnering en hoop: Geschiedenis en samenleving* (Leuven: Davidsfonds).

de Maesschalck, E. (2007) 'Geschiedenis op televisie', in A. Dhoest and H. Van den Bulck (eds), *Publieke televisie in Vlaanderen: Een geschiedenis* (Gent: Academia Press).

Dhoest, A. (2004a) 'Negotiating images of the nation: The production of Flemish TV drama, 1953–1989,' *Media, Culture & Society*, 26.3, 393–408.

Dhoest, A. (2004b) 'Quality and/as national identity: Press discourse on Flemish period TV drama', *European Journal of Cultural Studies*, 7.3, 305–24.

Dhoest, A. (2004c) 'Zichem versus Brideshead: The construction of national identity in Flemish and British period drama', *Film & History*, 2003 CD-ROM Annual.

Dhoest, A. (2007a) 'Ontspanning: Van bijkomende opdracht tot kerntaak', in A. Dhoest and H. Van den Bulck (eds), *Publieke televisie in Vlaanderen: Een geschiedenis* (Gent: Academia Press).

Dhoes, A. (2007b) 'Nostalgic memories: Qualitative reception analysis of Flemish TV fiction, 1953–1989', *Communications: The European Journal of Communication Research*, 32, 31–50.

Hesling, W. (2001) 'The past as story: The narrative structure of historical films', *European Journal of Cultural Studies*, 4.2, 189–205.

Higson, A. (1993) 'Representing the national past: Nostalgia and pastiche in the heritage film', in L. Friedman (ed.), *British Cinema and Thatcherism* (London: University College of London Press).

Monk, C. (2002) 'The British heritage-film debate revisited', in C. Monk and A. Sargeant (eds), *British Historical Cinema* (London: Routledge).

Popular Memory Group (1982) 'Popular memory: theory, politics, method', in R. Johnson, G. McLennan, B. Schwarz and D. Sutton (eds), *Making Histories: Studies in History-Writing and Politics* (London: Hutchinson).

Rosenstone, R.A. (1995) *Visions of the Past: The Challenge of Film to Our Idea of History* (Cambridge, MA: Harvard University Press).

Samuel, R. (1994) *Theatres of Memory. Volume 1: Past and Present in Contemporary Culture* (London: Verso).

Sorlin, P. (1998) 'Television and our understanding of history: A distant conversation', in T. Barta (ed.), *Screening the Past: Film and the Representation of History* (Westport, CT: Praeger).

Spigel, L. (1995) 'From the dark ages to the golden age: Women's memories and television reruns', *Screen*, 36.1, 16–33.

Taylor, H. (1989) *Scarlett's Women: Gone with the Wind and Its Female Fans* (London: Virago).

Theuwissen, D. (2002) *Uitgebeeld verleden: Geschiedenis op de Vlaamse televisie (1953–1974)* (Leuven: KULeuven).

White, T.J. (1997) 'The changing social bases of political identity in Ireland', in S. Sailer (ed.), *Representing Ireland: Gender, Class, Nationality* (Gainesville: University Press of Florida).

Wollen, T. (1991) 'Over our shoulders: Nostalgic screen fiction for the 1980', in J. Corner and S. Harvey (eds), *Enterprise and Heritage: Crosscurrents of National Culture* (London: Routledge).

Part IV

History Programming: Form, Genre, Technique

13
'I feel completely beautiful for the first time in my life'
Bodily Re-enactment and Reality Documentary

Jerome de Groot

This chapter is concerned with the interface between diet television and historical programming, a new hybrid style demonstrating what Annette Hill terms the continuing 'cross-pollination of genres' within documentary/reality practice (2008, p. 223). In particular, I consider the series *The Diets That Time Forgot*, screened by the BBC on Channel 4 in 2008. By demonstrating and performing historical otherness, and the physical difference between the historical body and the contemporary one, but further, by eroding that difference through clothing and dietary change, the show provokes disquieting questions. Put in the context of various theoretical discussions, the series allows us to meditate upon how historical documentary has evolved over the past decade, and, in particular, how the genre seems to be moving towards an explicit concern with the consequences of bodily affect on ways of defining subjectivity both contemporaneously and historically.

Diet television, reality television, history

Whilst not a new concern, weight loss as a cultural, social, political, economic and televisual phenomenon has never been a larger issue. The weight loss industry involves a range of products, media and institutions, from Weight Watchers meetings through to *Rosemary Conley Diet & Fitness Magazine*, and is worth an estimated \$60 billion per year in the US and Canada with more than 70 million people currently dieting.[1] This huge and unregulated industry has normally been publicly manifest on daytime television and in magazines. However, mainstream diet television has grown into a recognizable genre in the past decade. In many ways this is a reaction to news media concerns relating to the obesity in the West, and also government-led initiatives grappling with this concern. Diet television is also a reflective and constituent part of a culture obsessed with body image and, in particular, of the regulation of the female body through an aggressive discourse of constraint, discipline and public shame. Reality diet television interlinks particularly with the rise of women's magazine culture and the shift in this from an association of thinness with beauty and towards an equation of dietary control with public celebrity (best seen in the example of *Heat* magazine). Diet television cannot be considered outside of its cultural context; it is a product of particular concerns and reflective of certain contemporary anxieties. The increased visibility of body issues on television in the form of programmes relating to obesity and fatness seems a particularly contemporary phenomenon, and something that should be addressed at length.

Feminist concern with body image in public is not new – indeed, the ways that women have been constructed and interpolated physically has been part of the feminist critique from Mary Wollstonecraft onward; *Fat Is a Feminist Issue* is the title of Susie Orbach's 1978 book, but also a central concern from its very beginnings as a political movement. Yet feminist critique has often been concerned with the issues associated with thinness and with beauty, whereas these programmes are concerned with the loss of weight; the regulation of the body by displaying those wishing to publicly erase sections of themselves. It is apt, of course, that television seeks to address such issues, given that many health studies link excessive television viewing with dietary problems – particularly obesity.

Diet documentary series in the past decade include *Big Diet* (2001, Germany and Netherlands), *Fat Club* (2002), *Celebrity Fit Club* (2002–2006, UK and US), *Diet Trials* (2003), *Fat Nation* (2004), *The Fit Farm* (2004), *The Diet Doctors* (2006) and *Fat March* (2007, US). These programmes, and a multitude of daytime sections and series, have contributed to the creation of a type of television that is both voyeuristic and often judgemental. Furthermore, there are a tranche of programmes that might be argued to be analogous to diet television, or at least part of the same cultural matrix: *How to Look Good Naked* (2006–, UK; 2008–, USA), *What Not to Wear* (2002, 2003, UK and USA), *Extreme Makeover* (2002–2007, USA) and *Jamie's School Dinners* (UK, 2006) are the most obvious examples of this obsession with the issues of the transgressive, unhealthy, unbounded corporeal body in social and public space. Feminists and sociologists alike have commented upon the epistemic or psychological violence of such programmes (McRobbie, 2004). These shows have something in common with 'straight' sensationalist documentary about obesity such as the *Bodyshock* episode 'Half Ton Son' (Channel 4, 2009). They are not programmes that seek simply to disclose information but to introduce, as with all reality television, an element of competition, empathy and self-revelation. The question of the makeover, be it superficial or bodily, has become a strong central motif to most contemporary reality television. Early versions focussed on the 'journey' of the individual towards completeness, and this is now been enshrined in the actual format of shows about the makeover phenomenon. Diet television enshrines within it this constituent part of the makeover-reality show, depending as a genre on narratives of progress, improvement and moral aspiration (as well as on tropes of punishment, weakness, and failure).

Diet television is part of a new form of lifestyle programming, the development of which has been amplified by the growth of what is known as reality documentary or reality TV. Such forms are interested in autobiography, revelation, ordinariness, interactivity, confession and blurring the lines between public and private selfness. Reality TV has become fundamental to discussions of televisual culture over the past decade, demonstrating its continuing, evolving and pervasive influence. John Corner has influentially argued that documentary now is a fragmented, complex entity more concerned with playfulness than education or the more traditional aims of the genre. His theorization of a 'new ecology of the factual' has been supported by work on reception, particularly that of Annette Hill, who has demonstrated that 'Audience discussion of learning in contemporary reality programming highlights' how, as Corner argues, entertainment and diversion are key (Corner, 2002, p. 265; Hill, 2005, pp. 79–108). The transformation of the documentary form due to the influence of the reality phenomenon has been widely felt, from the evolution of historical programming to the rise of new genres such as makeover television (de Groot, 2008; Heller, 2007).

Critics have been split about the virtue and value of reality TV. Many see the involvement of formerly marginalized demographics as being a cause for celebration and possible social transformation. Jon Dovey argues for the empowering and positive aspect of reality TV and documentary: 'It addresses new formulations of a social subjectivity in which what was formerly private becomes an essential component of public speech' (Dovey, 2000, p. 86). Based on this formulation, reality TV is enfranchising because it allows direct access to new forms of subjectivity. The participatory element of reality allows the articulation of new, reflexive forms of identity. Others share Gareth Palmer's concern regarding privacy: 'It is not easy to be optimistic about the world as presented by reality TV. Across a wide range of subjects we have less control than ever over our public and, increasingly, our private identities' (Palmer, 2003, p. 39). In particular, the question raised here by Palmer relating to the definition and articulation of selfhood, or private identity, has been at the forefront of the discussion. Mark Andrejevic queries the dynamic between observation and self-definition: 'Underlying this euphoric rhetoric of enshrience is the equation of surveillance with self-fulfilment: that being watched all the time serves to intensify one's experiences, and thereby to facilitate self-growth and self-knowledge' (Andrejevic, 2004, p. 145). Additionally, Anita Biressi and Heather Nunn have linked reality TV with a newly therapeutic culture (2005, p. 107).

Reality diet television is a hybrid of daytime health and the new, increasingly complex genre of makeover television (Moseley, 2005). Of course, reality TV from the beginning had been concerned with transformation and the public revelation into selfhood; this has often been seen as part of its dissident potentiality (Palmer, 2004). As a phenomenon demonstrating the constant evolution of reality programming, makeover television offers an idealistic narrative of perfection and transformation, whilst being generally concerned with gender regulation and the rearticulation of various relationships of power: authority, class, body, gender. Most have a clear disciplinary structure, insofar as they seek to modify behaviour and to ensure the social-moral probity of the individual (Redden, 2007). This address to coherence and wholeness is common in reality television, particularly the historical genre, where immersion and abstraction from 'real' life leads to real-time advancement (de Groot, 2008, pp. 178–80). Makeover television is particularly interested in representing the importance of the expert and authority in the power relations of the shows; whilst these experts often seem approachable, they regularly take the role of disciplinarian, cultural gatekeeper, and in many cases are the enshriners of punitive measures (Weber, 2007). In particular, makeover television relating to weight loss presents a moral set of boundaries for the body, patrolled by meticulous and often invasive surveillance of that body. This generally involves a set of targets, a clear sense of before and after, and the constant monitoring of the physical form. There are two indexes of measurement: behaviour and the physical frame. Behaviour is modified through the intervention of experts and counsellors, but also through tests and tasks; the body is weighed, viewed, trained, measured, and sometimes cut.

In the discussion of transformation and revelation of self it is instructive to consider the most influential theories of social identity. Anthony Giddens is the most significant theorist of the contemporary social entity as something self-actualized. In post-traditional modernity, 'We are, not what we are, but what we make ourselves into', Giddens argued (1991, p. 75). Drawing conclusions from works of self-help, Giddens postulated that the keynote to identity was narrative: 'A person's identity is not to be found in behaviour, nor – important though this is -in the reactions of others, but in the capacity *to keep a particular narrative going'* [emphasis in the original] (p. 54). From this analysis, Giddens developed two key ideas – the 'trajectory' of the 'authentic' or self-authenticating self, and, further, the self-reflexiveness of identity. Importantly, this is linked to the physical entity: 'The reflexivity of the self *extends to the body*, where the body [...] is part of an action system rather than merely a passive object' [emphasis in original] (p. 78). Developing as a person is dependent upon the individual surmounting emotional obstacles, and the body is part of this process. Giddens' work has been critiqued by Beverley Skeggs, who argues that he 'sees class not as a modern identity, but as a traditional, ascriptive one, which has no place in a dynamic, reflexive and globalized world' (Skeggs, 2004, p. 52). Skeggs contends that the reflexive self is a liberal fiction preventing us from seeing that class is still a central discourse of society. Skeggs has developed her critical thesis regarding the continuing prevalence of class in the definition of self in modernity by turning to reality TV, which she sees as a crucible demonstrating the key concerns (Wood et al., 2008).

Historical reality television, or reality history, has rarely featured in discussions of the phenomena, despite it being a staple of most television channels and a clear demonstration of the shift in documentary style (de Groot, 2008, pp. 165–81). If reality television enables an interrogation of self, with varying consequences, then the complexity and downright oddness of this phenomenon is multiplied greatly when the selves being interrogated are performing historical otherness of some description. Reality history has been interested in exploring the physical dislocation of immersing participants in historical scenarios in shows such as *The Trench* (BBC2, 2002), *The 1900 House* (Channel 4, 1999), *The 1940s House* (Channel 4, 2001), *Edwardian Country House* (Channel 4, 2002), *Frontier House* (PBS, 2002), *Colonial House* (PBS, 2004), *Outback House* (ABC Australia, 2005), *Texas Ranch House* (PBS, 2006), *The Colony* (SBS Australia, 2005), *Pioneer Quest: A Year in the Real West* (PBS Canada, 2000), *Schwarzwaldhaus 1902* (SWR Germany, 2001–2002), *Quest for the Bay* (PBS Canada, 2002) and *Klondike: The Quest for Gold* (PBS Canada, 2003).

Historical reality television is interested in placing the contemporary self back in the matrix of 'traditional' identity and encouraging the diminution of a reflexive self by allowing it to be dissolved into a class-ridden, historical persona. If we follow Giddens' theory we can see how in some ways historical reality television, particularly that in which performance and immersive interactivity are constitutive parts, might be a space of resistance to the new reflexive selves of this late modernity; a desire to return to simpler times when the individual was not expected to self-construct. At the same time, the keen interest in individuality in reality TV – in the biography, the 'story' of the participant, the narratives of transformation – suggests that Giddens' reflexive self is a constituent part of the genre and thence of its historical manifestation. At the same time the performance of class that the historical shows allow demonstrates a fantasy of status mobility – as most of the participants are working- or middle-class, but they spend much of their time performing in aristocratic spaces. All such shows have explicit rules of etiquette and behaviour, and these particularly demonstrate the invisible workings of ideology; furthermore, in their conceptualization of the role particularly of women, these historical shows create a dissonance that again demonstrates the ways in which oppressive social forces work. The ability of historical shows to demonstrate the (to contemporaries) invisible workings of class and ideology might be seen, then, to critique the idea of the transformative, reflexive self. The modern subject is demonstrated to be fantasizing a freedom and mobility that clearly cannot be the case; the lurch into historicity that the television shows provoke demonstrates this clearly. So we might agree with Skeggs in that the historical shows demonstrate how class worked within history, and in their innate reflexiveness demonstrate how thinking of oneself within a classless society is a fiction.

The body in history/historical bodies

To complicate our discussion further, it is crucial to recall the importance of the body to contemporary feminist theory. It is important, furthermore, that we consider the importance of the regulation and subjugation of the female body in contemporary body/diet discourse. As Elizabeth Grosz argues, the body has often been associated with femaleness, both in terms of grotesque corporeality and also fragility. She contends that:

> The coding of femininity with corporeality in effect leaves men free to inhabit what they (falsely) believe is a purely conceptual order while at the same time enabling them to satisfy their (sometimes disavowed) need for corporeal contact through their access to women's bodies and services.
>
> (Grosz, 1994, p. 14)

What such feminists point out is that the body is a network of meanings, an expression of contemporary forms of power, and the signifier of types of subjectivity. The body is a 'social and discursive object, a body bound up in the order of desire, signification, and power' (Grosz, 1994, p. 19). Judith Butler argues for an awareness of the materiality of the subject, as something that demonstrates the influence and dominion of power. Theorists see the body as something both inscribed but also capable of dissenting and dissembling; as a space of epistemic violence but similarly an area that destabilizes and queers the rational and mainstream. Historical diet programmes might serve to reinsert the body into discourses of the past, providing a revelation of corporeal oppression through their ability to demonstrate the ways in which the female body is constrained. The association of dieting with women points to a fundamental weakness in the female body: a rational and corporeal incompleteness (or over-completeness), which, importantly, is somehow seen to be transhistorical.

Particularly significant for discussions of diets, which are often conducted at least partially as a public performance, is contemporary feminist and queer discussion of shame. In this formulation shame becomes something that might serve to individuate the body, to make it through an articulation of affect something phenomenologically particular. Affect, an unmediated individual response or experience, has been theorized as a dislocating potentiality, particularly related to the body: 'affect's difference from social structures that mean it possesses, in itself, the capacity to restructure social meaning' (Hemmings, 2002, p. 550). Discussion of shame has come within the context of work on the reification of the body and in particular the dislocation of the material and textured body from feminist discussion. Eve Kosofsky Sedgwick and Judith Butler have both written of the importance of recalling the materiality of the subject in order to resituate the female body at the centre of feminist argument (Butler, 1993; Kosofsky Sedgwick, 2002). Again this is important for a consideration of dieting, insofar as it is clearly significant to discuss the actual physical centrality of both the real body and the fantasized, idealized one to social, cultural and political discourse; and because the physical or psychological *affect* experienced by the participant might actualize and articulate a new type of subjectivity. It is a challenge to structures of power that allows for a newly inflected space of difference. Elspeth Probyn argues that 'shame as a very bodily affect has the potential to focus attention on the body as a vehicle of connection' (2000, p. 14). Thus the dieting body, particularly, in this analysis, the working-class dieting body, might serve to suggest a way of reintegrating the actual body into discourse, and thereby reconstituting the female self. Bodily shame, associated with dieting and the very public and visceral performance of the individual, lumpy, unique body, demonstrates a newly visible embodiment, and, importantly for our discussion, the fact that this is being conceptualized within an historical framework and nexus inflects the process still further. Though this is arguing against the grain somewhat, it is a standard resistant strain of feminist analysis: Kathy Davis has argued that there might be some agency involved in undergoing cosmetic surgery; Cressida J. Heyes has seen dieting as possibly something enabling; Su Holmes and Deborah Jermyn have considered *Wife Swap* to be potentially radical (Davis, 2002; Heyes, 2006; Holmes and Jermyn, 2008). If we consider the ways in which the body is individuated, and the experiences of the subject articulated, in makeover diet television, and, particularly, how the discourse of the historical expands this, we might see ways in which reality historical documentary, like historical fiction, allows for a dissident potential within what seems to be a conservative format. Historical dieting might be seen to allow women – and men – more purchase on their lives, and to feel more in control.

Furthermore, as Weber has argued about makeover shows, the introduction of the male body problematizes the gender regulation of the genre. It feminizes the man, insofar as it demands a passivity in front of a watching audience: he 'must be the object of the other's gaze and accept externally determined changes of his body and self-presentation' (Weber, 2006). The inclusion of men in makeover programmes, in particular using them in discussions of issues more usually culturally associated with women – clothing, weight, diet – means that they are exposed in new and interrogative ways. Dieting is a 'feminised realm', particularly, very rarely associated with maleness (Gough, 2006, p. 326). The use of men in makeover 'opens a fascinating cultural space where it is possible to see how male power and success is imagined and constructed, and how the discourses of health become implicated in gendered investments in masculinity' (Weber, 2006). The use of fat men raises questions relating both to gender construction and also to the ways in which masculinity has been ignored by feminist thought (Bell and McNaughton, 2007). The use of male participants in historical reality diet shows opens up this particular gendered problematic, and, by extension, suggests that this has been the case *through history*. What a consideration of the body in history demonstrates is its very insubstantiality as a taxonomizing system, the fluidity and flexibility of the body as a means of articulating anything. There is an ideal, and then there are the clear and present realities.

What of the historical diet shows, then, in the context of these various discussions of selfhood, the body, and dieting as a cultural phenomenon? These shows enable us to nuance our conceptualization of involvement in an historical reality show. Historical shows seem to demonstrate the *performance* of historicity. Participants recreate or re-enact past roles through costume, behaviour, and even in some cases what might be termed psychological transference. In *Edwardian Country House*, for instance, one claimed: 'I don't think I really like the 21st century [...] we've worked out from experience how to act in every situation, so now we think like Edwardians [...] we are the last living Edwardians' (*Edwardian Country House*, 2002). What historical diet shows seek is the physical, internal inscription of the past upon the contemporary body. There is a physical link between the contemporary dieters and their equivalents in the past, much more powerful and bodily than that of a re-enactor. Indeed, whilst both leisure and professional re-enactment is centred upon what Raphael Samuel called the 'fetish of authenticity', both types of activity are bedevilled by actual, physical problems in obtaining anything like 'realism' (Samuels, 1996, p. 191). Dieting, therefore, might allow a more sophisticated historical empathy and re-enactment to be undertaken.

The series also foreground interesting ideas about the body in history. Is the historical body similar to the contemporary body? Are the only differences dietary? In the comic documentary *The Supersizers Go...* (2008–9), diet becomes a bodily inscription of historical difference. Each week the two presenters, Giles Coren and Sue Perkins, lived on a particular historically specific diet to see exactly what effect the food had on their physical well-being. Invoking the campaigning fast-food film *Supersize Me* (Morgan Spurlock, 2004), the series was an intervention into contemporary concerns regarding obesity and a living history experiment. Each episode ended with a visit to the doctor to see how the week's diet had changed them physically. After each week they both lost weight and improved fitness, contrary to the opinions of their nutritionist and doctors. Conversely, there were more risks associated with their diets of developing cancer, gout, and not being able to process fat due to low fibre intake.

The presenters spent the week in period costume, in a period house, eating with old cutlery and crockery and trying various other historical activities such as diet cures, learn to dance, courting or going on a Plague picnic (*The Supersizers Go...*, 2008). Therefore they perform, live and digest history. Reality re-enactment of the past, here, actively articulates corporeal difference, conceptualizing the body as historically contingent. If we return to our discussion of affect, it seems here that the body might be reinserted into history and our understanding of the nexus of power and dependence that constructs and creates it might be interrogated through the individuated impact of diet upon the *individual* body. Diet allows us to see the way that the body works as a 'vehicle of connection', individuating experience in order to challenge the reification of the body and its disappearance, particularly in historical documentary, into the background (Probyn, 2000, p. 14). Furthermore, following Andrejevic, we might see that the bodily work of the participants puts their bodies into a nexus of capital/exchange and allows us as viewers to understand the potentiality of the body of the subject within this set of frameworks.

The Diets That Time Forgot was made in 2008 for Channel 4 by Silver River, a production company formed in 2005 that also made *The Supersizers Go...* for the BBC. Liz Hartford was executive producer, a veteran of innovative historical documentaries including directing episodes in the *Georgian Underworld* (2003) series and Simon Schama's *A History of Britain* (2001). Series producer Caroline Ross-Pirie had also worked on *Regency House Party* (2004) and *The Edwardian Country House* (2002). This confluence of production demonstrates the importance of previous experience but also in motif how the series was an evolution of successful formula reality history, namely the 'house' genre. The show followed nine overweight adults in an historical experiment to lose weight using diets from past time periods. Over 24 days, groups of three would follow a diet from a different period in history. The diets were relatively simple: the Victorian Banting diet, consisting of high protein, low carbohydrates; the Edwardian Fletcher 'chew chew' diet which allowed anything to be eaten as long as it was chewed 32 times; the 1920s Lulu calorie-controlled diet which allowed 1200 calories a day. The participants were taking part for a range of reasons, mostly to do with self-image and health; none were there, it seemed, so they might be involved *specifically* in an historical re-creation or experiment. When introduced to their foods the participants laughed in anxiety and disbelief at the things they were being asked to do, demonstrating a modern incredulity at the habits of the past. In addition the show created an 'institute of physical culture' where the participants lived, an educative institution run by Sir Roy Strong. The show therefore shadowed the format of the 'house' genre, placing the participants physically in a historical situation. Most reality history, and particularly 'house' shows, have clear historically specific rules, which can be argued to demonstrate the silent workings of dominant ideology; in their stead, this example had moral rules (act properly, do not cheat), physical rules (exercise) and historical rules (the various diet programmes). The house both allowed the participants to perform as aristocracy by having servants or wearing evening dresses, but also established a surveillance culture in which any transgression from the strict guidelines (not simply of eating, but of behaving) was punished.

The Diets That Time Forgot was part of a minor trend in historical programming, of focussing on the bodily experience of the past, and, in particular, different ways in which health in particular was conceptualized and maintained. This is exemplified particularly by Channel 4's *Bringing Up Baby* (2007), in which three different styles of childcare from the past were compared, although this show raised more ethical issues than *The Diets That Time Forgot*. The distasteful sight of a newborn child being the subject of a historical-reality experimental makeover show led to some media comment (Vine, 2007). Historical reality television has always, to some extent, exacted a physical effect on the participants. Members of *The 1940s House*, for instance, showed a distinct improvement in their fitness, weight, body fat and blood pressure. Conversely, some of the servants in *Edwardian Country House* began to develop breathing difficulties. Similarly, most reality TV is interested in physical privation of some description, and the changing of the life in question. Yet the extraordinary difference of these shows is in their concern with the physical development of the participant, and, moreover, the ways in which that may be linked (or not) to a particular type of historicity. Most commentators on reality history have pointed out its performative element, the ways in which it suggests pastness is both about costume and behaviour according to particular ideologically inflected rule sets. Yet what these shows foreground is a physical historicalness, an engagement with history that is bodily. *The Diets That Time Forgot* was a show that encouraged the participants to historically experiment upon their bodies. There were elements of living history recreation and re-enactment included this bodily manifestation, insofar as they also wear (diet-particular) period costume, have lessons in posture/movement and do exercise particular to their time periods. Not only are they weighed, but their organs are also measured by judging their levels of visceral fat. The level of visceral fat in the body can be used to express the metabolic age of the person, and a high metabolic age is a health risk. This introduces an odd sense of chronology and synchronicity, insofar as they bodily are defined as young/old, outwardly young but ageing inside. Fat can speed up time, take its toll on the body, and is unseen.

The show had a clear educational element. The matron argued in the first show: 'If we're going to stop the obesity epidemic today, I think we are going to have to go back to some of our old fashioned morals' (*The Diets That Time Forgot*, 2008, episode 1). Roy Strong bemoaned the 'age of self-gratification' and claimed, 'I believe you go back in order to go forward' (episode 1). As the authority in the programme and patriarch of the house, he outlined a very puritanical and ascetic approach: 'it requires an exertion of the mind, and a discipline, and a realisation that if you don't take control of it you're in trouble' (episode 1). Much of the first episode was given over to a discussion of the contemporary obesity epidemic in the West and meditated upon the bodily ways in which we might attempt to engage with and learn from the past. The historical perspective showed how the body is continually imperfect, but how models of idealized perfection differ through time. The peak of physical condition in the Victorian era is the thin waist and the huge bust, for instance. Indeed, the physical transformations that were desired by past dieters are not those of today, demonstrating that the purpose of dieting is superficial and not, actually, about health.

There is a certain pompous prissiness to the narration – a girl with spiky cut hair is regularly called 'tomboy Nikki', and she is regularly made to feel uncomfortable due to her inability to be feminine (episode 1). She is *too* modern, not ladylike, and hates the constraints of historical femininity. Lady Davenport, the costume and posture advisor, claims she must have 'an inner lady' that she has never seen, and forces her to dress accordingly (episode 1). Nikki, who 'hasn't worn a frock since she was a girl' according to the voice over, gives in: 'I think I look more feminine, and more ladylike' (episode 1). The show therefore invoked a type of femaleness in performance and projection, as well as bodily; she became *more* feminine through acting like an historical woman and losing weight, and is socially acceptable and more attractive. As Wood and Skeggs point out, signifiers of the authorized, proper 'self' in reality television are 'aesthetically appealing and thus competent femininity'; Nikki's transformation into a real girl allows her to become a 'real' person again (Wood and Skeggs, 2004, p. 206). The use of a hypnotherapist at the conclusion of the series demonstrates this therapeutic model. Both Nikki and Sophie Ridley-Smith articulate their sense of their former selves using self-help speak; for Ridley-Smith, her young, innocent, happy self 'got smacked around by life'; Nikki needs to get rid of her fear and find 'the real you' (episode 5). Engagement with an historical past allows the revelation of a particular, individual selfhood and an escape from the rigid, unnameable traumas of modern life.

Central to the series' purpose was the sense that the participants' engagement with history will leave an indelible mark (they will leave healthier) and have physical effect upon their lives *now*. Strong's words on discipline introduce a moral judgement on behaviour for the obese or fat which reflects the formulation of the new 'ethical self' that Wood and Skeggs see as the 'solution' offered by reality television: 'In opposition to the ethical self that can transform, tell and show its moral worth, is the self that does not know how to tell or display itself correctly and cannot claim or profess propriety' (Wood and Skeggs, 2004, p. 207). This unknowing self must be ordered, educated and controlled in order that it might transform. As is common in reality history, a central concept is self-revelation. One participant claims that she is

'Starting to love the pieces of me I hated, learning to love the pieces of me I hated'; a few weeks earlier she had claimed 'I don't like my body. I'm not attracted to it' (2008, episode 5, episode 2). The programme encourages the participants throughout to express their historical roles through costume, both as a way of ensuring they act properly but also to control them through means of uncomfortable clothing (particularly corsets). Strong argues that the 'clothes will actually begin to dictate how they move', and group members mention that 'I feel aristocratic for once' and 'I feel much more civilised' (episode 1). These two comments demonstrate the ways in which the historical makeover is designed to act, encouraging a sense of a nostalgic return to a lost world of rationality and order in which class, particularly, is key. In a society in which the links between obesity and socioeconomic status are clear, the participants' sense of a 'new' self being born from the old through the application of diet maps onto aspirations to escape from the hidebound structures of contemporary life into a fantasy of classlessness, or at least class that might be transcended.

At the same time, Strong's physical enforcement of behaviour maps onto the body a historically contingent disciplinary impetus. Sophie Ridley-Smith suggests: 'I feel completely beautiful for the first time in my life. It made me feel proud of my body and I want to treat it properly now, I don't want to put rubbish in it and abuse it' (episode 1). This sense of the physical revelation into an idealized selfhood, and the moral distinction between before and after, is significant. As the participants change into their historical clothes the camera lingers briefly on their semi-naked bodies, exposing them to the gaze of the viewer. This brief enaction of the violation-motif of the diet programme is repeated more passively at the end of each episode when the teams are gathered to be weighed and measured.

The show concludes with a gala in which all the participants do turns for their families and friends. This demonstrates the performative nature both of dieting and of historical reality television. The group present their 'new selves' to their families and celebrate the beginning of their 'new lives' (episode 5). Following Butler we might consider how this performance nexus might also seek to demonstrate how all bodily immanence – gender, historical situation, even physical proportion – is performative and thence suggest a troubling of the mainstream, a queering of the normal. By having a final set of roles at the conclusion of a series in which bodies have literally been on show underlines how the entire system of bodily definition subscribed to or challenged by the series is based upon a false sense that there is normalcy. The implicit point is that, whilst there is a sense of bodily perfection (which is historically contingent), *actual* bodies differ and shift and are complex and incomplete. Whilst bodies are obviously defined in a nexus of power and bounding rationality, they (particularly female ones) continually defy attempts to order and control them, even through clothing or diet or explicit punishment. Thus the return to centrality of the body within a consideration of history within this documentary provokes more questions and offers fewer answers than one might assume.

A note on availability

The Diets That Time Forgot is not available currently, although there is an hour of video on the Channel 4 website: http://www.channel4.com/programmes/the-diets-that-time-forgot. Accessed 15 August 2009. *Edwardian Country House* and *The 1940s House* are available on DVD from E1 Entertainment and Acorn Media, respectively.

Note

1. Figures from Market Research World: www.marketresearchworld.net. Accessed 17 June 2009.

Television

Edwardian Country House, episode 6, "Winners and Losers", Channel 4, 28 May 2002.
The Diets That Time Forgot, episode 1, 'Measuring Up', Channel 4, 18 March 2008.
The Diets That Time Forgot, episode 2, 'Great Outdoors', Channel 4, 1 April 2008.
The Diets That Time Forgot, episode 5, 'Extreme Measures', Channel 4, 22 April 2008.
The Supersizers Go…, episode 2, 'Restoration', BBC2, 27 May 2008.

Bibliography

Andrejevic, M. (2004) *Reality TV* (Oxford: Rowman & Littlefield).
Bell, K. and McNaughton, D. (2007) 'Feminism and the invisible fat man', *Body & Society*, 13.1, 107–31.
Biressi, A. and Nunn, H. (2005) *Reality TV* (London: Wallflower Press).
Butler, J. (1993) *Bodies That Matter* (London: Routledge).
Corner, J. (2003) 'Performing the real', *Television and New Media*, 3.3, 255–70.
Davis, K. (2002) 'From objectified body to embodied subject', in S. Jackson and S. Scott (eds), *Gender* (London: Routledge).
de Groot , J. (2008) *Consuming History* (London: Routledge).
Dovey, J. (2000) *Freakshow* (London: Pluto Press).
Giddens, A. (1991) *Modernity and Self-Identity* (Palo Alto, CA: Stanford University Press).
Gough, B. (2006) ' "Real men don't diet": an analysis of contemporary newspaper representations of men, food and health', *Social Science and Medicine*, 64.2, 326–38.
Grogan, S. (1999) *Body Image* (London: Routledge).
Grosz, E. (1994) *Volatile Bodies* (Bloomington, IN: Indiana University Press).
Heller, D. (ed.) (2007) *Makeover Television* (London: IB Tauris).
Hemmings, C. (2005) 'Invoking affect', *Cultural Studies*, 19.5, 548–67.
Heyes, C.J. (2006) 'Foucault goes to Weight Watchers', *Hypatia*, 21.2, 126–49.
Hill, A. (2005) *Reality TV* (Abingdon: Routledge).
Hill, A. (2008) 'Documentary modes of engagement', in T. Austin and W. de Jong (eds), *Rethinking Documentary* (Maidenhead: Open University Press).

Holmes, S. and Jermyn, D. (2008) ' "Ask the fastidious woman from Surbiton to hand-wash the underpants of the aging Oldham skinhead…": Why not *wife swap?'* in T. Austin and W. de Jong (eds), *Rethinking Documentary* (Maidenhead: Open University Press).

Kosofsky Sedgewick, E. (2002) *Touching Feeling* (Durham, NC: Duke University Press).

McRobbie, A. (2004) 'Notes on "What not to wear" and post-feminist symbolic violence', *Sociological Review*, 52, 106.

Moseley, R. (2005) 'Makeover takeover on British television', *Screen*, 41, 3, 299–314.

Palmer, G. (2003) *Discipline and Liberty* (Manchester: Manchester University Press).

Palmer, G. (2004) ' "The New You": class and transformation in lifestyle television', in S. Holmes and D. Jerm (eds), *Understanding Reality Television* (London: Routledge).

Probyn, E. (2000) 'Sporting bodies: dynamics of shame and pride', *Body & Society*, 6.13, 13–28.

Redden, G. (2007) 'Makeover morality and consumer culture', in D. Heller (ed.), *Makeover Television* (London: IB Tauris).

R. Samuel (1996) *Theatres of Memory, Volume 1* (London: Verso).

Skeggs, B. (2004) *Class, Self, Culture* (London: Routledge).

Stinson, K. (2001) *Women and Dieting Culture* (New Brunswick, NJ: Rutgers University Press).

Vine, S. (2007) 'Should you let your baby cry?' *The Times*, 20 September.

Weber B. R. (2006) 'What makes the man? Television makeovers, made-over masculinity, and male body image', *International Journal of Men's Health*, http://findarticles. com/p/articles/mi_m0PAU/is_3_5/ai_n27099054/?tag=content;col1.   Accessed 18 June 2009.

Weber, B.R. (2007) 'Makeover as takeover: Scenes of affective domination on makeover TV', *Configurations*, 15, 77–99.

Wood, H., Skeggs, B. and Thumim, N. (2008) "'Oh goodness, I am watching reality TV": How methods make class in multi-method audience research', *European Journal of Cultural Studies*, 11.1, 5–24.

14
(Re)constructing Biographies

German Television Docudrama and the Historical Biography

Tobias Ebbrecht

Television as public mediator of the past depicts various aesthetic and narrative strategies to communicate history. One major trend is the tendency to merge narrative forms from documentary and fiction to historical docudramas. 'Hybridization', 'blurring boundaries' and 'porosity' are frequently used terms to describe what happens when historical events are re-enacted on television. Television docudrama thereby has become one of the most important genres to represent history on the small screen. This tendency is closely related to a changing understanding of history, which is characteristic not only of the media but for historiography in general. The questioning of the narrative modes used to represent history has caused specific aesthetic reactions. The combination of documents, re-enactments and eyewitness testimonies are one result of significant methodological and epistemological shifts in historiography. Methods such as oral history as well as a change in the conception of memory towards more personal and fragmentary access to the past support changing attention granted to everyday life and ordinary people.

Nevertheless, television docudrama also utilizes traditional narratives in depicting history and reuses techniques from literature, theatre or classical cinema. One traditional mode of retelling the past is historical biography. Historical television biography – especially in the US and the UK – is a rich and longstanding TV genre. Telling history through the biographies of famous artists, politicians or other celebrities is not limited to documentary reconstruction or television reports. It also enables different modes of storytelling in the form of re-enacting personal life stories. Dramatized documentaries such as Ken Russell's *Elgar* (1962) about the famous British composer Edward Elgar made for BBC television became a popular form for dramatizing the past in the frame of biography. But the hybrid mode of docudrama storytelling was also suited to represent a past life combining more or less official film footage, interviews and re-enacted scenes. Today, the Biography Channel proves the ongoing popularity of the genre, the cinematic equivalent of which, the biopic, was defined by George Custen as a film 'that depicts the life of a historical person, past or present' (1992, p. 5). Custon also states that 'the definition of what constitutes a biopic…shifts anew with each generation' (1992, pp. 6–7). The notion of fame also differs over time. Therefore '[t]racing a code for the biopic is an exercise in reconstructing a shifting public notion of fame' (1992, p. 7).

This dynamic concept – reconstructing biographies in relation to changing conceptions of fame, social status and historical meaning – is of importance to my reconsideration of biographical docudrama on German television. I want to describe how biographic docudrama communicates different epistemological concepts of history, biography and memory. In the course of this chapter, I will consider different ways of depicting biographies in television docudrama, analysing three examples from German and Austrian television: *The Young Freud* (1976), *Colleague Otto* (1991) and *The Manns* (2001). These examples demonstrate not only the possibilities of how to tell about the past but also how to reflect the process of history telling itself. To frame these analyses the films have also to be parenthetically contextualized within the history of German television.

History on German television

In my cursory overview, I will focus on West German television, which influenced the following examples. The constitution of historical television in this context was mostly influenced by the controversial debate about how to deal with the Nazi era (Ebbrecht, 2008, p. 104). In West Germany's postwar era television became one of the most important agents in the process of coming to terms with the German past (Kansteiner, 2006, p. 132). Historical dramas and television features became dominant forms of communicating memories from the past. As Knut Hickethier observes, critical preoccupation with the Holocaust played a significant role in television dramas of the 1960s, especially those made by the NDR (Norddeutscher Rundfunk [North German Broadcasting Corporation]) and its department of television drama, headed by Egon Monk from 1960 to 1968 (Hickethier, 1979, p. 59). Monk was born in 1927 and had worked as an assistant to Bertolt Brecht. After the war he co-developed a new documentary drama aesthetic, strongly influenced by Brechtian theatre. These television dramas avoided the use of naturalistic décor and combined fictive scenes with documentary material that served to interrupt the narrative and disrupt the illusion for the spectators (Hickethier, 1979, p. 61).

Secondly, the public service television broadcasting structure in Germany is strongly linked to its federal constitution, leading to a cooperative network of regional public service television broadcasting stations (ARD) established in 1954. The second public broadcasting station (ZDF), founded in 1963, also engaged intensively in historical television programming. In contrast to the more journalistic and investigational perspective of historical television drama produced by the ARD, early ZDF television drama focussed on more entertaining stories. Historical documents served as basis for dramatic reconstructions (Keilbach, 2005, p. 113).

The third important aspect is the task of serving educational interests and values. According to Egon Monk, this included the duty to become a moral institution to communicate liberal and democratic values to the German population (Hickethier, 1998, p. 244). This strategy had to work for different generations of public television viewers. First, during the 1960s, it had to strengthen the audience's loyalty to the new state by educating them in democracy and tolerance (Hickethier, 1979, p. 58). This educational focus, accented by the governmental *Bildungsauftrag* [instruction for education], moved, during the 1980s, towards a critical and investigative journalistic television, which enhanced the styles and methods of television drama towards the hybridization of documents, testimonies and re-enactments. Christian Hißnauer calls this docudramatic mode a 'journalistic polit-television', strongly influenced by a media critical perspective (Hißnauer, 2008, p. 258). This version of television docudrama, which is in Germany foremost represented by Heinrich Breloer and Horst Königstein, transformed the educational focus into a critical perspective depicting controversial topics and reconstructing images and scenes behind the selective perspective of television news (Hißnauer, 2008, p. 259).

Nevertheless, the implementation of commercial television in Germany in 1984 changed the ways that history was depicted on the small screen. The shift towards more personal stories and the necessity of entertainment prepared the ground for new, more entertaining, modes of historical television in Germany, which also included biographies of famous, important or spectacular historic characters. In 1993, Heinrich Breloer created a biographical docudrama about the social democratic politician Herbert Wehner. In 1996, the important ZDF historian Guido Knopp launched the documentary series *Hitlers Helfer* [Hitler's Supporters], using a mixture of archive footage, testimonies and re-enactments to depict the biographies of the most prominent Nazis such as Göring, Himmler and Speer. In 2001, the prominent German producer Bernd Eichinger created a made-for-TV movie about the 1960s murder case against Vera Brühne with a German all-star cast. The biographical drama was first shown in two parts on the commercial channel Sat 1, re-cut into a feature film version in 2006, and spectacularly re-launched in a new version on ARD in 2008.

Docudrama and biopic

Docudrama and film biography share certain similarities. Both follow a narrative story structure and are based on facts. Similar to a general definition of docudrama, film biographies depict historic personalities or characters based on historic characters acting in a historic environment. Several additional signals situate biographical narratives in the context of docudrama. Derek Paget highlights, for example, captions and voice over (2004, p. 197). Both strategies, as well as the integration of documentary or archive footage into the narrative flow, are also often used in biopics (Straub, 2007, p. 17). In his extensive study of film biography as narrative system, Henry M. Taylor specifies that a biopic tells episodes from the life of an historic character or deals with its specific importance. Often but not always the person's real name is used. In contrast to the historical film genre, which focusses on circumstances and the actual historic situation, the film biography is centred on one personality (Taylor, 2002, p. 22). Similar to docudrama, the result is a more fragmented and episodic narrative structure. Both genres enable a variety of approaches to the past and are closely related to the ongoing shift towards personalized history. Therefore, the specific way of telling a historical biography as docudrama can fundamentally differ within a generic, historiographical and epistemological framework.

Biopics have flourished in recent years not only on television but also in cinema (Nieberle, 2008, p. 1). Cinematic stories 'based on facts' often depict biographical events from the life of more-or-less famous personalities. Recently, actor Tom Cruise portrayed Wehrmacht officer Stauffenberg in *Valkyrie* (2008), depicting the events of 20 July 1944 – the attempt to kill Hitler. The movie *Defiance* (2008) portrayed a group of Jewish brothers and their resistance to Nazi occupation and the deportation of the Jewish people in Eastern Europe. Both films use elements from the biopic genre and merge fact and dramatic fiction for an emotional reanimation of the past. Television is similar.

Paget describes this focus on people who experience, suffer, master or change the course of history as a significant element of the codes and conventions of docudrama. He states that docudrama, which is a re-telling of events from national or international histories, often does so by re-presenting the careers of significant national or international figures and, especially in recent years also focuses upon 'ordinary citizens' who have been thrust into the news because of some special experience (Paget, 2004, p. 196). Paget explains that the classical docudrama was intended to portray issues of concern to national or international communities in order to provoke discussion. More recent developments have often also provoked questions about its form (Paget, 2004, p. 196). Today, television docudrama depicts the life stories of those who have lived through history in order to create a certain re-experience of the past for the audience, which is intensified through personalized narration. Emotional addressing is therefore seen as an important element of historical docudrama. Borrowing a term from Guido Knopp, I describe these modes on German television as 'historical event television' (see Ebbrecht, 2007). One important aspect is that these docudramas capitalize on 'history as current event' because of anniversaries or rising public interest (Ebbrecht, 2008, p. 103). Additionally, they communicate the past in a clear personalized way. Often this is expressed by eyewitnesses, who are seen as mediators of past experiences (Keilbach, 2008, p. 165).

Furthermore, their testimonies can be enhanced through the performance of actors in re-enacted sequences (Ebbrecht, 2007, p. 42). While classical docudrama tries to create the impression of a fact-orientated representation of history through strategies of distancing the audience from the historic protagonists, historical event television changes the perception of historical authenticity, which is more and more linked to the expression of emotions. But not only ordinary citizens, as 'victims of history', have become protagonists in historical television docudrama, which was already intensified through the dominance of eyewitnesses as mediators of the past. Related to this personalization of history, the focus on famous people and 'great men' is changing. Historical television has become more and more centred on the 'private' aspects of a public person's life, as demonstrated by the increasing use of amateur images and private footage in historical television documentary series or the re-creation of 'private' shots, as in *Virtual History: The Secret Plot to Kill Hitler* (Ebbrecht, 2007, p. 46). This points towards the specific address of biographical docudrama, which on the one hand can *re*-construct history as re-experience for the present, not reflecting its own status and changing concepts of identity, history and biography, and on the other hand can address its own narrative and therefore broach the issue of constructing history for the audience.

Questioning biography as an educational model

In his analysis of biographies in popular magazines during the 1940s, Leo Lowenthal points out a series of characteristics that indicate the 'social need seeking gratification by this type of literature' (1961, p. 110). In general, Lowenthal describes the structure of popular biographies as success stories, which should function as 'educational models' (p. 113). At the same time the individual is seen as a 'product of his past' (p. 120), 'understood in terms of his biological and regional inheritance' (p. 119). Therefore, an 'element of passivity' (p. 120), even of weakness, towards the social environment is introduced, which is at the same time overwritten by the suggestion of strength and success. This originates in a certain narrative model, telling a life story as a 'road from childhood to maturity' (p. 124), while childhood 'appears neither as prehistory and key to the character of an individual nor as a stage of transition to the growth and formation of the abundant diversity of an adult. Childhood is nothing but a midget edition, a predated publication of a man's profession and career' (pp. 124–5). Similarly, George Custen highlights as a formal element of biopics that they focus on their character's progress from youth:

> The formulation 'young' in a film's title performs several functions. It seemingly permits the viewer to be present at the creation, witnessing the birth or the first display of the traits that will make the older version of the biographee famous. Second it also suggests that fame is often largely a genetic predisposition, present from a very early age.
>
> (1992, p. 51)

By highlighting this fateful character, the representation serves the 'pseudo-psychology of success' (Lowenthal, 1961, p. 125) as mythology, and a set of recurring stereotypes (p. 126). This corresponds with the accentuation of the factual base of the stories, in which 'the tendency to commute life data into facts to be accepted rather than understood becomes intensified' (p. 127).

In contrast, the television drama *Der junge Freud* [The Young Freud] from 1976, a co-production of Austrian public service television and the ZDF, directed by Axel Corti, subverts this kind of success story. Although the title indicates the conventionalized story from childhood to maturity, the docudrama starts with Freud's emigration from Austria after its annexation to the German Reich in 1938. The camera focuses on the elderly Freud, 82 years old, and a refugee showing him with his family in a train carriage leaving Vienna. Starting from this incident the biographic docudrama reverses the chronological order and sets up Freud's displacement as an explicit reference frame for the understanding of his biography and his intellectual work. Furthermore, the opening scene points towards the reflection of the film's own narrative. The dramatic re-enactment of Freud and his wife Martha leaning out of the train's window freezes and is followed by a historic photograph depicting the same situation. Although we hear the sound of a camera taking a photograph, this montage does not serve as authentication of the dramatization but makes us aware of its character as historical re-enactment. The following series of photographic portraits depicting Freud's biography in a reversed order, starting with an image of the old Freud and ending with a portrait of the famous psychoanalyst as a young boy, underlines the docudrama's critical approach towards the 'illusion of authentication' (Keilbach, 2005, p. 116). Instead of total illusion, the docudrama emphasizes its construction and the mode of speculation. Thereby it distances itself from the classical, chronological popular biography. Rather, and similar to Lowenthal's analysis, it follows a critical approach, helping the audience to understand the processes of history instead of creating a nostalgic reconstruction of a biographical life according to a 'timeless and passive image of modern man' (Lowenthal, 1961, p. 125).

To break up the impression of total illusion created by the dramatic re-enactments, the narration of *The Young Freud* is interrupted several times. Surprisingly, the first sequence of the retrospective sequence following Freud's emigration represents a paradox. Freud can be seen in this scene both as a boy and as an adult at the same time. Suddenly the diegesis is interrupted and a nonvisible narrator starts to interview Freud and the actor playing Freud, respectively. This technique produces a series of unexpected breaks and gaps causing a disturbance of the biographical order; the old Freud constantly comments on the actions, ideas and failures of the young Freud. This structure, producing a modus of retrospective interpretation, resembles the methods of psychoanalysis. Furthermore, the narrative structure of the dramatic reconstruction does not accord to the mode of a chronicle but rather creates a dialogue. This dialogue paradoxically transgresses the diegesis. As a nonvisible extra-diegetic narrator, the author of the docudrama, Georg Stefan Troller, a Jewish émigré himself, is intervening into the dramatic action by critically questioning Freud's theory, calling attention to the political circumstances and correlating Freud's biography to the history of anti-Semitism in Austria and Germany. As Judith Keilbach notes, these dialogues at some points suggest a kind of auto poetic soliloquy by the author himself.

Keilbach exposes the exceptional reflexive character of this docudrama, arranged in relation to interruptions and a dialogic structure of self-assessment. She calls this a 'mode of retrospection', which emphasizes the epistemological implications of historiography as well (2005, p. 122). But she also stresses that this reflection on the construction of characters in a television drama is not usual (2005, p. 124). Neither is it in historical biography. Already, during the 1930s, Leo Lowenthal and Siegfried Kracauer had discovered historical biography as a crucial phenomenon in the popular culture of the time. In 1932–1933, Leo Lowenthal wrote his first article on literary biographies, 'Die biographische Mode' ['The biographic style'], which was not published during the period. Focus on the genre originated in a specific interest in the fate of the individual. Retrospectively, Lowenthal explained that the genre of popular historical biography seemed to support the notion of individuality, but at the same time destroyed its emphatic sense (Göttlich, 1996, p. 113). In his article, Lowenthal describes the standardization and conventionalization of literary biographies. But he also touches on the social meaning of their form. He describes the aesthetical poorness of popular biographies as an expression of late liberalism, and a revision of the classic *Erziehungsroman* [educational novel]. In contrast to the popular biography, the novel creates a certain experience of subjectivity for the reader, which strengthens the individual in his or her interplay with society (Lowenthal, 1975, p. 49). Although in a distant manner, *The Young Freud* also emphasizes this notion of subjectivity, with its dialogic and fragmentary narration.

Interestingly, Lowenthal detects the difference between novel and biography in its specific use of documents. While documents in the classic novel were used as a resource for the historic imagination, popular biography tends towards a 'totality' of document materials, fixed data, events, names and letters, which supersede the social sphere (1975, p. 50). At the same time, the protagonists of these biographies, although represented as heroes, become nothing more than operational modes of historical progress while the particularities of the individual are lost (1975, p. 50).

The crisis of subjectivity and narrative crisis structure

In his analysis of literary popular biographies, Lowenthal finds an analogy for a more general crisis of subjectivity and modern identity, which is strongly related to certain concepts of history and memory. While modernist writing would be able to express this crisis of subjectivity, the popular biography conceals it behind standardized narratives and stereotypical characters. By doing so it compensates for factual uncertainties and turns it into a nostalgic approach to the past. Similarly, Lowenthal's colleague and friend Siegfried Kracauer touched on this connotation in his article, 'Die Biographie als neubürgerliche Kunstform' ['Biography as the art form of the new bourgeoisie']. Kracauer also highlights the crisis of the novel but suggests that it may be possible to develop an epic form in response to the world's confusion. In contrast, the biography condenses history into the life stories of its 'heroes' and sees it as a 'continent in the sea of the amorphous' (1963, p. 76). The biography serves as a backdrop, authenticated by facts and frozen in conventionalized forms.

Kracauer noted that in literary biographies of the time, leading motifs were escape and rescue (1963, pp. 78–9). In contrast to this nostalgic and compensating intention, he states that biography should touch on the breakages in the social construction of society without any ideological protective cover, to confront the problems and conflicts of social reality (p. 78). Similarly, in his last book about history, Kracauer questions the chronological order of time and states that '[a]ny period, whether "found" or established in retrospect, consists of incoherent events or groups of events' (1969, p. 147). He describes a 'paradoxical relation between the continuity of the historical process and the breaks in it' (p. 157). Negatively, Kracauer points out the necessity of focussing on such moments of fracture and ambiguity. These can also enable a more reflexive reason for adopting biographies, indicated by Kracauer in a later review of Orson Welles' *Citizen Kane*. In his first film review after his last-minute escape from France to the US, he highlighted the specific narrative structure of Welles' film, showing 'fragments of a vita'. This constructive aspect requests the particular participation of the spectator, to combine and understand the different fragments of the reconstructive puzzle of Kane's life

(Kracauer, 2004, p. 327). Similarly, Knut Hickethier describes the biographic mode of *Citizen Kane*:

> The cinematic dream, the documentary report and the biographic reconstruction effort – not only one of these narratives will assert oneself; the image of life results from the combination of what they constitute together.
>
> (1991, p. 294)

Citizen Kane served also as a narrative model for Heinrich Breloer's television docudrama *Kollege Otto – Die Coop Affäre* [Colleague Otto – The Coop Affair] made in 1992 (Breloer, 1994, p. 288). This docudrama reconstructs the biography of Bernd Otto, a member of the working class, then secretary of a German trade union, and finally the chairman of the supermarket cooperative owned by the union. The starting point of the reconstruction is a public scandal about Otto, who was responsible for the bankruptcy of the cooperative. The conflicts, crisis and tensions in this political biography open various narrative possibilities. The biography of Bernd Otto is, therefore, similar to Welles' approach in *Citizen Kane*; it is reconstructed from the perspective of others. It thereby evolves a patchwork structure, constituted by two differing perspectives. On the one hand, we find figures from the cooperative's management, on the other hand, members of the workers' council and the supervisory board (Breloer, 1994, p. 287). These testimonies are mediated by a 'reporter' personified in Heinrich Breloer himself who investigates 'Citizen Otto' (p. 288). Breloer and his colleague Horst Königstein describe this as being a detective (Königstein, 1997, p. 246). This character personifies the methods of research and investigation, which constitute the course of the film's narrative.

The testimonies are not seen as bits and pieces to illustrate a dramatic story. In contrast the portrait evolves out of differing perspectives. The re-enactments are constructed from remembered scenes. Both are merged afterwards in the process of montage. Breloer's aim is not to reconstruct or imitate the past. He wants to highlight the fragmentary nature of docudramatic construction. The actors do not need to look like their historical models, and do not have to imitate them but study their behaviour and manners. They should not become imitators but interpreters (p. 248). This is clearly shown in the opening sequence of the docudrama; the actor Rainer Hunold stands in front of a mirror in his dressing room to practice his performance of Bernd Otto. Otto's own 'appearance' in the drama is mediated through a letter he wrote to Breloer. This is also visualized in the dressing room indicating the transition between reality and re-enactment. Hunold/Otto reads Otto's words while we see the actor's face in the mirror, representing the absent protagonist. The crisis structure of the docudrama is therefore transferred to the biography and its reconstruction. We are not attracted towards a dramatic story but are repulsed by a puzzle of conflicting images, episodes and interpretations. No commentator organizes these fragments. Only the investigative movement of the 'detective' Breloer and his montage structures the reconstruction. Additionally, a clearly artificial character appears that interrupts the dramatic actions, addresses the audience directly and gives further information about the complex events (Hißnauer, 2008, p. 260). Breloer had condensed several anonymous witness reports in this character. Besides this narrative function, it also functions as an alienating effect in the Brechtian sense, calling the spectator's attention to the constructed structure of this political biography.

In Breloer's concept of biographic docudrama, both basic elements, documents and interviews as well as the imaginative and playful re-enactments have the same importance and value (p. 258). But his radical treatment in *Colleague Otto* also threatens to lose the docudrama's structure. In its failure to bring together a clarification of the facts and its deconstructive approach towards coherent interpretation, Breloer's docudrama indicates the paradoxical relation between the continuity of the historical process and breaks within it, described by Kracauer as a general aporia in historiography.

It runs in the family: biography as television event

To avoid this aporia and the consequences of losing a clear and coherent narrative structure, historical event television more often focuses on classical storytelling. This tendency and the changed institutional position of docudrama as television event also shaped the work of Heinrich Breloer and his conception of the hybrid form, described by Christian Hißnauer as journalistic polit-television. To conclude my discussion of biography and docudrama on German television I will explore some of the tensions, limits and boundaries of historical event television in relation to biographic docudrama, by analyzing Breloer's three-part television docudrama *Die Manns* [The Manns].

The Manns was screened in 2001 and reviewed in the context of an increasing number of made-for-TV biopics presenting the life and fate of more-or-less prominent historic figures from Germany's history (Seifert, 2001). Conforming to the codes and conventions of historical event television, *The Manns* was advertised as a national TV event, produced for prime-time broadcasting and framed by several extratextual events such as additional documentaries and media discussion. But in contrast to other biographic dramas on television, which like *Vera Brühne* focus on dramatic action, Breloer's *The Manns* is still dedicated to the hybrid docudrama form although with a clear tendency towards dramatized re-enactments (Zander, 2005, p. 161). According to a contemporaneous trend of cinematic biopics about artists, such as *Pollock* in the USA (2000, dir. Ed Harris) or, in Germany, *Brechts letzter Sommer* ['Brecht's last summer'] (2000, dir. Lars Schütte), *The*

Manns is much more focussed on the personal life, rather than on the artistic work, of its protagonist (Zander, 2005, p. 158). The docudrama therefore follows the perspective of popular biographies criticized by Lowenthal in his research. Illustrating the historic background with personal conflicts, love stories and crisis the film follows a classical strategy of condensing history into personalized stories.

At the same time, *The Manns* seems to correspond to the trend of earlier adaptations of Mann's novels for cinema and television, looking for auto-biographical evidence in fictional stories. According to Peter Zander, *The Manns* reverses this approach and builds a very special form of transfiguration between the artistic work and the biography. The biography is not extracted from the artwork, but instead the artistic work is repatriated in the biography (2005, p. 161). Therefore Breloer not only establishes a dialogue between the documents (visual documents such as photographs and film footage, and textual documents such as diaries and letters as well as interviews) and the fictional re-enactments. He also produces a dialogue within the re-enactments, moving them from simple illustrations towards imaginative interpretation of Mann's life through his poetic work. These echoes of Mann's own work in the reconstruction of his biography produce a space of transference similar to the hybrid character of docudrama. This causes a notion of 'in between' artistic imagination and historic reconstruction, which can exceed the limits of historical event television and its nostalgic and imitative position towards the past (Ebbrecht, 2008, p. 112). As a fourth perspective, alongside the testimony of Mann's daughter Elisabeth Mann-Borgese, who followed the traces of her father's life together with the film team, the visual and textual documents, and Breloer himself as 'investigator-detective' in the family history, Mann's poetic work constitutes an important counterpart to any 'closing' interpretation of this history.

Nevertheless, this notion of openness and intertextuality conflicts with the changed modes in Breloer's docudramatic technique. While earlier works like *Colleague Otto* demonstrated its fragmentary and artificial character, the montage of merging documents and re-enactments in *The Manns* seeks much more invisible transitions. Hiding the difference between archive images and dramatic action, for example, by showing Mann's son Klaus played by an actor sitting between other journalists after the war and then changing to archive footage of this specific historic situation, demonstrates a tendency to dissolve the difference between the past and its (nostalgic) re-invention. The ongoing 'perfection' of this method tends towards a decline of the epistemological potential of the docudrama to make us aware of the constructed character of the re-enactment and of history as well. This points towards the problem of personalization and emotional addressing – more precisely, the change from a distant and disturbing address towards more harmonious access to the past.

In *The Manns* this conflict is present as a tension between personal and public memory. Because Breloer presents the public figure of Thomas Mann through the frame of family history, which is represented by Mann's last remaining child Elisabeth, both perspectives compete in the films. This represents the tension between the investigative deconstructive mode, looking for gaps, conflicts and transgression, and the more harmonious mode of the family novel. Elisabeth Mann-Borgese's positive retrospective perspective on her father therefore dominates the perception of his biography, especially because she herself appears in the docudrama as a double of the audience. Fascinated by the reappearance of her childhood, we see her exploring the film sets where the sites of her family history are rebuilt. Therefore, sometimes it is not clear if we see the biographical reconstruction of Thomas Mann's life or of Mann-Borgese's memories. This has an idiosyncratic effect on the portrait of Thomas Mann in the film. Because of these conflicting public and private perspectives, the transfiguration of poetry into history and the dialogical structure of the docudrama, he is still an ambiguous figure. Although Thomas Mann is concretized in the presentation by the actor Armin Müller-Stahl, he remains artificial as a historic figure, inviting the audience to a more active interpretation.

Re/constructing biographies

The reconsideration of biographies in relation to docudrama as a hybrid form, and ambiguous access to the past, proves the potential and the limitations of this kind of historical television. Although the biographical docudrama is, according to recent trends, one of the more entertaining forms of re-enacting the past for the present, it is still able to call attention to its own form and also to the epistemological implications of representing history on television. The institutional changes in German television had noticeable effects on the possibilities and techniques of historical drama and docudrama. But they did not cause the limitations of conventional storytelling, as the possibilities of challenging journalistic polit-television during the 1980s and early 1990s prove, even after the introduction of private broadcasting in Germany. Furthermore, international trends in historical television tend towards more complex and partly also essayistic and fragmentary ways of depicting past events on the small screen, as Simon Schama's docudrama *Rough Crossings* (BBC, 2007) demonstrates. Entertainment, as well as emotional addressing, is not opposed to a reflexive mode of telling history. The question that still remains is: what motivations cause us to turn towards the past?

The biographical mode enables harmonic identification as well as an investigative access to the past through the life of a certain person. It can address a more nostalgic mood, looking for a mediated re-experience of the lost past through media experience. But it can also create modes of disturbance and an interest in history as an endless puzzle of different and partly conflicting perspectives, which together constitute a certain image of an historic biography that cannot be understood in terms of authenticity or originality but has to be seen as historic imagination. The porosity of the docudrama as narrative form is able to support this understanding of history as construction and process of interpretation. But it can also hide its own narrative from active reflection and create a biographic reconstruction motivated by rescue and escape, as Siegfried Kracauer noted during the 1930s. According to Kracauer, we still have to ask whether these historical reconstructions stick to a nostalgic and compensating intention, or if they try to touch the breakages in a biography to mark the influences of social construction in a broader society, therefore confronting through the artificial modes of docudrama the problems and conflicts of social reality.

A note on availability

Die Manns is available on DVD released by Euro Video in 2002 in a German version without subtitles. Regrettably, at the moment, a DVD or VHS version of *Der junge Freud* or *Kollege Otto* is not available.

Bibliography

Breloer, H. (1994) 'Spiel mit Fernsehen. Eine kurzgefaßte Arbeitsgeschichte', in P. Zimmermann (ed.), *Fernsehdokumentarismus: Bilanz und Perspektiven* (Konstanz: Ölschläger).
Custen, G.F. (1992) *Bio/Pics: How Hollywood Constructed Public History* (New Brunswick, NJ: Rutgers University Press).
Ebbrecht, T. (2007) 'Docudramatizing history on TV: German and British docudrama and historical event television in the memorial year 2005', *European Journal of Cultural Studies*, 10.1: 35–55.
Ebbrecht, T. (2008) 'History, public memory and media event: codes and conventions of historical event-television in Germany', in S. Nicholas, T. O'Malley and K. Williams (eds), *Reconstructing the Past: History in the Mass Media, 1890–2005* (London: Routledge).
Göttlich, U. (1996) *Kritik der Medien: Reflexionsstufen kritisch-materialistischer Medientheorien am Beispiel von Leo Löwenthal und Raymond Williams* (Opladen: Westdeutscher Verlag).
Hickethier, K. (1979) 'Fiktion und Fakt: Das Dokumentarspiel und seine Entwicklung bei ZDF und ARD', in H. Kreuzer and K. Prümm (eds), *Fernsehsendungen und ihre Formen: Typologie, Geschichte und Kritik des Programms in der Bundesrepublik Deutschland* (Stuttgart: Reclam).
Hickethier, K. (1991) 'Filmkunst und Filmklassik: *Citizen Kane* (1941)', in W. Faulstich and H. Korte (eds), *Fischer Filmgeschichte. Bd. 2* (Frankfurt a.M.: Fischer).
Hickethier, K. with P. Hoff (1998) *Geschichte des Deutschen Fernsehens* (Stuttgart: Metzler).

Hißnauer, C. (2008) 'Das Doku-Drama in Deutschland als Journalistisches Politikfernsehen – eine Annäherung und Entgegnung aus fernsehgeschichtlicher Perspektive', *MEDIENwissenschaft*, 03/2008: 256–265.

Kansteiner, W. (2006) *In Pursuit of German Memory: History, Television, and Politics after Auschwitz* (Athens, OH: Ohio University Press).

Keilbach, J. (2005) 'Geschichte als Geschichten: Koproduzierte Dokumentarspiele von ORF und ZDF', in S. Szely (ed.), *Spiele und Wirklichkeiten: Rund um 50 Jahre Fernsehspiel und Fernsehen in Österreich* (Wien: Filmarchiv Austria).

Keilbach, J. (2008) *Geschichtsbilder und Zeitzeugen: Zur Darstellung des Nationalsozialismus im bundesdeutschen Fernsehen* (Münster: LIT).

Königstein, H. (1997) 'Doku-Drama: Spiel mit Wirklichkeiten', in R. Blaes and G.A. Heussen (eds), *ABC des Fernsehens* (Konstanz: UVK).

Kracauer, S. (1963) 'Die Biographie als neubürgerliche Kunstform', in *Das Ornament der Masse* (Frankfurt a.M.: Suhrkamp).

Kracauer, S. (1969) *History: The Last Things Before the Last* (New York: Oxford University Press).

Kracauer, S. (2004) 'Ein amerikanisches Experiment', in *Werke. Bd. 1* (Frankfurt a.M.: Suhrkamp).

Lowenthal, L. (1975) *Notizen zur Literatursoziologie* (Stuttgart: Ferdinand Enke Verlag).

Lowenthal, L. (1961) *Literature, Popular Culture, and Society* (Palo Alto, CA: Pacific Books).

Nieberle, S. (2008) *Literaturhistorische Filmbiographien: Autorschaft und Literaturgeschichte im Kino* (Berlin: Walter de Gruyter).

Paget, D. (1998) *No Other Way to Tell It: Dramadoc/Docudrama on Television* (Manchester: Manchester University Press).

Paget, D. (2004) 'Codes and conventions of dramadoc and docudrama', in R.C. Allen and A. Hill (eds), *The Television Studies Reader* (London: Routledge).

Seifert, H. (2001) 'Familiendrama und Jahrhundertroman: Monumentaler TV-Dreiteiler über die Manns', *Neue Züricher Zeitung*, 30 November.

Straub, K. (2007) *Faszination Biopic: Entwicklungen und aktuelle Tendenzen populärer biographischer Filme* (Saarbrücken: Verlag Dr. Müller).

Zander, P. (2005) *Thomas Mann im Kino* (Marburg: Schüren).

15
Flog It!

Nostalgia and Lifestyle on British Daytime Television

Iris Kleinecke-Bates

Nostalgia, as has long been recognized, can have a powerful impact on the construction and reception of screen texts (e.g., Boym, 2001; Cardwell, 2002; Cook, 2005; Higson, 1993, 2003; Monk and Sargeant, 2002). Closely linked to the processes of memory production, it has become an important way of analysing the way in which representations of the past assume historically and nationally specific functions. While often associated with a kind of cultural conservatism, nostalgia has also been recognized as a legitimate part of historical narratives and an integral aspect of the act of remembering. As such, different ways of analysing its impact on British primetime television have emerged, going beyond its often-discussed manifestation in the heritage film and incorporating the many different forms in which representations of the past and history appear on the screen, as well as programmes that deliberately play with a nostalgia for television as a medium. These programmes[1] often explicitly play with notions of personal and public memory and nostalgia in ways which contextualize them not only historically and culturally but also institutionally through a deliberate address and meshing of private memory and a more public sense of collective remembered experience (e.g., Holdsworth, 2008, pp. 137–44).

The past and the individual's connection with it is also a preoccupation in daytime television, albeit often in different ways. Programmes like *Flog It!* (BBC2, 2002–), *Cash in the Attic*, (BBC1, 2002–) and *Car Booty* (BBC1, 2004–), although engaged in the negotiation of self and history, appear to counter, rather than celebrate, nostalgia. At first sight occupied with money and profit, and focussing on the finding and selling on of old items of value to finance family holidays and home improvements, they seem to embody what Nick Cohen has noted, in a recent article in *The Observer*, as the 'loss of love for the antique', as modern taste moves towards different preferences (2008, p. 32). Although not high-profile and hidden within the daytime schedule, these programmes tend to be long-running and popular. As Angela Piccini's research on history and archaeology programming on television has shown, a snapshot of the popularity of 'heritage programming' in 2005–2006 showed that 'some 13,000 programmes were transmitted and 98% of all adults saw at least one heritage programme during the year. Of these programmes, the top five made a 61% contribution to the amount of viewing in the study and all were about antiques' (2007, pp. 5–6). The apparent popularity of these programmes is important in the context of this chapter, because, situated within a television environment of 'primetime nostalgia', their popularity hints at a complex set of attractions that makes viewers favour these programmes, even over more high-profile primetime programmes such as *Coast* (BBC2, 2002–) or *Time Team* (Channel 4, 1994–).

My main interest in this chapter is the negotiation of the past and personal self-development as it emerges in these programmes. Do they advocate a letting go of the past in favour of cash, home improvements and holidays, or do they rather promote a shift of nostalgia from the home to the television screen, from private memory to collective remembering? Moreover, I want to investigate the way representation of object value, history and nostalgia can function as the site of class dynamics that is triggered by implicit judgements and viewer engagement. Although recently two studies of the *Antiques Roadshow* (BBC, 1979–) have been published (Bishop, 1999, pp. 1–27, and Clouse, 2008, pp. 3–20), indicating a shift of interest towards antiques programming, there is still a comparative lack of work in this area, in particular regarding my specific approach of analysing a set of hybrid daytime television programmes and their negotiation of memory, history and nostalgia. I will therefore, for my analysis, draw on a combination of scholarly work on nostalgia and the role of antiques, and more specific analyses of the programmes. Due to the length of the series, I am basing my work on a selection of programmes which serve as examples although they are in no way to be seen as representative of all the episodes within the respective series of *Flog It!*, *Cash in the Attic*, or *Car Booty*.[2]

Flog It!, *Cash in the Attic*, and *Car Booty* are a set of programmes on BBC1 and BBC2 which, in differing ways, centre on the sentimental and monetary value of antiques and heirlooms. *Flog It!* is similar to *Antiques Roadshow* in inviting members of the public to bring their antiques and heirlooms to have them valued. Owners are welcomed to explain the object's place within their family, and the expert offers information about the item's historical background, meaning that the viewer receives information about both sentimental and historical value. However, although it is possible to have items valued without selling them, the sale, as also illustrated by its *Radio Times* introduction, is an integral part of the show's narrative: 'the perfect antidote to those moments in *Antiques Roadshow* where, having discovered their dusty heirloom is worth a fortune, the owner insists they'll never sell it' (27 May 2002, p. 80).

Car Booty and *Cash in the Attic* also both revolve around the finding and selling of old objects. However, here the items are located in the home of the participants. The narrative centres on a team of presenters and specialists who help the participants find, so says the slogan of *Cash in the Attic*, 'hidden treasures in your home, and then sells them for you at auction'. The two programmes differ in their target area – while *Cash in the Attic* is aimed at high-value antiques to be sold at auction, *Car Booty* focuses on often low-value items that are sold at car boot sales, although more valuable collectables are also offered to specialist shops and collectors. However, for both programmes a set structure is repeated in each episode: the presenter introduces the area of the country for this particular episode, then introduces the participants. We learn about the reason they want to raise money – usually a goal that is linked to either a recreational ambition or else a lifestyle choice that is linked to a recent change in the person's life that acts as a catalyst for the desire to declutter. The team of presenters and experts comes to the home of the participants and looks through their possessions in search for valuables that can be sold. The participants are invited to recount the story behind chosen items; then the expert adds historical background and, finally, reveals a potential value. After that, the item is sold at auction or at a car boot sale, and the programme ends with the participants enjoying the fruits of their labour.

All three programmes share a focus on history and antiques, but the narratives appear dominated by an emphasis not on their celebration but rather on their transformation into cash, on what Ronald Bishop, in his article on the *Antiques Roadshow*, describes as a replacement of sentimental value by monetary value: 'Sentimental value is pushed aside by the discovery that the item is worth something – or nothing.[...] The narratives reconfigure how we place value on objects and on the personal history behind them' (1999, p. 13). *Flog It!*, with its emphasis on the element of the sale, seems to emphasize this consumerist take on heritage and history. Thus, often members of the public relate touching personal tales about the history of the valued object in their family, only to then happily sell said object at auction, such as a man who asks for a valuation of a bust of Pan (BBC, 22 November 2007). He narrates the history of the item, which is, in the family, known affectionately as 'Uncle Septimus'. However, despite the fond memories, and rather inexplicably, he is then happy to sell the bust.

As this example illustrates, while often sales seem to be determined by house moves or the realization that because of a lack of close remaining family the item cannot be passed down to the next generation, adding an element of nostalgia and loss, there are also participants who simply prefer to obtain money for other pursuits. This element of 'selling out' is also traceable in *Cash in the Attic* and *Car Booty*. Programmes such as *Cash in the Attic*, which advocate a kind of 'life-laundry'[3] in order to clear out the old and make money to purchase new consumer goods or to fund lifestyle choices, seem to complement the boom in lifestyle and also in many cases support the kind of upward class mobility inherent in the lifestyle narrative. As Jack Z. Bratich has discussed, makeover television, through its narrative of transformation, has an antecedent in the fairy tale. Drawing on analyses of the fairy tale by critics such as Zipes and Warner, he argues that the makeover narrative builds on a similar wish for transformation potentials in the world (2007, pp. 18-19). Although less overtly than makeover programmes such as *Extreme Makeover: Home Edition* (US, ABC, 2003–) which, according to Bratich, defines its project as 'making dreams come true' (2007, p. 19), shows like *Flog It!* and *Cash in the Attic* also build on this fairy tale notion of transformation. Thus, the 'Be On a Show' BBC website for *Flog It!* praises the magical transformation of ordinary items such as 'a ceramic bowl, bought for £4 at a car boot sale, which was sold for £1,500' ('Be On a Show, *Flog It!*' (n.d.)), emphasizing the transformative power of the programme, while *Cash in the Attic* claims that in order to help you raise money for 'something special', it will help you find 'those hidden treasures' ('Be On a Show, *Cash in the Attic*' (n.d.)). Money made in episodes of *Cash in the Attic* goes, for example, towards a new wardrobe for a woman who has managed to lose several stone through a diet, an MA in Fine Art (BBC, 4 December 2007), or a family outing to the Eden Project, which will allow a family to spend a day together (BBC, 22 November 2007). The epilogue, which is integral to shows like *Cash in the Attic*, revisits participants and shows them enjoying the fruits of their (decluttering) labour, further emphasizing the narrative of transformation by offering it as a point of narrative closure. It can thus be argued that the main attraction of these programmes lies in the transformation of sentimental value into monetary value to be transformed into consumer pleasures or, as presenter Jennie Bond puts it in an episode of *Cash in the Attic* (BBC, 26 December 2007), the selling of yet 'another set of family heirlooms' because 'quite simply – [the participants] wanna have some fun'. Tellingly, listings of *Flog It!*, *Cash in the Attic* and *Car Booty* all appear under the category of 'lifestyle' on the BBC website, emphasizing this transformation of family history into present-day self-improvement.

Not all objects have personal histories or sentimental value. Items may have been inherited, but histories have been forgotten, or else they may have been purchased very recently. In this, the makeover narrative is evident; with the lack of sentimental history the object becomes a treasure and an enabler of self through market value. What dominates is the individualist focus of the makeover show – what is important is the construction of a selfhood that is based on who the participant *wants* to be. As June Deery notes in 'Commodifying Self and Place' when talking about the reality makeover: '[W]hat makeover programming reflects is the extent to which the self is now regarded as a project and cultural construct, something that must be self-reflexively worked on and continually performed' (2006, p. 161). The sorting out, and selling, of unwanted heirlooms aids this process. While also present in the narratives of *Flog It!* when people are asked about their plans for the money raised by the sale of antiques, this narrative of improvement is particularly pronounced in the case of *Car Booty* and *Cash in the Attic*, where the narrative of self-improvement and realization is even implied in the structure of each individual episode, framed by information about the history of the location of each episode which places the individuals in question and their private lives within a wider historical context, and the revisiting and focus on the achieved goal of the participants at the end of the programme. There is a shift here from antiques and history programme, via the rite of passage of the selling of the items, to an expression of the participants' new and improved lifestyle.

At the same time, however, this structure also already hints at the potential tension between the two narrative strands, and I want to argue that although one aspect of these shows, the seemingly simple transformation of the family heirloom into ready cash is often more complex than it appears. Thus, as Bishop has suggested, the object's emotional value is altered through the knowledge of its monetary value; but while this narrative of transformation appears to sit well within a cultural and socioeconomic context that advocates a liquidating of stagnant wealth for the purchase of a chosen lifestyle, this replacement of sentimental value with monetary value is not always successful. Items may not sell on the day and participants are forced to take them back home with them as often happens on both *Car Booty* and *Cash in the Attic*, or participants may be disappointed when an item is worth less than they anticipated. Alternatively, as in an episode of *Cash in the Attic*, a participant may decide not to bring a family heirloom to auction because sentimental value outweighs potential monetary and transformative value after all (BBC, 22 November 2007). In either case, no straightforward transformation of value can take place. While it could be argued that in this case the object in question has been devalued by its failure to transform into the expected monetary value, the object's sentimental and historical background still functions to enrich and convey a value that is not linked to monetary worth and indeed highlights a tension between the lifestyle narrative and the narrative of history and nostalgia that is an undercurrent in both *Cash in the Attic* and *Car Booty*.

Moreover, even in the case of a successful transaction and sale, the way in which this stagnant wealth – the family heirloom – is selected and liquidated is in itself a matter of complex negotiation of memory, history and the care of the self. If, as Walter Benjamin has mused in his essay, 'Unpacking My Library: A Talk About Collecting', a collection harbours a 'chaos of memories...the chance, the fate, that suffuse the past...are conspicuously present in the accustomed confusion of these books' (2005, p. 486); the selecting of things in this manner becomes a metaphor for the sorting out of memories and the positioning of the self in relation to history. Thus, often items that are discarded are associated with relationships that are no longer intact and that the participants want to distance themselves from. What takes place then is a rewriting of the past through a selective discarding of items that are deemed not to have a place in the participants' life. Objects are stripped of their emotional power and reduced to monetary value as a kind of 'exorcism'. By being let go they become enablers of the future as the participants reject or transcend a past version of themselves and engage in an active remaking of the self, suggesting active agency as opposed to passive acceptance of selfhood.

Both *Cash in the Attic* and *Car Booty* bridge the gap between the heritage and antiques programme and the makeover programme, but they do not do so in the straightforward transformation of sentimental value into ready cash suggested by Bishop. Thus, the narrative of the makeover is still accompanied by an equally dominant narrative of history, memory, nostalgia and loss. Misha Kavka talks about what she sees as a specifically British obsession with both the past and with the makeover as follows:

> It is not just that décor and real estate can be probed for the secrets of interiority, but also that such objects are bearers of materialized history. [...] [P]art of the pleasure of watching what locals have dug out of the attic comes from the valuation expert who reads off the history of the object. As the cultural product of a nation self-admittedly obsessed with its history, the British home makeover is caught up not only with an aspirational future, but also with a national and personal past whose overhaul will itself become the material of heritage for the next generation.
>
> (2006, pp. 216–7)

Rather fittingly, *Flog It!*, *Cash in the Attic*, and *Car Booty* all combine both the national and personal past and what Kavka calls the 'aspirational future'. The result is a direct conflict between the forward-moving narrative of self-improvement and re-invention of the self, and the nostalgia that is generated by the items to be sold. This nostalgia, when disassociated from the personal, takes the form of a general longing that is juxtaposed with the narrative of progress embedded in the makeover formula. As Svetlana Boym notes in *The Future of Nostalgia*, 'nostalgia is rebellion against the modern idea of time, the time of history and progress. The nostalgic desires to obliterate history and turn it into private or collective mythology, to revisit time like space, refusing to surrender to the irreversibility of time that plagues the human condition' (2001, p. xv). While the participants may be invested in a forward-movement, the nostalgia that is inherent in the objects introduced in the programmes creates sentiments that are in direct conflict to this forward-drive. Although the surface narratives seem to confirm the selling out of personal memories and keepsakes for the sake of lifestyle changes, Clouse's claim that 'the narration of facts regarding the history and acquisition of objects provides the *Antiques Roadshow* with stories of human drama and history' (2008, p. 5) is also true of the three programmes discussed here. Despite, but also through, their narratives of moving on from the past, these programmes effect a sense of nostalgia and sentimentality.

At times, this conflict is shared by participants and audience alike, as is the case in an episode of *Cash in the Attic* in which a daughter is selecting items to be sold at auction to help her frail mother who is downsizing after the recent death of her husband (BBC, 23 November 2007). The narrative throughout is one of reminiscence and nostalgia, as the daughter picks out items and recounts their history and meaning for her in relation to the house she grew up in and the loss of her father. Despite the presence of a strong forward-drive provided both by the mother's moving on through her plans to downsize and through her wish to raise money to send her daughter, together with her best friend who also suffered a recent loss, to a health farm, the overarching sentiment of this episode is that of loss, as even the pamper weekend is revealed as a family tradition that mother and daughter used to enjoy together and that, due to the mother's frailness, cannot continue and is hence carried forward by her daughter and her friend. As the selected items go to auction the thrill of witnessing their sale for more than their estimated value is mingled with a strong sense of reluctance, loss and nostalgia.

This sense of reluctance and nostalgia is often present even when it is not shared by the participants, such as when a multitude of inherited antiques results in a loss of meaning for individual items as in the aforementioned *Cash in the Attic* episode which follows a family's money-raising efforts for a day at the Eden Project, and their choice to focus on their family's present rather than on what has become obscure family history. Similarly the case of a *Car Booty* participant deciding to sell his childhood collection of 1400 comic books, bought for him by his parents, one each day, between his 5th and 15th birthday (BBC, 20 December 07), to finance his wife's 50th birthday party may create a conflicted response. In both cases the worthwhile and commendable goal of a treat for the family vies with nostalgia produced by the items in question. Although the participants may be ready to let go of family heirlooms, souvenirs and keepsakes, this is not necessarily the case for the viewer, resulting in a tension between the pleasure of the lifestyle narrative and the witnessing of people fulfilling their dreams and ambitions and the narrative of family history. The consequence is a 'move sideways', in which the sentimental value is, via the telling of the object's story, passed onto the viewer, who seems to mourn the loss of it on behalf of the less sentimental participants. The knowledge of the item's history brings with it a different kind of nostalgia based on an awareness of the item's passage through both historical and personal time and space.

The result is a shifting of private memory to public and collective nostalgia which, for the audience, comes without any hindering of personal dreams and aspirations. Susan Stewart's distinction between the souvenir and the collection is useful here. The souvenir, she says, 'involves [a] displacement of attention into the past' (2003, p. 151) that discredits the present. The evaluation and sale of the item becomes a rite of passage in which the role of souvenir as private memory is replaced by a new identity as collectible, which, emotionally accessible not to one but to all, becomes synonymous with the history it embodies as an antique object. The past, now, rather than making us turn our gaze backwards, lends significance to the object, which becomes imbued with a wider sense of treasure lost and found. As Stewart puts it: 'The collection does not displace attention to the past; rather, the past is at the service of the collection, for whereas the souvenir lends authenticity to the past, the past lends authenticity to the collection' (2003, p. 151). In the act of transferring personal and historical value from the individual to the public, the souvenir or heirloom becomes part of a public collection and thus of a wider sense of nostalgia for the past.

The narrative of these programmes is twofold: on the one hand, it is a story of wish-fulfilment or the remodelling of the self, and on the other, it is the making of a collective and shared history through the publicizing and the historical contextualization of the personal; a transformation of personal, sentimental value into 'official' history and historical value.[4] Stewart notes that 'the function of the heirloom is to weave, quite literally by means of narrative, a significance of blood relation at the expense of a larger view of history and causality' (2003, pp. 136–7). While this would imply that the personal history cancels out the wider historical significance of a personal artefact, here, the combination of both creates a step-by-step process in which the items in question are brought out into a realm of public nostalgia and ownership as personal and 'official' histories are merged. Thus, even while the programme may promote the fulfilling of personal dreams through the selling of family heirlooms, the selling does not signify a selling out of the past but a shifting sideways, turning the items from personal memory into public heritage. Knowledge of the 'hidden history', the sentimental value of the item and its private history magnify audience reactions, and reactions to the sale can at times, as for example in the case of the head of Pan, become personal as the object becomes a 'treasure' ill-treated by its unappreciative owners. While the participants of the show may sell the object and replace sentimental with monetary value, the witnessing and recording of sentimental value on screen means that the viewer can cherish and be-mourn the object on behalf of the participants. Personal memory is thus replaced with a collective post-memory and nostalgia about what is lost to our modern lives and lifestyles, even while the item is successfully exchanged for short-lived pleasures. The role of the expert as the person who unlocks the object's historical value is here similar to the role Holdsworth attributes to the curator: 'An an understanding of the context/use/history of the object, as narrated by the curator [...] reinserts the object with a memory' (2008, p. 141). The narrative of 'official' history as conveyed by the expert imbues the object with a 'sense of time and memory' (2008, p. 141).

Although viewing pleasure is derived from the transformation and transfer of sentimental value into monetary value and the narrative of self-improvement that it accompanies, the question that always remains is if the selling is, in the eye of the viewer, a positive decision and improvement, or rather a selling out for short-sighted amusement, and even when the transfer of emotional into monetary value is completed the sense of loss provoked by the recording of the histories of the sold object again reaffirms the importance and impact of sentimental value. Here, the narrative of transformation and the narrative of history and nostalgia collide, as participants and their goals are, as Bratich puts it, 'judged according to their deservingness' (2007, pp. 18–19). This element of judgement is important because, as Clouse notes, objects are 'socially dynamic' (2008, p. 3) and linked to the construction of identity, meaning that they can trigger very personal reactions as judgements about the participants are made.

As Mihaly Csikszentmihalyi notes, everyday objects are relevant for the construction of the self in various ways. They do not only demonstrate the owner's power and place in a social hierarchy and give evidence of the place of the self in a social network of symbols, but also situate and 'reveal the continuity of the self through time' (1993, p. 23). Through their cultural construction, objects provide meaning and value on different levels and imply a distinction of class and taste. While clearly present in the case of souvenirs and other items of little monetary or historical value in *Car Booty*, this judgement on the basis of knowledge of symbolic value is emphasized in the case of antiques, because of the special function of antiques as signifiers of taste and social class. As Baudrillard notes, antiques are not simply signs of an upward social mobility, where the purchasing of antiques highlights the moving up into the lower upper classes. If this upward mobility can be signalled in other ways through the purchase of modern consumer goods, why, as Baudrillard asks,

> is the reference to the *past* so often chosen as a vector of status? All acquired value tends to metamorphose into inherited value, into a received grace. But since blood, birth and titles of nobility have lost their ideological force, the task of signifying transcendence has fallen to material signs – to pieces of furniture, objects, jewellery and works of art of every time and every place.
>
> (2005, p. 89)

The appraisers/experts in this context function as benchmarks or, as Clouse calls it, as 'arbitrators of taste, value and significance' (2008, p. 15), with judgement hinging on the dynamic between participants, experts, and audience which situates them within a system of symbolic value that serves as a signifier of class and taste. This is particularly the case when family heirlooms are sold that come with a long family history, yet appear unappreciated by the owners. The juxtaposition is one of knowledge and (often) taste, as the experts recognize and acknowledge the symbolic worth of objects that the participants, in an apparently ill-judged move to replace heritage with new lifestyle choices, have decided to sell. The juxtaposition underlines the pre-existing tension inherent in the format of the programme: the antiques/history versus the lifestyle/life-laundry narratives which sit uneasily and allow the viewer to associate more with one or the other, depending on a perceived 'deservingness' of individual participants. Enjoyment of the thriftiness and resourcefulness of the participants in raising money for their needs and dreams and the pleasure and satisfaction of the lifestyle narrative vies with dissatisfaction with their lack of knowledge about the symbolic value of what they are selling. The expert, in this situation, serves to highlight a class tension implied by the frequent juxtaposition of middle-class, 'informed' appraisers and 'clueless' owners,[5] and is created by on the one side a perceived lack of respect the owners show towards their family heirlooms and on the other side the expert and the 'official' historical and monetary value. The fact that often participants are presented as unaware of the historical importance or monetary value of the objects 'found' in their homes is significant in this context, as, in the case of an 'undeserving' participant, it allows the viewer to form a judgement based on a distinction of taste and education that is the outward sign of a process of identification and positioning of the self. The viewer is at once learning about the object and, by allying him/herself with the appraiser, enabled to feel 'superior' in the face of the owners' apparent lack of knowledge and taste. Moreover, by juxtaposing the (via the appraiser) legitimized aesthetic, historical and monetary value of the object with the taste of its owners, the programmes also invite another question: how would we react? Would we sell the item? The narrative of the sale then also poses questions about the viewer and his/her own class aspirations, again personalizing the process of transformation from nostalgic to monetary value.

If, as Csikszentmihalyi has claimed, objects aid the construction of the self through situating the individual in space and time, how do programmes such as *Flog It!*, *Cash in the Attic*, and *Car Booty* resolve the tension between their 'life-laundry' narratives which seem to promote a 'selling and moving on' mentality and the inherent nostalgia that the objects and their stories convey? Antiques programmes such as *Flog It!*, *Car Booty* and *Cash in the Attic* are hybrids whose narratives oscillate uneasily between past and future, nostalgia and makeover, as participants and viewers are situated as cultural constructs continually remade within a matrix of interconnected discourses about the self in time and space, as rooted in personal and public history. Lifestyle aspirations and the remodelling of the self clash with notions of personal history and national heritage; the two models of selfhood that can be traced – of self as part of a larger whole and as independent and self-styled entity and maker of one's own destiny – remain unconsolidated.

Programmes such as *Cash in the Attic* try to unravel the link between self and object by posing the self differently, as an entity not held back by the past but actively constructed, but the recording of the objects' histories already allows them to work as situating agents, even if they are then willingly disposed of and invite an active engagement of judgement and self-positioning in relation to what is seen. The resulting tension appears unresolved but, in a television environment torn between a celebration of history and the makeover, it is perhaps also a reflection of a wider unresolved malaise; of selfhood suspended between the individual and the collective, between a lingering in the memories and traditions of the past and a moving forward into the promise of a seemingly unfettered and 'lighter' future. As the heirloom is transformed into the public collection and personal memory becomes public nostalgia, perhaps Cohen's claim that Britain's love for the antique is waning is not a contradiction. In a society in which sleek and minimalist modern lifestyle has replaced the old, perhaps audiences simply prefer to look at antiques on the screen, to engage in a public mourning of the loss of personal history without having to 'clutter' their own houses and lives with the mementoes of the past. It remains to be seen how the current economic climate of recession will affect these programmes, but the thriftiness of the decluttering and selling narrative may even increase their popularity further as a means of both holding on to the past and aspiring to a modern consumerist lifestyle.

A note on availability

Regrettably, at the moment, DVD or VHS versions of *Flog It!*, *Cash in the Attic*, *Car Booty*, *I Love the '80s* and *Life Laundry* are not available. *The 1940s House*, *Ashes to Ashes*, *Coast*, *Dr. Who*, *Life on Mars* and *Who Do You Think You Are?* are all available on DVD. A selection of programmes from *Antiques Roadshow* is available through Acorn Media UK Ltd, and there are several DVD compilations of *Time Team*, which are available through 4DVD. A selection of episodes from *Extreme Makeover: Home Edition* is available in Region 1 format through Walt Disney Videos.

Notes

1. I am referring here to a wide range of programming, from history documentaries, to re-enactments and reality television shows such as *1940s House* (Wall to Wall, 2001), to nostalgia programming such as *I Love the '80s* (BBC, 2001), to family history programming such as *Who Do You Think You Are?* (BBC, 2004–), to recent drama such as *Dr. Who* (BBC, 2005–), *Life on Mars* (BBC1, 2006–2007) and *Ashes to Ashes* (BBC, 2008).
2. The fourth programme, *Bargain Hunt*, which, with its game show structure and the lack of personal history linked to the items found and sold, is less associated with

notions of memory and nostalgia than the programmes discussed here, is excluded from the analysis.

3. The term here deliberately refers to the BBC programme of the same name, *Life Laundry* (BBC, 2002–2004), which involves participants who, at a point of crisis in their lives, decide to declutter their houses (and lives) to make room for a fresh start.

4. And at times also back into the personal via the television screen. Thus, the discovery and evaluation of these objects is accompanied by another, secondary, discovery, in which the viewer may recognize in these items part of his or her own history and memory, long forgotten and now triggered. While the discovery of the value attached to these items now may lead to a frantic searching for forgotten clutter stored away in the attic to then sell and make quick money, it also, I suspect, very often just leads to a trip down memory lane, a pleasure in the rediscovery of what was deemed lost.

5. This does not mean to imply that the participants on programmes such as *Cash in the Attic* or *Flog It!* are usually working class; the reverse is the case, adding a further twist to the issue of judgement and position of the viewer in relation to distinctions of class and taste by signalling an implied upward social mobility on behalf of the viewer who is made to feel 'better' or 'more informed' than the middle-class participants.

Teleography

1940s House, Wall to Wall, Channel 4, UK, 2001.
Antiques Roadshow, BBC, UK, 1979–.
Ashes to Ashes, Kudos Film and Television, BBC1, UK, 2008.
Car Booty, BBC1, UK, November 2004–.
Cash in the Attic, BBC1, UK, November 2002–.
Coast, BBC2, UK, 2002–.
Dr. Who (new series), BBC, UK, 2005–.
Extreme Makeover: Home Edition, ABC, US, 2003–.
Flog It!, BBC2, UK, May 2002–.
I Love the '80s, BBC, UK, 2001.
Life Laundry, BBC2, UK, 2002–2004.
Life on Mars, Kudos Film and Television, BBC1, UK, 2006–2007.
Time Team, Channel 4, UK, 1994–.
Who Do You Think You Are?, BBC, UK, 2004–.

Bibliography

Baudrillard, J. (2005) *The System of Objects* (London: Verso).
'Be On a Show; *Flog It!*', BBC, available at: http://www.bbc.co.uk/showsandtours/beonashow/flogit.shtml. Accessed 3 April 2009.
'Be On a Show; *Cash in the Attic*', BBC, available at: http://www.bbc.co.uk/showsandtours/beonashow/cash_attic.shtml. Accessed 3 April 2009.
Benjamin, W. (2005) 'Unpacking my library: a talk about collecting', in H. Eiland, G. Smith and M.W. Jennings (eds), *Walter Benjamin: Selected Writings, Vol. 2, Part 2, 1931–1934* (Cambridge, MA: Harvard University Press).
Bishop, R. (1999) 'What price history? Functions of narrative in television collectibles shows', *Journal of Popular Culture*, 33.3, 1–27.

Bourdieu, P. (1984) *Distinction: A Social Critique of the Judgment of Taste* (Cambridge, MA: Harvard University Press).

Boym, S. (2001) *The Future of Nostalgia* (New York: Basic Books).

Bratich, J.Z. (2007) 'Programming reality: control societies, new subjects and the powers of transformation', in D. Heller (ed.), *Makeover Television: Realities Remodelled* (London: I.B. Tauris).

Cardwell, S. (2002) *Adaptation Revisited: Television and the Classic Novel* (Manchester: Manchester University Press).

Clouse, A. (2008) 'Narratives of value and the *Antiques Roadshow*: "A game of recognitions"', *The Journal of Popular Culture*, 41.1, 3–20.

Cohen, N. (2008) 'Our worrying loss of love for the antique', *The Observer*, 9 October, 32.

Cook, P. (2005) *Screening the Past: Memory and Nostalgia in Cinema* (Abingdon: Routledge).

Csikszentmihalyi, M. (1993) 'Why we need things', in S. Lubar and W.D. Kingery (eds), *History from Things: Essays on Material Culture* (London: Smithsonian Institution Press).

Deery, J. (2006) 'Interior design: commodifying self and place in *Extreme Makeover*, *Extreme Makeover: Home Edition*, and *The Swan*', in D. Heller (ed.), *The Great American Makeover: Television, History, Nation* (Basingstoke: Palgrave).

Heller, D. (ed.) (2007) *Makeover Television: Realities Remodelled* (London: I.B. Tauris).

Higson, A. (1993) 'Re-presenting the national past: nostalgia and pastiche in the heritage film', in L. Friedman (ed.), *British Cinema and Thatcherism: Fires Were Started* (London: UCL Press).

Higson, A. (2003) *English Heritage, English Cinema: Costume Drama Since 1980* (Oxford: Oxford University Press).

Holdsworth, A. (2008) ' "Television resurrections": Television and memory,' *Cinema Journal*, 47.3, 137–44.

Kavka, M. (2006) 'Changing properties: The makeover show crosses the Atlantic', in D. Heller (ed.), *The Great American Makeover: Television, History, Nation* (Basingstoke: Palgrave).

Monk, C. and A. Sargeant (eds), (2002) *British Historical Cinema: The History, Heritage and Costume Film* (London: Routledge).

Piccini, A. (2007) 'The stuff of dreams: archaeology, audience and becoming material', *Televising History: Memory, Nation, Identity* conference, University of Lincoln, 13–15 June.

Radio Times (2002) 'And the best of the rest: *Flog It!*', 27 May, p. 80.

Stewart, S. (2003) On Longing: Narratives of the Miniature, the Gigantic, the Souvenir, the Collection (London: Duke University Press).

16
Who Do You Think You Are?

Family History and Memory on British Television

Amy Holdsworth

> The British now love family history research as much as they love gardening or DIY.
>
> (Vanessa Thorpe, *The Observer*, 10 October 2004)

The popularity of family history research as a national pastime has been successfully adopted by British television over the last five years, with *Who Do You Think You Are?* (*WDYTYA*), produced by Wall to Wall Media Ltd, pioneering the employment of family history and memory as a televisual narrative strategy. The first series aired in Autumn 2004 to popular and critical acclaim, becoming one of the highest rated shows on BBC2. It was promoted to BBC1 in 2006 and is currently in its seventh series. The success of the format, which follows the genealogical investigations of various television personalities as they track down the stories behind their family trees, may indeed have convinced commissioners that, according to *WDYTYA* alumni Ian Hislop, 'family history is not dull, but a surprisingly watchable commodity' (in Rowan, 2005, p. 12). Indeed, the format has found international success, selling to broadcasters across Western Europe and beyond, and has been followed by a glut of programming that uses family history research as an investigative narrative structure, including other Wall to Wall productions including *Not Forgotten* (Channel 4, 2005), *Empire's Children* (Channel 4, 2007) and *You Don't Know You're Born* (ITV1, 2007).

WDYTYA was billed by its producer Alex West as a mix of 'history today and *Heat*' (in Deans, 2004), and quickly came 'to symbolise the kind of programme the newly public service focused BBC should be doing: serious-minded, but also accessible and popular'.[1] Part of the programme's populist address lies in its use of celebrities, but can also be found in its focus on the desire to experience history at a personal and affective level, on the part of both the investigator and the audience. As such, *WDYTYA* clearly corresponds with one recent trend in historical programming, which has been described by British historian and broadcaster, Tristram Hunt as 'reality history.'[2] By placing the personal at the centre of understanding of public or social histories, the series uses family history and memory as a conduit between the past and present. Wall to Wall describes *WDYTYA* as a show that 'features famous names [...] as they venture on a journey of discovery into their ancestors' pasts to ultimately find out more about themselves, their family, and also our shared social history' (Wall To Wall press release, 2006). By remaining 'serious minded' and demanding personal stories that 'dovetail with big themes – Caribbean immigration, Indian Independence, World war, Industrial revolution' (Brown, 2004), the programme makers also weave the genealogical investigations of its various personalities, clearly chosen to offer a more encompassing vision of 'Britishness' into a potentially more inclusive history of Britain and British national identity.

The generic blending at work in *WDYTYA*, along with its stress upon emotion and experience as modes of knowledge, have been at the heart of its success in the terms of circulating BBC promotional discourses. However, we might also relate these characteristics to the emphasis on memory within the series. Kerwin Klein writes: '[W]e sometimes use memory as a synonym for history to soften our prose, to humanize it, and make it more accessible. Memory simply sounds less distant, and perhaps for that reason, it often serves to help draw general readers into a sense of the relevance of history for their own lives' (2000, p. 129). Memory narratives in formats like *WDYTYA* might be viewed as a way of 'softening' social history documentary, employed as a populist strategy and as part of the increasing centrality of emotion in contemporary British television. By focusing my analysis on some of the textual and narrative conventions of *WDYTYA*, for example, the trope of the 'journey' and the use of family photography, I examine the ways in which the series represents memory and memory work. In the light of Myra Macdonald's work on television documentary conventions and how they can both enable and constrict memory work, I argue that the format simultaneously opens up a vision of a multicultural British heritage whilst closing down or 'taming' our relationships to difficult and contested areas of history and identity by the stress on an affirmative cultural citizenship. Whilst this book seeks, in part, to analyse the representation of history on television, we might also bear in mind how the analysis of a text such as *WDYTYA* allows us to consider what I refer to as 'televisual memory', to begin to open out an examination of the representations and forms of memory on television.

This chapter will focus predominantly on the first two series of the show as broadcast on BBC2 in 2004 and 2006. Coinciding with the period of the BBC's most recent charter renewal and license fee negotiations, the celebrations of *WDYTYA* and the specific nature of its address must be viewed in relation to the renewed public service ethos of the BBC in this period.[3] It is within this climate that I wish to suggest that an additional layer of memory is at work in the *WDYTYA* 'campaign'. Whilst the programme uses strategies of memory work to reaffirm personal and national identities, the BBC uses *WDYTYA* to secure its own sense of identity and remind the viewer of its role as an effective and relevant public service broadcaster.

Emotional journeys

Helen Weinstein has spoken of how the 'emotional hook' provided by human interest stories has become central to the motivational and creative decision making of television history producers.[4] It is important to acknowledge that the stress on emotion and experience, the blurring of 'hard' and 'soft' generic forms, and the merging of private and public spheres form part of a wider trend in television programming and have been much discussed in television scholarship on the talk show (Shattuc, 1997), factual programming (Bondjeberg, 1996; Brunsdon et al., 2001) and reality TV (Biressi and Nunn, 2005), forms that have all clearly influenced *WDYTYA*.

Whilst these features are not new to the presentation of history on television, what is remarkable is the populist appeal of *WDYTYA* and the emotionalism and sensationalism inherent in its presentation and marketing. What these programmes exhibit is how, rather than viewing these categories as a marker of the 'dumbing down' of television, the elicitation of emotion, at least within BBC discourses, became the key to their value. It was the attention on the emotional revelations of Bill Oddie's and Jeremy Paxman's stories and personalities that offered a point of media focus and promotion and opened the first and second series of *WDYTYA*, respectively.[5] Rather than reading the interruption of the personal and the emotional and the incorporation of celebrities – in Catherine Johnson's summary of the popular argument – as part of the 'decline of factual programming and a concession to populism at the expense of the BBC's public service remit' (2001, p. 41), generic blending becomes a point of renewal and success. John Willis's speech at the Factual Forum on 18 March 2005 remarked upon the qualities of *WDYTYA* amongst other recent BBC 2 documentaries:

Last month BBC2 had *Auschwitz*, *Tribe*, and *The Lost World of Mitchell and Kenyon*, riding high simultaneously. They were all very different, all attracted brilliant reviews and all surpassed expectation of audience size significantly. These programmes – and others like last autumn's hit from Wall to Wall – *Who Do You Think You Are?* – demonstrate that there is a clear audience appetite for traditional documentary virtues like strong narrative and genuine insight but illuminated in ways that feel modern and relevant, whether using celebrities or dramatic reconstruction.

(Willis 2005)

Both celebrity and emotionality are central to the promotion of *WDYTYA* and are seen to function as a sign of the BBC's appeal to a more popular market, delivering programmes that are both 'serious' (traditional documentary virtues) and 'entertaining' (use of celebrities).

The incorporation of both celebrities and 'real people', the positioning of the celebrity as a 'real person', viewed at home with their families, and the programmes' reliance upon personal memory and emotional revelation links the format with a series of recognisable television genres outside of historical programming – the confessional talk show, the celebrity talk show and, perhaps less obviously, the makeover show. Framed within an investigative narrative structure the celebrity embarks upon a physical and emotional journey. Whilst narratives of transformation and improvement pervade lifestyle television, *WDYTYA* attempts to encourage a reading of the journey to self-knowledge, both historical and emotional, as a means to self-improvement, charting how self-revelation leads to self-awareness.[6] The show's therapeutic aspects in its employment of a form of post-memory work is beneficial for some of its celebrity participants – as Bill Oddie states 'this isn't curiosity, this journey – it's self-help' – whilst others, though spectacularly revealed as an emotional being are more resistant to the prescribed reading: as Jeremy Paxman comments – 'What did I learn from the delving into my family background? I got a strong impression that the producer wanted me to say the experience had somehow changed my life. It didn't' (Paxman 2006, p. 19).

Mark Lawson commented in *The Guardian* that *WDYTYA* has 'the feel of a version of *Great Railway Journeys* in which the geography is personal' (Lawson, 2004). It is perhaps the trope of the journey that is the most significant for the show. The format charts the mundane aspects of the quests of its investigators: the physical journeying across the country and even the globe in some episodes, the arrival at libraries and archives, and the negotiation of the dusty corridors of history. The journey in *WDYTYA* is also meant to be read as having a metaphorical significance – as an emotional journey of self-discovery. As Meera Syal comments at the end of her journey in India, 'Even if you only go back one generation, you will experience a lot just on the journey'.[7]

In the first episode of the first series of *WDYTYA*, Bill Oddie's investigations into his family history focused on the story of his mother Lillian. Suffering from severe mental illness, Lillian was hospitalized during Oddie's childhood and remained in an institution for the majority of her life. Knowing little of his mother's history, and remembering less, it is the family photograph that is presented as a source of anxiety for Oddie, and prompts his search for personal meaning and memory. It is significant that it is in the representation of journeying and the beginning of Oddie's investigations, that the four images that Oddie has of his mother are inserted into the documentary, where the view of a grey Birmingham suburb from inside a moving car is interrupted by the black-and-white image of the young Oddie with his mother, fragmented from its context so as to focus on this relationship and sliding into the frame from right to left. The movement into the frame is accompanied by a familiar 'rushing' sound as when two cars pass each other. Placed against the travelling shot, the movement of the image into the frame and the accompanying noise gives the impression that the image forms another part of the landscape/cityscape viewed from the car; that in this case the geography has literally become personal. This image is followed by another three photographs of Oddie's mother; the quality, colouring and composition of the images clearly mark them as amateur family photographs but also place them into a biographical timescale. The family album is perhaps a practice of photographical collection/exhibition that many of us recognize, and it attaches an image-narrative to our personal memories. What is interesting in Oddie's case, revealed through both the dialogue and the presentation of these few images, is that Oddie's own sparse family album is seen to reflect his own lack of memory or knowledge in relation to his mother and his mother's story. For Oddie, the lack of narrative meaning is a cause of anxiety, unrest and the drive for meaning. Oddie's own mental health problems are disclosed at the start of the programme, and Oddie himself speculates that his relationship with his mother might lie at the root of his depression. One might argue that this anxiety, the lack of and desire for understanding or 'closure' is revealed in the presentation and movement of the photographs in the sequence, allowing us to position the significance of the images for Oddie and the documentary in relation to a therapeutic discourse.

The effect of the zoom into the image accompanied by the switch of image which pulls back each time to an increased length of the shot scale gives the impression of an object that although one might be moving towards it is continually out of reach. This effect is heightened by the alternating movement of the images, the first sliding into the frame from the right to the left, a movement that reverses with each new image, and the repetition of the piano riff on the soundtrack which emphasizes the sense of continuity without climax or conclusion.

It is important to note that this sequence does not stress Lillian's experience, locked within the images, but Oddie's experience of these photographs; what is revealed in the dialogue is how they become his memory of the photographs rather than them being photographs of a memory. As Oddie himself remarks, 'When I look back at my childhood, I have about four images which involve my mother. They are like a scene out of a movie, y'know, they're like here's the best of…this is the trailer as it were. But I never did see the film.' The enigma photograph, the image without a clear indexical link, is often central to the investigative drive of *WDYTYA*. As a documentary format that functions as both an investigation of aspects of our social history and as narratives of self-discovery, the image of a national landscape is built up via the personal and the emotional. This point is revealed in this sequence by the interruption of a personal geography into the frame.

Empty space and memory work

The investigative activities of the television personalities in *WDYTYA*, the piecing together of the puzzles presented to them, might be seen to correlate with Annette Kuhn's delineation of 'memory work'. She writes in *Family Secrets* that:

> The past is gone forever. We cannot return to it, nor can we reclaim it now as it was. But that does not mean it is lost to us. The past is like the scene of a crime: if the deed itself is irrecoverable, its traces may still remain [...] Memory work has a great deal in common with forms of inquiry which – like detective work and archaeology, say – involve working backwards – searching for clues, deciphering signs and traces, making deductions, patching together reconstructions out of fragments of evidence.
>
> (1995, p. 4)

The investigative strategies of 'memory work' are clearly reminiscent of the practices of genealogy and the lines of inquiry the celebrities' journey down. As part of this journeying the show places a great deal of emphasis upon *sites of memory* that are significant for the investigators' family narratives. It is an emphasis that illuminates the potential for the interaction between place and memory within this particular television documentary format.

In Myra Macdonald's study of the 'performance of memory' in a series of documentaries from the 1990s that focus on the 1960s, she analyses how television documentary conventions both vivify and constrict memory work. For Macdonald, drawing on Kuhn, the 'specificity of place' has the potential to act as a 'powerful stimulus of memory' (2006, p. 336). However, in Macdonald's examples, 'by routinely filming interviewees against interior backdrops that lack precise indices of cultural or geographical context' the documentaries 'miss opportunities to experiment with the interactions between place and memory' (2006, p. 336). *WDYTYA*, however, places emphasis on the idea of origin and belonging and stresses the attachment between place and memory; however, the memory workers of *WDYTYA* are often faced by the empty spaces and weeds of memory and history. A desire for a sense of continuity between past and present is often expressed by the celebrity investigator and indeed by the family history documentary itself; a desire to see, through ancestral connections, how we got to where we are today. This, however, is often complicated by the fact that, as Kuhn states, the past is gone forever and there is often nothing to see.

History, by definition, has gone. What we are left with is the search for presence in absence. Perhaps it is an aesthetic of absence that might more broadly characterize history on television, as Simon Schama notes: 'we are in the business of representing something that is no longer there' (cited in Champion 2003, p. 116).

This problem is partly resolved by what we might refer to as an 'iconography of memory'; graves, ruins, memorials, weeds – as Jeremy Clarkson responds to the absence at the site of his ancestor's former glassworks that most of industrial history is now *'just weeds'*.[8] Kerwin Klein writes that 'such memorial tropes have emerged as one of the common features of our new cultural history where in monograph after monograph, readers confront the abject object: photographs are torn, mementos faded, toys broken' (2000, p. 136). Television, however, is left with the problem of filling this empty space. There are various strategies, detailed by several of the contributors to Roberts and Taylor's collection *The Historian, Television and Television History* (2001), to overcoming the dominance of this absence, through the appeal of storytelling to the imagination. However, I want to suggest that this empty space is key to the representation of memory and significant for the emotional pull of a programme such as *WDYTYA*.

Significantly, for the programme, a photographic archive is no longer enough in terms of evidence; this perhaps reflects a desire for unmediated experience which necessitates a return to the sites of memory and the origin of the specific photograph. However, our investigators are often met with absence, and the empty spaces they encounter often resonate with the knowledge that something was once there. This is often achieved by the use of image matches, between the 'then' of the photograph and the 'now' of the investigations. This strategy is employed to encourage a direct comparison between the then and now, to offer both an examination of how things have changed, where empty space resonates with the knowledge that something meaningful was once there, and to validate the existence of that something meaningful.

In an example from Ian Hislop's episode of *WDYTYA*,[9] he visits the site of a Boer War battle in which his grandfather fought. The events of the battle, including the massive casualties sustained by the British Army, are related by the battle historian who accompanies Hislop. At this point, a photograph depicting a trench of bodies, killed in the battle, is matched against the image of the grave as it is today. The shot scale and camera position of the original image is reproduced so the content of the 'then' is transposed onto the image of the 'now', revealing what horrors lie in the quiet and sunny grave. In Clarkson's episode, he returns to the town where his ancestors, the Kilners, had their first glass factory. We cut from a long shot taken from the hill overlooking a Northern town, a square of houses outlining a large field in the centre of the frame where the factory would have been, to a nineteenth-century illustration of the factory, held in front of the camera by Clarkson, who exclaims as the scene progresses, that such a huge factory is 'just sports pitches now.' By matching the images of the 'now' and 'then' in the centre of the frame, through this juxtaposition we are invited to read into the significance of the comparison as the ghosts of both Clarkson's and Britain's industrial heritage echoes in the space of the frame.

Image matches are not always used to highlight the more disruptive or erosive examples of historical change but to stress the sense of a continuity, particularly in the relationship between the investigators and their ancestors. The desire for a continuum is continually stressed by the revisiting of significant ancestral sites and the retracing of ancestral steps, in the search for memory and historical significance. There are examples in *WDYTYA* where the re-creation of the content of the photographic image is used to forge a link between past and present, immediate and ancestral family relations. In Stephen Fry's episode,[10] he returns with his mother to her childhood home, and the pair explore the present-day garden, searching for the locations of the photographs they have and then setting up lines of continuity rather than rupture between the then and now. In one example, with the camera positioned behind Fry and his mother, he holds up the black-and-white image of her and her sisters as children are positioned on the garden steps and sit on a stone urn. The photograph is held up by Fry in the centre of the frame and is matched against the lines of the steps and the edge of the garden. The lush green of the present-day garden almost seamlessly merges into the black-and-white tones of the photograph, and it is almost as if we are peering across time, through the centre of the image and into the past. Rather than juxtaposing the images of past and present, preferring to have them exist and blend in the same frame establishes a strong sense of continuity.

As the scene progresses, Fry and his mother reproduce the positions of people in another family image, where she and her father stood in front of the house ('so you were standing just there and in fact if we go round we could reproduce it'), with Fry taking the place of his grandfather (which, he quips, is a 'Freudian nightmare') and his mother placed back in her childhood position, standing in front of Fry. Fry then holds the photograph in front of the pair to confirm the match for the cameras, once again stressing continuity rather than juxtaposition by placing the investigator where the ancestor was pictured. The attachment to a site of memory arguably encourages a sense of belonging that reaffirms the investigators' search for their place in history.

Closed space? Home and nation

The domestic lives of the celebrity investigators and their interactions with family and friends are often featured in *WDYTYA*. Our celebrities are often positioned at home at both the beginning and end of their respective journeys, often returning to their families with the information, images, and even relics or mementoes they have gathered while exploring their family histories. Meera Syal returns from tracing her grandfather's story in India to her parent's home in Epping Forest with a brick taken from her mother's family home. Stephen Fry returns to a family gathering to reveal the fates of the related Lamm family who were discovered to have perished at Auschwitz. Amanda Redman's journey also concludes with a family gathering, though this time it is more celebratory, as she introduces some long-lost cousins to the family. Lesley Garrett is viewed returning from Yorkshire to her London home and an enthusiastic reception from her children, whilst David Baddiel returns home to his mother and daughter to celebrate his fortieth birthday. In Jeremy Paxman's episode, the return to familiar surroundings, and arguably to his more familiar television personality, is marked by his return to the *Newsnight* studio, whilst Moira Stewart returns from the lapping shores of the Caribbean to the River Thames and the familiar cityscape of the London embankment.

The cyclical nature of these journey narratives and the insistence on the return home or at least to familiar surroundings and iconography seems suggestive of, contrary to the aesthetic of empty space, a way of closing down imaginative investment. Memory work as process is illuminated by the trope of the journey, but an insistence on affirmation and a stress on completion and closure is emphasized in the dénouement of the various stories. The loss of family members and ancestors is often filled by the discovery of distant relations and new familial connections. For example, whilst David Baddiel is unable to ascertain the fate of his uncle, he encounters new, albeit distantly related, family members in London's Jewish community. In Macdonald's analysis of the codes and conventions of television documentary that 'act both to vivify but also to constrict "memory work"' (2006, p. 327), she concludes that 'television too often finds ways to integrate, and subdue, the performance of witnesses' memories within its own narrative and visual requirements. Commentary and archive footage, with their directing or generalizing capacities, tend to smooth away the rough edges of potential moments of disruption or tension in memory evocation' (2006, p. 344). The return to the safety of the home is suggestive of one of the ways in which television is often involved in a process of 'taming' difficult material.

WDYTYA has undoubtedly been successful in its campaign objectives, prompting through a multiplatform approach an increase in the genealogical enquiries of the British public.[11] Whilst the format was designed to 'dovetail' with larger themes and histories, it arguably creates a more inclusive and affirmative vision of our national identity. The content of the histories represented in *WDYTYA* might be seen as a negotiation with, for example, Britain's post-colonial identity reflected in the selection of television personalities such as Meera Syal, Moira Stewart, Colin Jackson and Ainsley Harriot. An image of a 'New Britain' is arguably realized through the personal narratives of emotion and experience, charting social, industrial, colonial and wartime family histories. However, it is the presence of these big themes and difficult histories that raise a series of concerns. Firstly, the affirmations and melodramatic gestures of the format might be seen to preclude further investigation into these difficult histories, and secondly, they return us to the insistence on the traumatic content of memory and history.

The dramatizing gestures, the stress on emotional engagement and experiential knowledge all, according to Helen Weinstein, are effective ways of delivering audiences for 'UK TV history products' to broadcasters. But these must be situated within wider concerns surrounding a 'contemporary confessional culture in which the key attraction is the disclosure of true emotions' (Aslama and Pantti, 2006, p. 167), which begs the question of whether 'crying citizens make good citizens?' (Pantti and van Zoonen, 2006). Whilst in some ways the programme opens up a productive engagement with personal and national history and memory, the overemphasis on catharsis and closure – the endpoint of the therapeutic narrative – closes down further investigation into the more difficult stories. We might question whether certain forms of televisual memory re-engage audiences with their private and emotional engagements with memory and history at the cost of the exorcism of the irreconcilable and the problematic, returning us to, as Paul Gilroy writes on post-colonial melancholia, familiar patterns of collective remembering and forgetting.[12] Alison Landsberg also points to this concern in her account of the success of Alex Haley's *Roots* in 1970s America:

> While it enabled many whites to see through black eyes for the first time, what emerged from the experience of *Roots* was not so much a critique of white oppression as an appreciation of the importance and power of genealogy [...] Rather than forcing white Americans to take a look at their own attitudes toward race, rather than forcing them to own up to the crimes of slavery, the mass media stimulated instead a fascination with the project of genealogy.
>
> (2004, pp. 105–6)

In some senses, the family history documentary may suffer from an emptying out of meaning, replaced by the fascination with celebrity revelations or with the private genealogical investigations of the viewer.

Conclusion: Remembering public service broadcasting

Narratives of transition and crisis have become increasingly prevalent during a time of dramatic technological change and uncertainty over the future of television. Increased commercialization, competition and the fragmentation of the television audience has brought into question the efficacy of public service broadcasting as a form of 'social cement'. As Philip M. Taylor comments, 'the idea that television, as a medium which enjoys near universal social penetration, can unite a nation is in decline. The likelihood of an affirmative answer to the question "did you see on TV last night?" has diminished in less than a generation' (2001, p. 174). However, a show such as *WDYTYA* might be seen to reinvigorate those qualities that Taylor laments. A ratings success for the BBC, often with sensationalist appeal, the programme is also significant in its exploration of national history and identity, as it attempts to re-imagine British identity through the investigations of personal history, memory and identity, and employing the significant popular appeal of family history research itself as a form of 'social cement'. One might argue that, in its careful construction of a portrait of 'New Britain', *WDYTYA*, alongside projects such as *A Picture of Britain* (BBC, 2005) and *Coast* (BBC, 2005–2007) marked a renewed PSB ethos that focused on the construction of 'Britishness' and national identity; PSB as nation-building rather than nation-binding.

The consumer and audience research report on the first series of *WDYTYA* outlined, via quantitative data on the 'success' of the website and related family history events, how the BBC had fulfilled its campaign objectives. According to the report, 7 per cent of UK adults claimed to have started researching their family history for the first time in the two months after the transmission of the first series. Sixty-one per cent of www.bbc.co.uk/familyhistory users said that they were new users to family history on the Web, whilst there was an 18 per cent increase in first-time visitors to the National Archive website (in the last quarter of 2004 versus the last quarter of 2003). *WDYTYA,* as the forerunner of the genealogy show, may certainly have 'come to symbolise the kind of programme the newly public service focused BBC should be doing: serious-minded, but also accessible and popular' (Brown, 2004); at least this is the assessment within BBC discourses.

I want to conclude by suggesting how *WDYTYA* is tied to a complimentary form of television memory, one that we might refer to as BBC nostalgia. It is perhaps not surprising that the programme was promoted as a jewel in the BBC crown throughout the period of the recent licence fee negotiations. Along with ratings success, the interactive platforms attached to the programme produce a form of public service that is tangible and quantifiable, in which the relevance of the BBC can be clearly visualized via statistics. *Who Do You Think You Are?* is perhaps a key example of the BBC's attempts to secure and re-affirm its own identity through a period of transition and uncertainty. The show is arguably as much about our memories of, and nostalgia for, effective and relevant public service television as it is about family memory and national history.

A note on availability

Currently in its seventh series on BBC1, Wall to Wall has recently been commissioned to make two more series of *Who Do You Think You Are?* Series 1–5 of the programme are available on DVD, released by Acorn Media.

Notes

1. '...and crucially in the slimmed down BBC, made by an independent production company. Little wonder, then, that the director general Mark Thompson as been citing it in is recent speeches' (Brown, 2004).
2. Hunt cites *1900 House*, another Wall to Wall production, as 'the pioneer programme in this 'experiential history' genre [...] with its easy invitation to empathy, reality history failed to invite more searching questions about the underlying structure of the past' (Hunt, 2005). In recent years, Hunt has also attacked *WDYTYA*, arguing that 'television history is now more about a self-indulgent search for our identity than an attempt to explain the past and its modern meaning' (Hunt, 2007).
3. After the perceived slippage of public service provision in a period of increased competition, commercial pressures and the battle for ratings (see Catherine Johnson's summary of the familiar argument below), along with the shift towards 'Digital Britain', the year 2006 saw intense debates around the 10-year Royal Charter review and the future of the BBC. It is within the context of this period that the BBC attempts to revalidate its role as a public service provider and justify the continuation of, and argue for, an above-inflation increase in the licence fee.
4. 'Narrative strategies and emotional engagement: how genre and format deliver audiences in UK TV history products', *Televising History: Memory, Nation, Identity* conference, University of Lincoln, 13–15 June 2007.
5. The *Daily Mirror* TV Guide remarked, 'This is famously the programme that made telly toughie Jeremy Paxman cry' (Anon., 2006, p. 19), whilst Ciar Bryne wrote in *The Independent*, 'It is a sight few people would have expected to see on television – Jeremy Paxman, that most ferocious of political interviewers, reduced to tears' (2005, p. 5).
6. As Alex Graham stated in 2004, 'It's not a very complicated proposition. It is about people you are interested in, and taking them, perhaps, on unpredictable emotional journeys' (in Brown, 2004).
7. *WDYTYA*, series one, episode nine (BBC 2, 7 December 2004).
8. *WDYTYA*, series one, episode four (BBC2, 2 November 2004).
9. *WDYTYA*, series one, episode five (BBC2, 9 November 2004).
10. *WDYTYA*, series two, episode three (BBC2, 25 January 2006).
11. The BBC campaign objectives for the first series of *WDYTYA* were stated as the following: '(1) To enable and encourage 150,000 ABC1 50+ BBC2 audiences to start researching their own family history for the first time; (2) To bring new users to archives and genealogical websites; (3) To give people a meaningful sense of their personal connection with history' (in Sumpner et al., 2005).
12. Gilroy himself calls for more 'complex and challenging narratives' (2004, p. 131), whilst Tobias Ebbrecht, in his analysis of a different form of TV history, has noted how the closed narration of docudramas about the Third Reich produces a definite history of period, closing down what is 'controversial and inconsistent' (2007, p. 50).

Bibliography

Anon. (2006) 'Review: *Who Do You Think You Are?*' *Daily Mirror* TV Guide, 11 January, 19.

Aslama, M. and Pantti, M. (2006) 'Talking alone: Reality TV, emotions and authenticity', *European Journal of Cultural Studies*, 9.2, 167–84.

Biressi, A. and Nunn, H. (2005) *Reality TV: Realism and Revelation* (London: Wallflower).

Bondebjerg, I. (2000 [1996]) 'Public discourse/private fascination: hybridization in "true-life-story" genres', in Newcomb, H. (ed.), *Television: The Critical View*, 6th edition (Oxford: Oxford University Press).

Brown, M. (2004) 'Television goes back to its roots', *The Guardian*, 13 December. Available at:http://media.guardian.co.uk/mediaguardian/story/0,7558,1372234,00.html. Accessed 25 October 2005.

Brunsdon, C., Johnson C, Moseley, R. and Wheatley, H. (2001) 'Factual entertainment on British television: The Midlands Television Research Group's "8-9 project" ', *European Journal of Cultural Studies*, 4.1, 29–62.

Byrne, C. (2005) 'Paxman reduced to tears by journey into his past', *The Independent*, 8 December, 5.

Champion, J. (2003) 'Seeing the past: Simon Schama's *A History of Britain* and public history', *History Workshop Journal*, 56, 153–74.

Deans, J. (2004) 'Oddie found sister through BBC genealogy show', *The Guardian*, 28 July. Available at: http://media.guardian.co.uk/broadcast/story/0,7493,1270988,00.html. Accessed 25 October 2005.

Dowell, B. (2007) 'Genealogy show has lost its roots, says expert', *The Guardian*, 8 June. Available at: http:// media.guardian.co.uk/bbc/story/0,2098823,00.html. Accessed 27 June 2007.

Ebbrecht, T. (2007) 'Docudramatizing history on TV: German and British docudrama and historical event television in the memorial year 2005', *European Journal of Cultural Studies*, 10.1, 35–53.

Gilroy, P. (2004) *After Empire: Melancholia or Convivial Culture?* (London: Routledge).

Hunt, T. (2005) 'Whose story?' *The Observer*, 19 June. Available at: http://media.guardian.co.uk/broadcast/story/0,7493,1509770,00.html. Accessed 25 November 2005.

Hunt, T. (2007) 'The time bandits', *The Guardian*, 10 September. Available at: http://media.guardian.co.uk/mediaguardian/story/0„2165609,00/html. Accessed 17 September 2007.

Klein, K. (2000) 'On the emergence of memory in historical discourse', *Representations*, 69, 127–50.

Kuhn, A. (1995) *Family Secrets: Acts of Memory and Imagination* (London: Verso).

Macdonald, M. (2006) 'Performing memory on television: documentary and the 1960s', *Screen*, 47.3, 327–45.

Pantti, M. and Van Zoonen, L. (2006) 'Do crying citizens make good citizens?' *Social Semiotics*, 16.2, 205–24.

Paxman, J. (2006) 'Jeremy Paxman', *Radio Times*, 7–13 January, 18–19.

Roberts, G. and Taylo, P.M. (eds) (2001) *The Historian, Television and Television History* (Luton: University of Luton Press).

Rowan, D. (2005) 'Interview: Ian Hislop, Private Eye', *Evening Standard*, 16 November. Available at: http://www.davidrowan.com/2005/11/interview-ian-hislop-private-eye.html. Accessed 10 September 2007.

Shattuc, J. (1997) *The Talking Cure: TV, Talk Shows and Women* (London: Routledge).
Sumpner, C., Roberts, Armitage, R.U. and Cross, J. (2005) *Who Do You Think You Are? 360 Audience Feedback* (MC&A: Audience and Consumer Research for the BBC).
Taylor, P.M. (2001) 'Television and the future historian', in G. Roberts and P.M. Taylor (eds.), *The Historian, Television and Television History* (Luton: University of Luton Press).
Willis, J. (2005) 'John Willis' speech in full', *Broadcast Now* 21 March. Available at: http://www.broadcastnow.co.uk/news/multi-platform/news/john-willis-speech-in-full/1021625.article. Accessed 15 October 2005.

Conclusion

Broader Themes and Televisualization

Erin Bell and Ann Gray

> Europe [...] is a continent in which one can easily travel back and forth through time. All the different stages of the twentieth century are being lived, or relived, somewhere. Aboard Istanbul's ferries it is always 1948. In Lisbon it is forever 1956. At the Gare de Lyon in Paris, the year is 2020. In Budapest, the young men wear their father's faces.
>
> (Geert Mak, 2007, p. xii)

Themes evident in this collection demonstrate the links in Europe between the representation of the past and cultural – including broadcasting – developments, allowing us to place the scholarly insights raised in the chapters in this wider context in order to consider how television modes, forms and imperatives have mediated the way in which the past is portrayed. Whilst it is useful to look at this collection as a gathering together of important articles about the current state of history programming on television in Europe, we can also provisionally identify the modes of televisual mediation applied to history and in this way examine how television itself shapes representations of the past.

Although by no means a systematically representative sample of history programming – and this collection makes no such claim – it is interesting to note that the key themes emerging from the pieces in this collection can be identified in the history programming discussed. These themes are:

- hidden or unspoken: social history and traumatic historiography;
- oral histories and testimony;
- reality television and re-enactment;
- biography;
- topography: landscape;
- national political history and broader contemporary issues; and
- pan-national sources, politics and memory.

We will now discuss these themes and then consider the absences, or the stories, using examples, which are not told through history programming.

Hidden or unspoken: social history and traumatic historiography

History on television is often criticized, sometimes legitimately, for its reliance upon certain tried and tested ways of representing the past including a tendency to claim that the events represented were formerly 'secret' or 'unknown' (see, e.g., Bell and Gray, 2007a). Television producers and commissioners are constantly looking for interesting and revealing 'new' stories, but it is often the case that an appropriate period of time must elapse after events before certain stories can be told and experiences can be spoken about. Jeremy Isaacs refers to this, in his account of the making of *The World at War* (Thames TV, 1973–1974), which, unlike previous programmes on this topic, drew on the eyewitness accounts of lower-ranking officers and ordinary civilians, as a time when people were prepared and able to talk about their experiences.[1] The forthcoming 20th anniversary of the collapse of the Berlin Wall will no doubt provide additional impetus for such programming. In relation to broader scholarship, it is useful to note that televised history often attempts, and succeeds, in engaging in traumatic historiography, as defined by historian of the Holocaust Saul Friedländer. This allows the voices of victims to break up the smooth narrative of a historical text as 'any number of different vantage points' may be used in order to represent a traumatic past (1992, p. 53). Several of the chapters in this collection (see, e.g., Rohringer, de Leeuw, Winston, Blaney) consider aspects of the representation of pasts that were for many years 'hidden' or silenced, from different national and cultural perspectives, and televised accounts have made the wider population aware of them.

Oral histories and testimony

Necessarily closely bound to the theme of traumatic historiography is the use of oral history and the significance of the relatively recently developed field of memory studies. As Karen Till notes, 'Over the past decade, memory studies has emerged as an interdisciplinary field in its own right, with specialist journals and degree programmes' (2006, p. 326). Unlike history, memory studies is deliberately interdisciplinary, and in part because of this it has been seen by some scholars, such as Susannah Radstone, as offering both opportunities and risks by consolidating the memory research of historians, social scientists and psychologists, amongst others, into one broad area (Radstone, 2008, p. 31). In 2008, this culminated in the first issue of the international academic journal *Memory Studies*, which publishes articles on the 'social, cultural, cognitive, political and technological shifts affecting how, what and why individuals, groups and societies remember, and forget'.[2] Television is undoubtedly one of these shifts affecting how we remember, and in particular the use of oral testimony, of individuals appearing to remember onscreen, possibly triggering the memories of some audience members (Smither, 2004, p. 62) and certainly representing a far larger generation, is very significant.

Indeed, testimony and eyewitness accounts are a staple of television. Its intimate and domestic mode of address and ability to dwell on the 'talking head' produces compelling and accessible viewing. Whilst several university-based historians interviewed by Erin Bell in the course of the project expressed their appreciation of history programming based around oral testimony as an authentic way to access the past, and indeed for audiences to understand historical research to some extent, the media professionals also interviewed by Bell and Gray demonstrated instead a greater awareness of the way in which testimony may offer an affective route into the past for audience members. Those who watch are invited to share intimate memories and as such this is a highly specific televisual mode. The work of historians and producers such as Steve Humphries demonstrates the kinds of programming that can be made; his Testimony Films remains one of the chief UK-based sources of oral history-based series, such as his *The Secret World of Sex* (BBC, 1991) and different forms of testimony, from eyewitness to that of actors in drama-documentaries, are considered by a number of the volume's contributors (see, e.g., Bell, Holdsworth, Rohringer and Ebbrecht). Such types of programming can, in addition, give a voice to the silenced. The work of Myra MacDonald in this area (1998) has been crucial to a reconsideration of the uses of women's testimony in history documentaries, amongst other genres, and some of the chapters utilize specifically feminist approaches in order to explore this further (see, e.g., de Groot and Rohringer).

Reality and re-enactment

Related to the issues raised by the chapters considering testimony, in recent years the declining number of eyewitnesses to the major events of the twentieth century has been recognized as potentially problematic, not least because the presenter-historian and the 'archive and eyewitnesses' format have dominated for many years (Downing, 2004, p. 10). Furthermore, developments in 'factual' television have been transported into history programming and as such the latter shares some of the history of this development. A parallel tendency in television is the use of so-called 'ordinary people' in entertainment and factual genres, and this can be perceived in both the use of testimony, and reality and re-enactment genres. In re-enactment series, which predate the current 'crisis' of testimony, 'ordinary' individuals live in an environment that to some degree re-creates life in the past and the value lies as much in the contrast between the two periods than in the authentic replication and living-through of an earlier era. Re-enactment as a historical pastime also predates television (see, e.g., Horwitz, 1999) and in its televised form in Britain, nonactors playing people of an earlier generation appeared in *Culloden* in the 1960s, *Living in the Past* in the following decade, and in a range of series from the later 1990s in Europe, North America and Australasia. Re-enactment can also take other forms: Collingwood's idea of mental re-enactment has been used by historians directly involved in televised re-enactments, but it may also be used as a means to consider other ways in which historians and celebrities are seen to empathize with people living in the past (see, e.g., de Groot, Corner and Holdsworth).

Biography

The appeal to television producers of recognizable and engaging characters from the past inevitably engages the 'Great Men' mode of history, but increasingly television seeks to look into the private lives of such characters. Whilst the idealized figure of the woman is one key area of discussion for those using feminist approaches in the collection, the idealized figure of the national hero, or heroine, is common in televised accounts of the past, as is the villain. In some cases, such figures have maintained their status as referents despite political currents and changes. In transcending contemporary trends an analysis of the role they play as part of a master narrative of a nation's history and identity is worthwhile (see, e.g., Veyrat-Masson). Televised accounts of the past have also, though, sought to consider the biographies of nonelite individuals, and several of the contributions here outline the role biography plays in creating and sustaining gendered ideals of behaviour in the present.

Topography: landscape

The importance of the visual and the enduring nature of landscape is an attractive feature of much factual television – e.g., *Coast* (BBC, 2005 – present), David Dimbleby's *A Picture of Britain* (BBC, 2005) and Corner in this volume. Idealized and mythologized as much as individuals or their homes, a national or regional landscape may come to stand for the character traits of those who live in it and represent their history and memory. In 1995, Simon Schama's groundbreaking *Landscape and Memory*, published to accompany the BBC2 series of the same name, suggested the historical, cultural and political roots of perceptions of the natural environment and human activity within it. Several contributors outline the enduring significance of the landscape to televised representations of the past, although the way in which the landscape is utilized in each case differs, reflecting its role in different national identities (see, e.g., Corner, Hanna and Dhoest).

National political history and broader contemporary issues

Two of the commissioning editors interviewed by Ann Gray in the course of the research for the 'Televising History' project spoke of the need for history programming to be relevant to the contemporary world in order to appeal to their target (younger) audience. Such programmes should, they suggested, 'say' something about the present day. Unsurprisingly, key national issues of significance in the past are often also related to those in the present. They may refer to former and current conflicts, the significance of key national figures, or current political identities. The frequent reference to key events and figures in a nation's history on television may encourage some film-makers to represent them in different ways or even to leave out elements of past events in the light of current political, cultural or other circumstances; for others, common interpretations of past events – or earlier ways of representing the past – should not be viewed as unquestionable, and has led to alternative representations that seek, depending on the political perspective of the filmmaker and indeed of the scholars commenting on the work, to provide an alternative perspective, sometimes with the intention of persuading those in authority to act in response. Certainly, political transition and identity politics, as Till asserts (2006, p. 327), are often fruitfully analysed together, and many of the chapters in this collection allow this to be done (see, e.g., Gray, Blaney, Veyrat-Masson, Hernández Corchete, Rohringer, Dhoest and Winston).

Pan-national sources, politics and memory

The collection underscores the importance of international audiences for television programming, and particularly that of co-production between European nations. This is a relatively recent development, although, for example, BBC series have been sold overseas for some years, and the almost constant broadcasting of Thames TV's *The World at War* (1973–1974) across the globe is now well known. Often a series such as Laurence Rees's 2005 *Auschwitz: The Nazis and the Final Solution* (BBC, 2005) uses archive material based in several other countries, is sold abroad and offers both home (in this case, British) and overseas audiences a fulfilling viewing experience, in part because of shared, although differing, memories in Europe (see, e.g., Cigognetti and Sorlin, Winston, Holdsworth, Ebbrecht and Rohringer).

In addition, many of the chapters, particularly those in the 'Televised history and national identity' section, make reference to the idea of collective or cultural memory, seen by Maurice Halbwachs as the selective memorialization – or indeed construction – by different groups of people of aspects of the past, shaped and chosen by their concerns in the present (Coser, 1992, p. 25). Although bearing some resemblance to the desire of commissioning editors for history programmes to be relevant to the contemporary world, cited in the previous section, not all of the authors in this collection would concur entirely with Halbwachs. Certainly, several historians have questioned the validity of claims made as part of the recent surge of interest in Memory Studies (Kansteiner, 2002), preferring the issue to be considered more in terms of public history rather than collective memory, because the latter infers, they suggest, an unproblematic, shared and consensual understanding of the past and, we might extrapolate, of the present (Page, 2001). However, Halbwachs' assertion that the past is constructed in the present, and reflects present-centred concerns, appears to be the case when key historical events and actors are commemorated in the television programmes outlined by the authors in this and other sections (see, e.g., Veyrat-Masson, Hanna, Hernández Corchete). This may reflect the selectivity of commissioning editors at least as much as that of programme makers, and more than that of viewers, and is considered in the following section.

Absences: stories that are not told

In many ways, and perhaps for obvious reasons, the scholarly agenda as evidenced in this collection is based on the history programmes that *do* appear on television. Throughout our research we have become aware of both the complexity of the commissioning and production process behind the screen and, to a certain extent, the ways in which the imperatives of television and other wider pressures restrict the range of topics covered in television history programming. Thus, contentious subjects and narratives of the past that unsettle the dominant national narratives are rarely seen. Margit Rohringer's chapter in this collection is an excellent example of scholarly engagement with the desire of filmmakers to address these issues and unsettle dominant narratives, and there are many other examples, some of which received international comment. A documentary on Max Merten and the Holocaust in Greece from which, in 2003, the Greek public channel ET-3 reportedly decided to withdraw funding, despite support for the film from the Simon Wiesenthal Center, is one such case. The same channel, the following year, withdrew from transmission *The Other Side*, an award-winning documentary on Turkish Cypriots in the 1960s. In both instances, political commentators have suggested that this was the result of Greek nationalism and, we may extrapolate, the related desire to preserve a particular way of representing Greek, and related, pasts.[3]

An example of a contentious documentary made and aired, despite attempts to prevent this, is *Congo: White King, Red Rubber, Black Death* (2004). Directed and written by Peter Bate, it was co-produced by Australian, British, Belgian, Canadian, Danish, Dutch, French, Finnish and German broadcasters, and caused considerable controversy in Belgium where there were calls for it to be banned because of its representation of the monarchy

(Ceuppens, 2007). The film considers the abuse and murder of millions of Congolese in the Congo Free State, an independent corporate sovereignty ruled directly by Leopold II from 1885 to 1908, resulting from his desire for colonial expansion and economic development through rubber plantations, in parallel with the similar, albeit earlier, colonialism of other European nations. The programme was broadcast on European channels including ARTE (France/Germany), ZDF (Germany) and YLE (Finland), then sold to the US company ArtMattan. *Congo* is in some respects, then, representative of recent developments, such as the shared production and funding of programmes by European broadcasters, which are also of interest to audiences and media companies overseas, particularly in the US (Bell and Gray, 2007b).

Like *Congo*, many of the chapters in this collection stretch beyond the boundaries of nation in terms of their production, distribution and consumption, and also at times the broader political significance of the histories represented. This is hardly surprising given the increasingly globalized nature of the media industries and international nature of the Internet, whilst in parallel the EU supports collaboration between EU nations, although of course not all of the chapters discuss EU nations alone. This helps to highlight the transnational nature not only of the programmes themselves, but also of many of the primary visual sources used within them. One possible response to Roger Smither's question (2004), 'why is so much television history about war?', apart from the availability of a wealth of film archive, could well be because historically it is a shared experience, binding nations and even continents. The focus on the First and Second World Wars in many of the studies in this collection reflects both the interest of television producers and to some extent their audiences in these topics, and underlines the continent's shared history, but also the need for careful consideration of the ways in which these key events are represented, in order to avoid perpetuating the same stereotypes – or silences – in future.

Notes

1. Isaacs also reminds us of the contribution television researchers make to the documenting of oral testimonies and eyewitness accounts as well as the hunting down of film archive and other historical documents.
2. See Sage, *Memory Studies,* website: http://mss.sagepub.com/.
3. We greatly appreciate the help of Dr. Minna Rozen, University of Haifa; Prof. Samuel Hassid, Israel Institute of Technology; and Katie Anagnostopoulou, Millcreek Films, in collating this material, although errors and opinions are entirely our own. See the Greek Helsinki monitor website: www.greekhelsinki.gr/special-issues-antisemitism.html. Accessed 1 July 2009. Details of the debates surrounding the withdrawal of funding can be found on the

European Free Alliance website: www.florina.org/news/2004/2004_ghm_greektv_censors_documentary.asp. Accessed 1 July 2009. For further details of Max Merten's trial see: http://hcc.haifa.ac.il/Departments/greece/events/holocaust_greece/Samuel_Hassid.pdf. Accessed 1 July 2009.

Bibliography

Bell, E. and A. Gray (2007a) 'History on television: charisma, narrative and knowledge', *European Journal of Cultural Studies* 10.1, 113–33.

Bell, E. and A. Gray (2007b) *'Rough Crossings*: documentary and drama in history programming on British television', conference paper. Visible Evidence XIV, Bochum, Germany, 18–21 December.

Ceuppens, B. (2007) ' "U bent mij vergeten, I presume?": De actualiteit van de koloniale geschiedenis', *Mondiaal Nieuws Magazine*: http://cas1.elis.rug.ac.be/avrug/forum_0702/bambi2007_01.htm. Accessed 25 June 2009.

Coser, L.A. (1992) 'Introduction', in M. Halbwachs (ed.), *On Collective Memory* (Chicago: University of Chicago Press).

Downing, T. (2004) 'Bringing the past to the small screen', in D. Cannadine (ed.), *History and the Media* (London: Palgrave MacMillan).

Friedländer, S. (1992) 'Trauma, transference and "working through" in writing the history of the *Shoah*', *History and Memory*, 4.1: 39–55.

Horwitz, A. (1999) *Confederates in the Attic* (New York: Vintage Books).

Kansteiner, W. (2002) Finding meaning in memory: A methodological critique of collective memory studies, *History and Theory*, 41.2, 179–97.

MacDonald, M. (1998) 'Politicizing the personal: women's voices in British television documentaries', in C. Carter, G. Branston and S. Allan (eds), *News, Gender and Power* (New York: Routledge).

Mak, G. (2007 [2004]) *In Europe: Travels Through the Twentieth Century* (London: Harvill Secker).

Page, M. (2001) 'Radical public history in the city', *Radical History Review*, 79, 114–6.

Radstone, S. (2008) 'Memory studies: for and against,' *Memory Studies*, 1.1, 31–9.

Smither, R. (2004) 'Why is so much television history about war?' in D. Cannadine (ed.), *History and the Media* (London: Palgrave MacMillan).

Till, K. (2006) 'Memory studies', *History Workshop Journal* 62.1, 325–41.

Author Index